# Financial Markets and Institutions

## PEARSON

At Pearson, we take learning personally. Our courses and resources are available as books, online and via multi-lingual packages, helping people learn whatever, wherever and however they choose.

We work with leading authors to develop the strongest learning experiences, bringing cutting-edge thinking and best learning practice to a global market. We craft our print and digital resources to do more to help learners not only understand their content, but to see it in action and apply what they learn, whether studying or at work.

Pearson is the world's leading learning company. Our portfolio includes Penguin, Dorling Kindersley, the Financial Times and our educational business, Pearson International. We are also a leading provider of electronic learning programmes and of test development, processing and scoring services to educational institutions, corporations and professional bodies around the world.

Every day our work helps learning flourish, and wherever learning flourishes, so do people.

To learn more please visit us at: **www.pearson.com/uk**

# Financial Markets and Institutions

Robert Webb

Sanjukta Brahma

**PEARSON**

Harlow, England • London • New York • Boston • San Francisco • Toronto • Sydney
Auckland • Singapore • Hong Kong • Tokyo • Seoul • Taipei • New Delhi
Cape Town • São Paulo • Mexico City • Madrid • Amsterdam • Munich • Paris • Milan

Economics Express

**PEARSON EDUCATION LIMITED**
Edinburgh Gate
Harlow CM20 2JE
United Kingdom
Tel: +44 (0)1279 623623
Web: www.pearson.com/uk

First published 2013 (print)

The Financial Times. With a worldwide network of highly respected journalists, The Financial Times provides global business news, insightful opinion and expert analysis of business, finance and politics. With over 500 journalists reporting from 50 countries worldwide, our in-depth coverage of international news is objectively reported and analysed from an independent, global perspective. To find out more, visit **www.ft.com/pearsonoffer.**

ISBN:      978-0-273-77606-2 (print)
         978-0-273-77609-3 (PDF)
         978-0-273-78556-9 (eText)

**British Library Cataloguing-in-Publication Data**
A catalogue record for the print edition is available from the British Library

**Library of Congress Cataloging-in-Publication Data**
Webb, Robert, 1959–
  Economics express: financial markets and institutions/Robert Webb. – First Edition.
    pages cm
  Includes index.
  ISBN 978-0-273-77606-2
  1. Financial institutions.   2. Capital market.   I. Title.
  HG173.W3957 2013
  332.04–dc23

                         2013019176

10 9 8 7 6 5 4 3 2 1
16 15 14 13

Print edition typeset in 9.5/12.5 pt Scene std by 71
Print edition printed in Great Britain by Henry Ling Ltd., at the Dorset Press, Dorchester, Dorset

# Contents

# Supporting Resources

→ **Understand key concepts quickly**

Printable versions of the **Topic maps** give an overview of the subject and help you plan your revision

Test yourself on key definitions with the online **Flashcards**

→ **Revise effectively**

Check your understanding and practise for exams with the **multiple choice questions**

→ **Make your answers stand out**

Evaluate sample exam answers in the **You be the marker** exercises and understand how and why an examiner awards marks

**All this and more can be found at www.pearsoned.co.uk/econexpress**

# Introduction – Economics Express series

## From the series editor, Professor Stuart Wall

Welcome to *Economics Express* – a series of short books to help you to

- take exams with confidence
- prepare for assessments with ease
- understand quickly
- and revise effectively

There has never been a more exciting time to study economics, given the shock to so many individuals, institutions and countries in 2007/8 when long-established economic certainties were suddenly brought into question. The so-called 'credit crunch' overpowered both financial and non-financial organisations. Government bail-outs of banks and businesses became the order of the day in many countries, with massive increases in government expenditures to fund these bail-outs, quickly followed by austerity budgets aimed at restoring national debts and budget deficits to pre-credit crunch levels. Looking forward, there is as much talk about 'triple-dip' recessions as there is about recovery.

As you embark on your economic journey, this series of books will be your companions. They are not intended to be a replacement for the lectures, textbooks, seminars or further reading suggested by your lecturers. Rather, as you come to an exam or an assessment, they will help you to revise and prepare effectively. Whatever form your assessment takes, each book in the series will help you build up the skills and knowledge to maximise your performance.

You can find more detail of the features contained in this book and which will help develop your assessment skills in the 'Guided Tour' on page ix.

# Series editor's acknowledgements

I am extremely grateful to Kate Brewin and Gemma Doel at Pearson Education for their key roles in shaping this series. I would also like to thank the many lecturers and students who have so helpfully reviewed the key features of this series and whose responses have encouraged us to believe that many others will also benefit from the approaches we have adopted throughout this series.

*Stuart Wall*

## Publisher's acknowledgements

We are grateful to the following for permission to reproduce copyright material:

Examples and evidence on pp. 47–9, taken from 'Much will depend on how RBI capitalizes on its good start', *The Economics Times*, 18 December 2012, Times of India (Gupta, A.); Examples and evidence on pp. 78–81, taken from 'In search of natural velocity', *The Economist*, 11 December 2012; Examples and evidence on pp. 170–2, taken from 'The fear gauge: share prices are breaking records. Are investors too complacent?', *The Economist*, 11 May 2006; Examples and evidence on pp. 200–3, taken from 'Slim pickings for AAA-rated Government bonds', *Morningstar* (Garcia-Zarate, J.); Examples and evidence on pp. 233–8, taken from 'Futures market set for another glorious decade?', *Futures and Options World*, 20 July 2009, Euromoney plc (Packham, C.); Examples and evidence on pp. 262–4, taken from 'Put out: the risks posed by CDOs should have been familiar to Wall Street's finest', *The Economist*, 6 December 2007; Examples and evidence on pp. 359–60, taken from '£1m isn't rich anymore: the rise and fall of investment banking', *New Statesman*, October 2012 (Preston, A.). All rights reserved.

In some instances we have been unable to trace the owners of copyright material, and we would appreciate any information that would enable us to do so.

# Guided tour of the book

→ **Understand key concepts quickly**

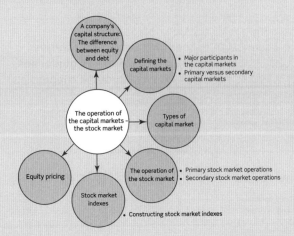

Start to plan your revision using the **Topic maps**.

Grasp **Key definitions** quickly using this handy box. Use the flashcards online to test yourself.

**Key definitions**

**Bond**

A fixed interest financial security issued by large companies, financial institutions and governments whereby the investor (lender) gives money to the issuer (borrower) for a defined time period in return for a fixed rate of interest.

**Fixed income securities**

A type of security where the issuer promises to make fixed payments of a fixed amount during a fixed time scale until maturity.

**Equity**

A type of financial security that in return for cash provides part ownership of a company, with each individual share representing individual ownership of a very small portion of the company.

→ **Revise Effectively**

**✱ Assessment question**

A well-developed capital market is essential for the proper functioning of an economy.

(a) Explain the difference between the primary and secondary capital markets. (40 marks)

(b) Discuss the steps involved in valuing equities, including any drawbacks to the methods utilised. (60 marks)

Can you answer this question? Guidelines on answering the question are presented at the end of this chapter.

**✱ Assessment advice**

Understanding the money markets goes hand in hand wi~~th~~ the capital markets so ensure that you understand both m~~arkets~~ enable you to contrast both of them when answering a qu~~estion~~ that you also know the basics of capital markets: the m~~arkets,~~ their maturities; the difference between brokers and marke~~rs;~~ operation of the primary and secondary markets. The actua~~l~~ stock markets changes rapidly and the textbook your tutor may have used could well be out of date – to show you have up-to-date information check out the websites of the key markets. For example, the London Stock Exchange has an excellent site as well as the FTSE share indexes. Another tip is to get hold of textbooks used in the industry, such as the ones published by the Chartered Institute for Securities and Investment (CISI) as these tend to get updated regularly. When discussing the return on equities remember that the dividend used or any growth rate or **required rate of return** are 'judgement calls'.

Prepare for upcoming exams and tests using the **Assessment question** and **Assessment advice** at the start of each chapter.

## Answer guidelines

### ✳ Assessment question

Derivative markets have witnessed a remarkable growth during the past two decades.

(a) Describe the features of the main derivative instruments. (50 marks)

(b) Examine how futures and swaps can be used to manage risky situations. (50 marks)

### Approaching the question

Begin this question by showing that you understand what is meant by a derivative. Explain the spot market and what going long and going short mean. You should then introduce the main derivative instruments: forwards, futures, swaps and options. Provide an explanation of each before going into a more detailed description of them – provide full explanations of their key features. Avoid using bullet points as this looks like a list and fails to give you the opportunity to analyse or describe in detail. Explain the key differences between each derivative instrument. Part (b) requires you to examine the use of futures and swaps. Begin this part by linking the main features discussed in part (a) with the oncoming discussion: you should relate futures and swaps to risk management. Provide a definition of risk. The rest of this section should concentrate on examples of how futures and swaps can help manage risk. These should be fully explained.

### Important points to include:

- Key definitions.
- An explanation of each type of derivative instrument – avoid bullet points and take time to describe in full.
- A definition of risk and how this can be managed using derivatives.
- As many numerical examples of how futures and swaps can help manage risk.

Compare your responses with the **Answer guidelines** at the end of the chapter.

## → Make your answers stand out

Check out the additional tips to **Make your answer stand out** at the end of the chapter.

### Make your answer stand out

Ensure that you have fully explained each derivative instrument and contrasted the differences clearly – to make an answer stand out in this type of question you must get the basics right. You will see your grade

### Examples & evidence

DIVERSIFICATION is always cited as a good thing when investing. Spread your bets, and you will not be exposed to a sudden collapse in a single company, sector or economy. But for equity investors the task is getting harder and harder. International markets seem to be increasingly correlated.

In part, this may be down to the diversification process itself. Investors buy an exchange-traded fund based on the MSCI world index, or US mutual funds venture into more exciting emerging markets. Either way, a loss of confidence among such investors may cause a worldwide sell-off (as research shows: http://www.economist.com/node/21528640).

But it may also be that companies have diversified themselves. The table, from Orrin Sharp-Pierson at BNP Paribas, shows the proportion of corporate revenue that comes from various countries. So, for example, Canadian companies get 11.5% of their revenues from Europe; UK companies get 20% of their revenues from emerging markets.

Using real-world examples can raise your marks during an exam or assessment. Read the **Examples and evidence** boxes in each chapter.

#### Corporate revenue exposure by area

| % | Emerging markets | Developing Asia | Japan | Europe | North America | Implied revenue |
|---|---|---|---|---|---|---|
| GDP*, 2012 forecast | 11.1 | 7.0 | 0.9 | 2.5 | 2.5 | — |
| Canada | 9.2 | 0.6 | nil | 11.5 | 78.7 | 3.32 |

# 1 The financial system

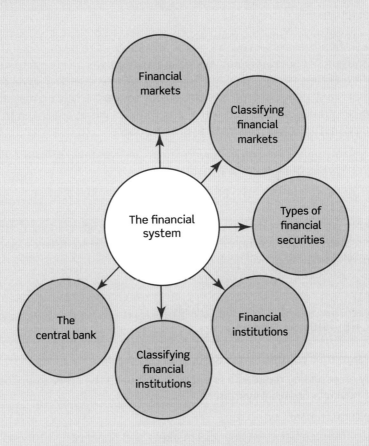

A printable version of this topic map is available from **www.pearsoned.co.uk/econexpress**

## Introduction

All western-style capitalist economies strive for an efficient, well-functioning financial system. This is because all economies aim to increase the wealth and prosperity of their entire population. To understand how a well-functioning financial system helps to build growth, first imagine an economy without a financial system and ask yourself how would the economy function? How would you purchase goods or services? How would you determine the value of your transactions with other individuals? How would you save for the future? Financial systems answer these questions by mobilising funds and getting those funds working in the most efficient ways. So if someone were to ask you for just one reason why a financial system exists, then the best answer would be: to allocate resources efficiently, which means quickly and at the correct price. The faster and more efficiently this is completed, the more an economy grows, increasing the overall national wealth and living standards of the population.

So, a basic financial system allows goods and services to be priced and traded. As the system becomes more advanced it allows trades on claims to future wealth. It achieves this in a myriad of different ways and recent advancements mean that many financial products traded are now extremely complicated. However, all products have common characteristics which are linked to levels of liquidity, maturity and risk. The aim of this chapter is to:

- give you an understanding of how the financial system is delineated into different types of markets and institutions;
- make you aware of the main products traded within the system.

One theme we will be returning to again and again is that financial systems rely upon three factors, namely information, money and confidence, and that all financial transactions will have some level of risk.

---

### → Revision checklist

*Make sure that you both understand and can define:*
- why an economy requires a financial system and the consequences of not having a financial system;
- the term transaction costs;
- the difference between financial markets and financial institutions (how they differ in terms of cost and risk);
- the different types of financial market;

- ❏ financial assets traded within a financial system and the differences between them;
- ❏ asset transformation and the difference between a broker and an asset transformer;
- ❏ the different types of financial institutions;
- ❏ the role of the central bank.

 **Assessment advice**

### Use descriptive data

It looks impressive if you can remember and analyse the key components of the financial system. This would involve your remembering the size of the different financial markets; new issues of financial instruments; or the size of different financial institutions (for example, what are the total assets of Barclays Plc?).

### Remember the basics

The basics are often overlooked – when preparing for the exam make sure you know the difference between a money market and a capital market or a unit and investment trust.

**Assessment question**

Critically analyse the role played by a financial system in an economy. Define the different types of financial securities available to borrowers and lenders and the differences between them.

Can you answer this question? Guidelines on answering the question are presented at the end of this chapter.

## The financial system

Financial systems are generally characterised by distinguishing between financial markets, where households (or individuals) and companies deal directly with each other, and financial institutions, where parties decide to deal through an institution acting as an intermediary. Most textbooks will distinguish between types of financial markets and types of financial institutions. **Financial markets** are commonly distinguished by the time to maturity of the instruments traded within them. **Capital markets** are used to buy and sell long-term debt and **money markets** trade short-term financial instruments. In most cases short term means less than one year and long term is greater than one year (however, usually it is a much greater period than a year, for example long-term bonds are frequently issued for time periods of five and ten years).

**Financial institutions** are more difficult to categorise but one way is to think of the large banks, which usually dominate the retail consumer market, and the rest. In this way you can think of major banks and then non-bank financial intermediaries. Major banks in Europe include: Crédit Lyonnais in France, Santander in Spain and Barclays in the UK. However, all these banks have global operations. Depending on the country, non-banks can be categorised in many ways, such as by the sector of the economy they serve or by the type of business they undertake. An example of the former is the UK building societies, which deal mainly with lending for house purchase; examples of the latter are insurance companies, pension firms or unit and investment trusts. A further category of bank that has come to prominence recently is the investment bank. These financial institutions may or may not be part of a larger commercial bank and focus mainly on two areas within the financial system: underwriting and trading securities. Examine Figure 1.1 on the structure of the financial system.

The overall functions of a financial system are to:

- clear and settle payments (the payments system);
- aggregate (pool) and disaggregate wealth and flows of funds so that both large-scale and small-scale projects can be financed (collection and parcelling);
- transfer economic resources over time, space and industries;

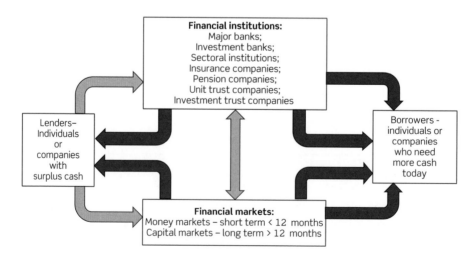

**Figure 1.1** The financial system.

- accumulate, process and disseminate information for decision-making purposes;
- provide ways for managing uncertainty and controlling risk;
- provide ways for dealing with incentives and asymmetric information problems that arise in financial contracting.

## Test yourself

**Q1.** If you won £1 million on the Lottery, where would you choose to invest it? In a bank, or would you use the financial markets? Why? If you set up your own company, where would you choose to obtain finance? Why?

**Q2.** How does the financial system help allocate resources?

**Q3.** What is meant by asymmetric information?

**Q4.** List the main functions of a financial system.

## Key definitions

**Financial market**

This refers to a place, which can be physical or virtual, where IOUs or financial claims are issued and traded.

**Money market**

A type of financial market where short-term financial claims are issued and traded. Short-term refers to maturities of less than one year. Examples of money markets are the Treasury Bill or Interbank market.

**Capital market**

A type of financial market where longer-term financial claims are issued and traded. Long-term refers to maturities of more than one year. Typical capital markets are markets for equity (shares) or bonds.

**Financial institution**

A general term to cover institutions that deal with those wishing to borrow and those wishing to save and/or offer financial advice.

Lenders and borrowers have different requirements and the financial system makes these transactions easier. A question that is often asked is what are the differences between transacting with financial markets and financial institutions? Or why would households or companies choose markets over institutions? Remember that when issuing IOUs on the financial markets they come with a commitment to pay off the interest plus principal (the principal refers to the original amount borrowed). When purchasing IOUs you are providing cash directly to the company issuing the instrument and this involves the risk that the company may not pay the cash back – this is known as default risk. Apart from default risk there are other issues with lenders and borrowers dealing with each other directly:

- **Lenders generally demand:** high returns or yield; liquidity, certainty of value and minimisation of risk.
- **Borrowers generally demand:** cash at a particular time; cash for a specified period of time; low costs (interest rate); cash for long periods of time.

Financial markets and institutions solve these problems but in different ways and at different costs. Financial markets solve them via direct transactions, whereas choosing a financial intermediary means that you have chosen to place an institution between you as a borrower or lender. Financial institutions take ownership of risk from their customers and manage risk for profit. For doing this they charge customers a fee either directly or via an interest rate.

Factors you must consider when choosing to transact directly, or through an intermediary, are:

- speed;
- ease of the transaction;
- price;
- risk;
- liquidity; and
- maturity.

## Financial markets

Financial markets exist to facilitate, at low cost, the:

- placing;
- pricing; and
- trading of financial assets.

Financial markets solve transactions by offering direct transactions – where borrowers take cash directly from lenders in exchange for securities or financial instruments, in a sense an IOU on the future profitability of the borrowing entity. This is cheaper than using an institution, but as a lender you bear all the risk and as a borrower you increase uncertainty in obtaining a stream of funding. Companies that are considered less risky will find it easier to obtain funding directly as lenders can assess their riskiness more easily.

If you buy a security, you have an asset; if you sell a security, you have created a liability for yourself which must be paid back at some time in the future. Major players include households (you and me), businesses, governments and foreign companies. Transacting directly requires the use of a broker – someone who brings you into contact with the markets and helps sell or buy securities. Brokers do not hold the securities and do not take on risk.

## Classifying financial markets

In order to cater for household, business and government financing require-ments there are many different types of financial markets which can be classified in a myriad of ways. The most common way to distinguish between financial markets is by maturity – however, a number of other factors can be used to distinguish between the many types of financial markets.

Financial markets are commonly classified by:

- maturity and type of financing;
- type of issue;
- type of securities that are traded;
- their trading procedures/organisation.

Remember that there is some overlap here and instruments may belong to a number of these classifications.

## Classifying financial markets by maturity

These are markets where short-term debt instruments with a maturity of less than one year are traded on money markets.

Money market examples:

| Certificate of deposit market | Treasury Bill market | Gilt repo market | Interbank market |
|---|---|---|---|

Markets where long-term debt instruments are traded are classified as capital markets – this is where long-term debt is issued and traded, such as long-term bonds and equity (company shares).

Capital market examples:

| Bond market | Equity market |
|---|---|

## Classifying financial markets by type of financing

Debt markets are where debt instruments are traded (and will include the money markets). In the longer-term debt markets such as the bond market, the debt instruments usually carry an agreement by the borrower to pay back the purchaser of the debt at regular intervals. This includes a portion of the original amount plus interest. It is issued for a fixed period of time known as the maturity of a debt instrument – this is the date when the instrument has been promised to be paid off in full.

Another method is to issue equity onto equity markets. The issuer of equity does not pay back any interest or principal but sells ownership rights to their company in exchange for cash. Purchasers of equity own a portion of that company. Companies that issue equity may pay a dividend out of any end-of-year profits but this is not compulsory.

Type of financing examples:

| Debt markets | | Equity markets | |
|---|---|---|---|
| Bonds | Certificates of deposit (CDs) | Common equity | Preference shares |

## Classifying financial markets by type of issue

**Primary markets** are where new issues of debt or equity are put up for sale by companies or governments who want to borrow or obtain funding. The instruments are sold at prearranged prices/levels of interest/maturity and issues of new debt are usually heavily marketed by investment banks, which are employed to sell the instruments:

- **Debt** is usually sold at fixed maturity and comes with an interest rate that is paid by the issuer either throughout the time to maturity or in full at maturity.
- **Equity** is sold to the primary market and comes with a price per share (with purchasers also being aware of the total amount being issued).

**Secondary markets** are where these instruments are traded, making the instruments more liquid; that is, the initial purchaser of the instrument can sell the instrument in the secondary market for cash. Remember, equity is never paid off – it is traded in the secondary market with the share price being the price at which the holder can sell one share (or equity) in the market. It does not help raise capital for the company which issued the equity – profits/losses are borne by the buyers and sellers in that market.

## Classifying financial markets by securities that are traded

There are a myriad of financial assets (see below); in many cases markets are referred to by the products that are traded on these markets. Derivatives markets are one example. A derivative is a financial instrument that 'derives' its value from some underlying asset. Derivatives markets are organised around financial instruments that give you an obligation or choice to buy or sell the underlying asset at some future date. Remember that markets are commonly referred to by the type of instrument traded, for example the bond market.

Product market examples:

| Derivatives markets (futures or options market) | Foreign exchange market | Bond market |
| --- | --- | --- |

## Classifying financial markets by how they are organised

Secondary financial markets can also be classified as being either exchanges or over-the-counter (OTC) markets. Exchanges have one physical location where buyers and sellers meet to trade. In contrast, OTC markets are virtual exchanges where brokers are ready to trade securities as they are demanded or supplied (sell or buy). OTC markets include all types of securities and can include types of bonds, negotiable CDs, or commodities.

Examples of OTC versus organised exchanges:

| OTC markets | | Physical exchanges | |
| --- | --- | --- | --- |
| Negotiable CDs | (Some) bonds | Equity markets | Futures market |

### Test yourself

**Q1.** What are the different ways of classifying financial markets?

**Q2.** What is the difference between a formal exchange and an OTC market?

### Key definitions

**Debt**

This usually refers to bonds, which are fixed interest financial security issued by large companies, financial institutions and governments, whereby the investor (lender) gives money to the issuer (borrower) for a defined time period in return for a fixed rate of interest.

**Equity**

A type of financial security that in return for cash provides part ownership of a company, with each individual *share* representing individual ownership of a very small portion of the company.

> **Primary market**
> The market where financial securities are first issued.
>
> **Secondary market**
> The market where financial securities, once issued, are traded.

## Types of financial securities

There are many types of financial security that are traded every day within financial markets in any financial system.

Key characteristics of financial securities:

- Those that issue a security have created a **financial liability**.
- Those that purchase a security have bought a **financial asset**.
- A financial asset is a claim against something real; this could be a tangible (physical) asset (for example, a house) or an expected income stream (for example, the future profits of a company);
- Purchasing a financial asset means that you expect some kind of compensation, or return, or yield from the asset – usually expressed as an interest rate. This is the price of borrowing cash today for the issuer of the financial security – the price being expressed as a percentage of the whole amount being borrowed;
- All financial securities have a degree of **risk**, because the future is uncertain: a degree of **liquidity**, which is a term used to denote how quickly the security can be turned into cash; and a **maturity**, which is the time until the financial security pays off in full.
- Risk, liquidity and maturity will help derive the securities price in the market. The lower the perceived risk, the higher the liquidity, and the shorter the maturity, the lower the return from a security.

Financial securities are split into two types: debt and equity.

Purchasers of debt are classed as creditors and do not have ownership rights on a company. Debt holders have purchased:

- a financial security which provides them with a flow of interest payments at specific times in the future (and a specific time when the total amount of the instrument will mature or will be paid off).

Equity does not have a maturity date, or an interest rate, and is never paid back by the issuing company (unless it decides to buy back its own shares on the secondary market). Instead, purchasers of equity have bought themselves:

- legal ownership of the company, giving them the right to have a say in company strategy;
- a claim on the profits of the company, which may be paid in the form of a dividend each year by the company.

If you recall, financial securities are traded on either the money markets, which are short term (less than one year), or the longer-term capital markets. Money market instruments tend towards being easily sellable, liquid and low risk. This is because the market participants are less risky and the instruments are short term. Short term lowers risk because investors receive their money back more quickly, increasing certainty. Capital markets are where longer-term, less liquid and riskier securities are traded.

## Key definitions

**Financial liability**

A financial obligation to somebody else.

**Financial asset**

A financial obligation that somebody owes to you.

**Liquidity**

The ease with which a financial security can be exchanged for liquid assets, usually cash.

**Maturity**

The time it takes for a financial security to pay back in full.

**Risk**

The potential for an issuer of financial securities to have inadequate funds to meet their financial obligations can also be viewed as the variance in return on a financial asset and the potential for loss.

## The main securities (debt instruments) traded on the money markets

## Key definition

**Treasury Bills (Tbills)**

Short-term debt instruments issued by a country's government in order to help finance the country and/or manipulate the amount of cash in the economy. Issued in the UK:

in minimum denominations of £5,000 at a discount to their face value for any period not exceeding one year. Although they are usually issued for three months (91 days), on occasion they have been issued for 28 days, 63 days and 182 days. They are issued:

- by allotment to the highest bidder at a weekly (Friday) tender to a range of counterparties;
- in response to an invitation from the Debt Management Office to a range of counterparties;
- at any time to government departments.

(Bank of England website)

Key features:

- pay a set amount at maturity;
- have no interest payments;
- sell at a discount, that is a price lower than you will receive at maturity (effectively, this becomes the interest rate)– for example, you buy a 91-day Tbill for £4,700 which can be redeemed for £5,000;
- most liquid of all financial securities;
- most actively traded;
- almost no risk as it would require the government to default (Tbills are often referred to as the risk-free rate of return);
- bought and sold mainly by banks.

### Key definition

**Certificates of deposit (CDs)**

Financial security sold by a bank. Short-term CDs (91 days) are highly marketable – in contrast longer-term CDs are less marketable. Used along with retail deposits by retail commercial banks to obtain funding to enable them to operate their business.

Key features:

- pay an annualised interest rate;
- at maturity pay back the original purchase price;
- the bank does not redeem the CD before its maturity date;
- larger CDs are negotiable, which means that they can be sold to another investor if the original owner requires liquidity (cash).

### Key definition

**Commercial paper (CP)**

Issued by large, high-reputation companies in order to obtain short-term funding to cover short-term obligations.

Key features:

- issued at a discount like Tbills;
- has a maturity of between 1 and 270 days;
- is unsecured (no assets specifically backing the issue of CP);
- is low risk due to the high reputation of the companies issuing this form of security and due to its short-term nature.

## Key definition

**Bankers' acceptances**

Slightly different in nature to the other securities listed here. A non-financial firm which owes money at some point in the future contacts its bank asking it to 'accept' to pay on behalf of the firm. If the bank accepts, it is then the bank's responsibility to pay off the holder of the acceptance – which will now be an IOU – that is, a promise to pay a set amount in the future.

Key features:

- they have a maturity of less than 182 days;
- low risk – as they are linked to the bank's credit rating (not the initial firm);
- they sell at a discount;
- used widely in international trade – where there is less transparency as to the creditworthiness of the customer.

## Key definition

**Repurchase agreements (repos)**

A popular way of obtaining a return on excess cash for large reputable companies. Such companies purchase Tbills from a bank (providing liquidity to the bank) with an agreement that the bank 'repurchases' the Tbills at a slightly higher price sometime in the near future – say, one week. The rise in price equals the interest rate charged by the lender for borrowing.

## The main securities (debt instruments and equity) traded on capital markets

## Key definition

**Government bonds (known as gilts in the UK)**

According to the UK's Debt Management Office (DMO) website:

A gilt is a UK Government liability in sterling, issued by HM Treasury and listed on the London Stock Exchange. The term 'gilt' or 'gilt-edged security' is a reference to the primary characteristic of gilts as an investment: their security. This is a reflection of the fact that the British Government has never failed to make interest or principal payments on gilts as they fall due.

(See **www.dmo.gov.uk/index.aspx?page=Gilts/About_Gilts.**)

Key features:

- come in two different types: conventional (which form the majority) and index linked;
- can also be issued by local governments to fund expenditure. In the United States they are called municipal bonds.

*Conventional:*

- they guarantee to pay the holder of the gilt a fixed cash payment (coupon) every six months;
- long term;
- issued with a specific maturity date, for example 4% Treasury Gilt 2016;
- in the above example the coupon is 4% and the principal will be repaid to investors on 7 September 2016;
- issued mainly with 5-, 10- and 30-year maturities.

*Index linked:*

- semi-annual coupon payments and the principal are adjusted in line with the UK retail prices index (RPI);
- both the coupons and the principal paid on redemption of these gilts are adjusted to take account of accrued inflation since the gilt was first issued.

## Key definition

**Corporate bonds**

Similar to gilts but issued by large corporations. They come in different types. Secured corporate bonds are less risky as they are 'secured' against some form of asset. Unsecured corporate bonds, or debentures, have no security and are therefore riskier. 'Subordinated' debentures have a lower priority claim than debentures if the company fails.

Key features:

- like gilts they pay a coupon twice a year and return the face value on maturity;
- can be risky, specifically suffering a default risk, which is the chance that the issuer cannot repay either the coupon or face value;
- can be issued as 'convertible' bonds which allow the bondholders to 'convert' their bond holding into equity;

- a thriving international bonds market where you may purchase bonds from international issuers. Bonds that are issued not in the local currency are known as Eurobonds.

## Common stock or equities or shares and preferred stock

Purchasers who have bought a 'share' in a company have thus bought a part ownership of the company. Common equity also gives voting rights at the company's annual general meeting. Public limited companies are owned by their shareholders but controlled by a board of directors which is elected by the shareholders. The board of directors selects the managers who then run the company on the shareholders' behalf.

Key features:

*Common stock:*

- buyers have bought a part share of the company;
- does not pay interest;
- does not mature;
- shareholders may receive a dividend paid from retained profit – but the board may choose not to pay a dividend;
- once issued on the primary market, shares can only be sold on the secondary market at the prevailing market price – this price does not directly affect the company;
- indirectly – a falling share price can signify poor company performance and increase the cost of future financing (debt or equity);
- share price multiplied by shares in issue = market capitalisation and is an indication of the total worth of the company, thus a falling share price will make the company attractive for a takeover bid;
- incentives to own shares are to buy at a lower price than you can sell at a later date, or to receive any (annually paid) dividend.

*Preferred stock:*

- pays the holder an annual return similar to a debt instrument;
- again, does not 'mature';
- does not come with voting rights;
- holders have priority over any unpaid dividends;
- in the case of liquidation preferred stockholders are paid back ahead of common stockholders;
- in some cases can be converted into common stock.

### Recap

All the securities discussed above can be classified into one or more of the financial market classifications outlined above. Derivatives are slightly different and come in four main types.

## The main instruments traded on derivatives markets

Remember, derivatives are different to other financial securities because they are contracts to allow something to happen in the future and they 'derive' their value from some underlying asset. They can be split into forwards, futures, swaps and options:

Key features of forwards:

- two parties agree to exchange a real or financial asset on a prearranged date in the future for a specified price;
- private agreements between two parties – not negotiable, no secondary market;
- customised to the specific needs of the parties;
- informal communication networks (OTC) market.

Key features of futures:

- the contract is negotiable, therefore trades on organised markets;
- carries standardised terms, amounts and maturities;
- liquid (unlike forwards) due to tradability;
- can trade through **brokers**;
- initial margin required (2–10% of value of contract) and variation margins usually activated;
- so, as the price moves, they (the current loser) must pay a counterparty each day a variation margin based on the day end settlement price (marking to market);
- the payment credits the counterparty's (the current winner) account;
- all potential losses have to be paid on a daily basis, which limits risk exposure;
- futures have a clearing house that sits between the parties guaranteeing the contract (lower counterparty risk).

Key features of swaps:

- an agreement between two parties to exchange two differing forms of payment obligations;
- swap market dominated by interest rate swaps and currency swaps;
- used by large multinational corporations (MNCs), financial institutions and governments to manage risk and gain cheaper finance.

Key features of options:

- options give the holder the right, but not the obligation, to buy or sell an underlying security at a specified price;
- the value of the option is derived from the price of the underlying asset in the cash market;

- contract to buy = call option;
- contract to sell = put option;
- this market allows investors to transact for real (or financial) assets but they do not have to exercise that option.

## Financial institutions

The major financial institutions in an economy are the large deposit-taking institutions commonly referred to as the major commercial or retail banks. They add value to the economy by taking money from those with surpluses and lending it to those who require cash to invest. However, in contrast to financial markets they transform the characteristics of their liabilities as they become assets – making them more attractive to borrowers – and by doing so bear risk for both lenders and borrowers. The most important asset transformers are the major retail banks. Major bank liabilities are dominated by deposits which tend to make up 60–70% of total liabilities. In contrast, loans dominate assets making up around 60-65%. Asset transformation is outlined in Figure 1.2: deposits tend to be short term and have the characteristics outlined in the left hand column of the figure; loans tend to be long term and have the characteristics shown in the right hand column of the figure.

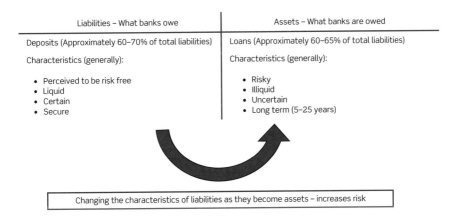

| Liabilities – What banks owe | Assets – What banks are owed |
|---|---|
| Deposits (Approximately 60–70% of total liabilities) | Loans (Approximately 60–65% of total liabilities) |
| Characteristics (generally): | Characteristics (generally): |
| • Perceived to be risk free<br>• Liquid<br>• Certain<br>• Secure | • Risky<br>• Illiquid<br>• Uncertain<br>• Long term (5–25 years) |

Changing the characteristics of liabilities as they become assets – increases risk

**Figure 1.2** Basic asset transformation on a retail bank's balance sheet.

## Banks and asset transformation

Referring to Figure 1.2, banks transform assets in four ways:

- **Risk:** the main bank liability, deposits are perceived to have no or very little risk; in contrast, their main asset, loans are very risky.
- **Maturity:** deposits can be short term with many being able to be withdrawn overnight; loans are commonly longer term, maybe five years or more.
- **Liquidity**: deposits are extremely liquid; loans can be extremely illiquid.
- **Size:** deposits are gathered in small denominations; loans tend to be much higher in value.

**Asset transformation** and risk management are the major benefits that retail banks bring to the economy. Asset transformation can be a costly trick for banks as it requires a large branch network and control of the money transmission mechanism. Banks know that not all depositors will require cash at the same time and, in addition, there will be a daily dynamic between cash being deposited into the bank and cash being withdrawn.

This is where a large branch network reduces risk and allows banks to operate asset transformation – the more branches, the more certain a bank can calculate its daily cash requirements. This is what the textbooks refer to as the 'law of large numbers'. The sheer size of a bank will allow it to calculate with some certainty what is being deposited and what is being withdrawn across all its branch network: the more observations (that is, branches), the more accurate the estimation. However, branches are costly.

Asset transformation can also be performed because large retail banks have a privileged position within the economy, operating the payments mechanism (which is the way money is circulated around the economy) and dominating the deposit and loan business. For example, in the UK the largest five banks (Barclays, Lloyds, RBS, Santander and HSBC) have approximately 80% of all retail deposits and so can be fairly sure that as cash is spent it will be retained among themselves, allowing them to reduce the amount of cash they need to hold on a day-to-day basis. Think about what happens when you spend cash in a shop. Your money is transferred from your bank account to the bank account of the shop. If you both bank at the same bank then the liquidity at the bank is unaffected – money is just transferred from your account to the shop's account at the same bank. In addition, the bank can also calculate how much cash will be coming in from asset investments (what a bank is owed). For example, its loans will be being paid off and it will receive cash (most likely) on a monthly basis, which it can retain as cash. Banks can therefore asset transform and 'create credit' for the economy but must be aware of the risks to which they are exposed. Of course there will be some withdrawals from the retail sector, for example cash going abroad to a non-domestically owned bank.

**Q1.** How do major retail banks transform their assets?

**Q2.** How do they achieve this without going bankrupt?

## Key definitions

**Broker**

An entity that brings individuals together to enact trades. Brokers do not hold risk.

**Asset transformation**

A process that involves banks 'transforming' the characteristics of their liabilities as they become assets. They do this in four ways: risk, size, liquidity and maturity.

## Classifying financial institutions

Think of the financial institutions sector as being hierarchical, where, at the top, is the central bank. All advanced economies have a lead bank at the top of their financial system which is usually owned or controlled by the government. In the UK it is the Bank of England, in Germany it is the Deutsche Bundesbank, in France it is the Banque de France and in the United States it is the Federal Reserve. The Bank of England in the UK is owned by the UK government, having been nationalised in 1946; it has a monopoly on the note issue in England and Wales, and is committed to maintaining a stable and efficient monetary and financial framework. Central banks in any jurisdiction tend to be involved in similar areas of the economy and usually focus on controlling inflation (a general rise in prices) while helping the economy to grow. Central banks also deal directly with the largest banks in the economy in order to aid in these goals.

For example, the Bank of England has three core purposes:

- maintaining the integrity and value of the currency;
- maintaining the stability of the financial system;
- seeking to ensure the effectiveness of the UK's financial services.

Beneath the central bank an economy has many other financial institutions. There are numerous ways to categorise them – one way is to think of bank financial institutions (BFIs) and non-bank financial institutions (NBFIs). Another way of categorisation is between those that primarily take in deposits being classified as deposit-taking institutions and those that are investing institutions – in the list below, these are the insurance, pension, unit trust and investment companies.

## Typical classification of banks operating within an economy (including all those that hold a banking licence)

### High street commercial banks

Major players dominate the retail deposit markets and today offer a full range of services including: loans, mortgages, investment banking and insurance business. They tend to have large branch networks, work with both individuals and businesses, and participate in the UK clearing system.

### Investment banks

Once separate institutions, many have now merged with a commercial bank. Their core business is to underwrite new issues (sell new issues of shares on the financial markets). They are also involved as secondary market traders; consultants selling financial data; agents/advisers/deal makers in mergers and acquisitions (for fee income); merchant bankers; investment councillors for high-net-worth individuals; brokers; mutual funds and money managers for pension funds and proprietary traders, where they trade/invest their own money for profit. Investment banks are known for being opportunistic and innovative.

### Foreign banks

Business is dominated by foreign currency and interaction with financial markets. They also facilitate businesses from their home/domestic market.

Some traditional differences between large retail commercial banks and investment banks:

- a small number of large retail banks but a large number of smallish investment banks;
- retail banks transact with less knowledgeable clientele – the majority of investment bank transactions are completed with knowledgeable corporate clients;
- retail banks have wider margins than investment banks, which have slim margins due to knowledgeable clientele and greater competition;
- investment banking is dominated by foreign currency.

## Non-bank financial institutions

### The building societies

In many countries, sectoral institutions (depending on the country) concentrate upon a certain sector of the economy. For example, it is common to have institutions to provide capital for house purchase. In the UK these are called building societies; in Germany they are called Pfandbrief banks. In the UK, building societies are 'mutuals', which means that they are owned by their members – those that have deposits or loans with the society.

## Insurance companies

Insurance comes in many types including car insurance, home insurance, health insurance and life insurance. Insurance companies are generally categorised into life insurance companies which concentrate on life and pension business, and non-life/general insurance companies which concentrate on all the other categories. Think of the difference being term based, with life insurance as long term and general insurance as short term and renewed annually.

## Pension companies

Much like life insurance companies, these companies offer individuals the opportunity to invest long term (by allowing them to pay a certain amount each month for, say, 20 years) to accumulate proceeds for a pension on retirement.

## Unit trust and investment trust companies

Much like pension companies, these institutions allow individuals the chance to invest in a diversified portfolio of assets, reducing risk but attaining attractive returns. They tend to be medium to long term. A unit trust is 'open ended' and it contracts and expands with demand for its units. In contrast, investment trusts are actual public limited companies and to invest in them you must purchase shares in that investment trust. As these are limited, investment trusts are deemed 'closed ended'.

Life insurance companies, pension companies, and unit and investment trusts offer lenders a chance to buy into a diversified portfolio of assets and benefit from a more efficient risk return trade-off. They achieve this by pooling funds and then implementing current portfolio management techniques that individuals could not replicate with their limited funds, invested monthly. They are important to the economy because they invest heavily in the financial markets, buying equity and debt. This increases the efficiency of the financial markets, meaning that they help to increase the speed and accuracy of asset pricing within financial markets.

### Test yourself

**Q1.** What is the main purpose of a central bank?

**Q2.** Explain the difference between a retail bank and an investment bank.

### Examples & evidence

The protracted debate over how to clean up after the financial crisis – and how to reform our accident-prone financial system to prevent another such episode – is stuck on the problem of how to regulate markets without undermining the benefits they bring. What is sorely missing is any real discussion of what function our financial system is supposed to perform and how well it is doing that job – and, just as important, at what cost.

The crucial role of the financial system in a mostly free-enterprise economy is to allocate capital investment towards the most productive applications. The energetic growth and technological advance of the western economies suggest that our financial system has done this job pretty well over long periods. The role of start-up companies in this process – Apple, Microsoft, Google and many others – testifies to the success not just of our entrepreneurs, but of our financial markets too. The financially triggered Great Recession of 2008 blemishes this record but does not wipe it away.

Apart from the recession, it is important to ask how much this once-admired mechanism costs to run. If a new fertiliser offers a farmer the prospect of a higher crop yield but its price and the cost of transporting and spreading it exceed what the additional produce will bring at market, it is a bad deal for the farmer. A financial system, which allocates scarce investment capital, is no different.

The discussion of the costs associated with our financial system has mostly focused on the paper value of its recent mistakes and what taxpayers have had to put up to supply first aid. The estimated $4,000bn of losses in US mortgage-related securities are just the surface of the story. Beneath those losses are real economic costs due to wasted resources: mortgage mis-pricing led the United States to build far too many houses. Similar pricing errors in the telecoms bubble a decade ago led to millions of miles of unused fibre-optic cable being laid.

The misused resources and the output forgone due to the recession are still part of the calculation of how (in)efficient our financial system is. What has somehow escaped attention is the cost of running the system.

What makes a more efficient financial system worthwhile is not that it allows us to achieve greater production and economic growth, but that the rest of the economy benefits. The more the financial system costs to run, the higher the hurdle is. Does the increased efficiency that our investment allocation system delivers meet that hurdle? We simply do not know.

Economic decisions are supposed to turn on weighing costs and benefits. It is time for some serious discussion of what our financial system is actually delivering to our economy and what it costs to do that.

*Source:* Benjamin Friedman in *The Financial Times*, 26 August 2009

## Questions

On reading the textbooks it may appear that a financial system brings only benefits. This may not always be the case:

1. What are your thoughts on this article?
2. Write down a list of benefits and drawbacks of a financial system.
3. In what ways do you believe the financial system could be improved?

## Chapter summary – pulling it all together

By the end of this chapter you should be able to:

| | Confident ✓ | Not confident? |
|---|---|---|
| Know the benefits that a financial system brings to an economy | | Revise pages 1–6 |
| Understand the difference between financial markets and financial institutions | | Revise pages 1–7 and 17–19 |
| Define the role of financial markets | | Revise pages 6–7 |
| Classify financial markets and know which markets should be placed in which classification and why | | Revise pages 7–8 |
| Discuss the different types of financial securities that trade in the financial markets | | Revise pages 8–17 |
| Explain fractional reserve banking and asset transformation | | Revise pages 17–19 |
| Know the difference between the financial institutions that exist within a financial system – including the role of the Bank of England | | Revise pages 19–22 |

Now try the sample question at the start of this chapter, using the answer guidelines below.

## Answer guidelines

### ✳ Assessment question

Critically analyse the role played by a financial system in an economy. Define the different types of financial securities available to borrowers and lenders and the differences between them.

## Approaching the question

Begin by taking into account the question asked. Refer to the issues posed by barter (high in transaction costs) and the rise of financial markets and institutions. Mention a financial market in the UK or abroad and its role. Similarly, mention a large bank and its operations.

## Important points to consider

- Allude to the problems of risk within financial transactions.
- Explain the main features of financial markets in placing, pricing and trading financial securities.
- Explain the benefits of financial institutions, the role of barter and asset transformation and link these to the role of financial markets.
- Discuss how both financial markets and institutions manage risk.
- Thoroughly analyse the various securities, discussing their main features. Who uses the security? What is its risk, liquidity and maturity?

## Make your answer stand out

Begin to link together cohesively the various components discussed above. For example, do financial markets and institutions link together? How? To what benefit? In addition, give empirical information on the size of the markets, the balance sheets of banks. For example, how many deposits do large UK banks have? How many CDs have they issued? (Both are readily available from the various financial market websites and individual bank's websites (see investor relations section on their websites).) Use key journals such as the *Journal of Banking and Finance* and quote the main authors.

## Read to impress

### Textbooks

There are many books that explain the main features of a financial system. Find the one that makes most sense to you. The ones that I like and use are:

Bodie, Z., Kane, A. and Marcus, A.J. (2010) *Essentials of Investments*. McGraw-Hill.

Mishkin, F.S. (2012) *The Economics of Money, Banking and Financial Markets*. Pearson Education.

Ritter, L.S., Silber, W.L. and Udell, G. F. (2008) *Money, Banking and Financial Markets*. Pearson Education.

Santomero, A. and Babbel, D. (2000) *Financial Markets, Instruments and Institutions*. McGraw-Hill.

Saunders, A. and Cornett, M.M. (2011) *Financial Markets and Institutions*. McGraw-Hill.

### Journal articles

Journal articles are a good source of up-to-date information by key academics. Again, some will make more sense to you than others. Here are a few that link well to this chapter:

Goodhart, C.A.E. (2011) The changing role of central banks. *Financial History Review*, Vol. 18 (2), pp. 135–54.

Levine, R. (1997) Financial development and economic growth: view and agenda. *Journal of Economic Literature*, Vol. XXXV, pp. 688–726.

Mayer, M. (2008) Trust in financial markets. *European Financial Management*, Vol. 14 (8), pp. 617–32.

Rajan, R. and Zingales, L. (2002) Financial systems, industrial structure, and growth. *Oxford Review of Economic Policy*, Vol. 17 (2), pp. 467–82.

Scholtans, B. and Wensveen, D. van (2000) A critique on the theory of financial intermediation. *Journal of Banking and Finance*, Vol. 24 (8), pp. 1243–51.

### Website

Due to the recent financial crisis there are many reports that have been written – some sponsored by the government. One of the better ones is the:

Independent Commission on Banking (2011)

You can find it at: **http://bankingcommission.independent.gov.uk/**

## Data sources

Check out the websites of the following for data on financial markets and institutions:

Bank of England

British Bankers Association

European Central Bank

Individual banks

London Stock Exchange

The City UK

UK Debt Management Office

## Companion website

Go to the companion website at **www.pearsoned.co.uk/econexpress** to find more revision support online for this topic area.

## Notes

# 2

# General characteristics and pricing of financial securities

## Topic map

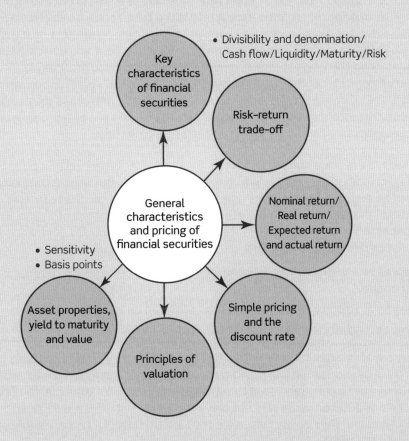

- Divisibility and denomination/ Cash flow/Liquidity/Maturity/Risk

Key characteristics of financial securities

Risk–return trade-off

General characteristics and pricing of financial securities

Nominal return/ Real return/ Expected return and actual return

- Sensitivity
- Basis points

Asset properties, yield to maturity and value

Principles of valuation

Simple pricing and the discount rate

A printable version of this topic map is available from **www.pearsoned.co.uk/econexpress**

## Introduction

The previous chapter introduced the financial markets and institutions that operate within a financial system. This chapter will concentrate upon the key characteristics and pricing of financial assets that are issued and traded within a financial system. Remember that **financial securities** are a claim on the future production of those issuing the security so that issuers create a financial liability for themselves (that is, something that must be paid off at a future date) and purchasers a financial asset.

In order to provide capital (money) to companies, those that buy financial securities require some kind of compensation. This can be referred to as a **return**, yield or interest rate. The expression return or yield tends to be used when discussing the 'return' the investor demands in 'return' for their money investment. In contrast, the interest rate is usually used when discussing the issuer of debt, where the interest rate is the price for borrowing money. However, the terms are commonly used as substitutes. An interest rate will eventually be expressed in money terms, so, for example, if you borrow £100 for a year and the interest rate charged is 10% per year you must pay back to the lender £110 at the end of the year. So the price you paid for borrowing £100 was £10 in exactly the same way as buying a pair of trainers may cost you £50. The interest rate on a financial security is the price of borrowing and compensates purchasers for giving up their spending today.

However, there are a number of factors that can affect the level of interest or yield on a financial security which may be specific to the issuing company or may be external. You must be able to distinguish between these factors, which will then help you to understand how the characteristics of financial securities influence the interest rate, yield or return. The most common characteristics referred to in the finance books are the financial security's:

- degree of risk (the risk associated with the issuer being able to pay back the money);
- degree of liquidity (how quickly the security can be turned into money);
- time to maturity (the longer the maturity, the higher the risk).

These are all internal factors. External factors which may affect the levels of return will be associated with conditions within the economy which will affect companies differently (and so in turn their issued debt). For example, the financial crisis of 2008 onwards was not only created by, but affected all, financial institutions and their ability to service their issued financial securities (known as debt instruments).

Investors also have to be aware of the level of inflation. That is, how much will your return be worth when you eventually receive both the money you lent to the company and any interest payments? **Inflation** reduces the spending power of money within an economy and so **investors** must be aware of how much their invested funds will be able to purchase after taking account of inflation. The chapter begins by taking a look at the various characteristics of securities, all of which combine to affect the riskiness and price of the security.

## Revision checklist

*Make sure that you understand:*

- ❑ The relationship between a security's risk, liquidity and maturity, and its return;
- ❑ That as risk increases so does (expected) return (and vice versa);
- ❑ The difference between nominal return, real return, expected return and actual return;
- ❑ And can calculate simple interest and compound interest;
- ❑ Present value and how to calculate the present value of a security;
- ❑ That present value is calculated using a yield to maturity which is the market's 'best guess' rate given the characteristics of the security;
- ❑ That yield and a security's price have an inverse relationship – if investors demand a higher yield due to changing market conditions then the present value of each cash flow decreases in value and so does the current price;
- ❑ Sensitivity, which examines how changes in the variables of the present value formula affect the price of the security.

## Assessment advice

This chapter covers the basics of financial assets – make sure you understand what affects the pricing of assets. This understanding can then be used throughout any exam questions that you undertake. For example, remember that: every financial asset has certain key characteristics that affect its pricing; generally risk is related to (expected) return in a linear fashion, that is as one goes up so does the other; and that as the market increases the discount rate then the current price of an asset goes down. Again, remember the basics: understanding the logic of this chapter will help you understand the pricing of all financial instruments. How is maturity linked to yield? What is a basis point?

**Assessment question**

Define the key characteristics inherent in all securities. Critically examine why £1 today is not worth £1 in two years' time. Your answer should include a thorough examination of the use of present value calculations.

Can you answer this question? Guidelines on answering the question are presented at the end of this chapter.

## Recap

The interest rate on a financial security is the price of borrowing and compensates purchasers for giving up their spending today. The most common characteristics that will affect the interest rate on a security are:

- degree of risk (the risk associated with the issuer being able to pay back the money);
- degree of liquidity (how quickly the security can be turned into money);
- time to maturity (the longer the maturity, the higher the risk).

## Test yourself

**Q1.** What is a financial security?

**Q2.** List the three most common characteristics evident in all financial securities.

## Key characteristics of financial securities

You have already been introduced to the myriad of financial securities that trade on the various financial markets (see Chapter 1). All these financial securities have key characteristics which when combined make them more or less attractive to purchasers (known as investors) or issuers. These characteristics help determine the securities demand, supply and return (yield or interest rate). As a result, before moving on in later chapters to examine the dynamics and pricing aspects of financial securities traded on the various financial markets it is beneficial to understand their key characteristics. These are explained below.

## Moneyness

Assets that can be used as a direct medium of exchange are known as money. Financial assets are therefore classified as being money or near money. Near money assets can be transformed into money without much cost, delay or risk. Moneyness is also used widely when discussing options. Investors are termed as being *in the money* if by exercising an option they will gain; *out of the money* if they will lose; and *at the money* if they will break even.

## Divisibility and denomination

Divisibility refers to the minimum size at which a security can be traded. Think of this as the minimum denomination for which the security can be bought and sold in the market. Many retail transactions with individuals will be infinitely divisible (no set denomination) as there is no minimum amount, for example your current account. However, in the wholesale market securities are commonly denominated into set amounts before being sold. For example, bonds are sold at £1,000 par (par referring to the initial contribution (or selling price) per bond) whereas certificates of deposit may be denominated and sold at £100,000 par.

## Cash flow

This refers to all the money that an investor will finally receive when holding a financial security. As we know from the previous chapter this can be realised in different ways, for example by purchasing discounted bonds or buying a security that pays a **coupon** twice a year. The cash flow refers to the repayment of principal, which is the initial amount invested plus any cash received throughout the holding period.

## Maturity

As mentioned above, the maturity of a security is the period of time before the security provides its final payments of principal plus interest. Some financial instruments allow their owner to demand liquidation – these are known as demand instruments, an example being a savings account. Maturity can be overnight or decades with some UK gilts being perpetual, that is having no final pay-off date of the principal but paying interest indefinitely.

## Convertibility

An interesting concept which allows a financial security to be converted into another type of financial security. There are many examples: certain types of bonds can be converted into other types of bonds with different characteristics; convertible bonds can be changed into equity; and preferred stock can be converted into common stock.

## Liquidity and reversibility

Ensure that you understand the difference between these two characteristics. Reversibility is the cost of purchasing and then selling the same financial asset. Certain financial securities are known to be highly reversible because when buying and then redeeming the security is close to costless. If the security is traded on a financial market with market-makers offering a bid–ask spread (the difference between the price at which the market-maker will buy and sell the financial security) then the greater the bid–ask spread, the lower the reversibility. Liquidity usually refers to how costly (or cheap) it is to convert a security into cash immediately.

Both reversibility and liquidity will depend on a number of the other characteristics listed above but also on the dynamics of the financial market on which the securities are traded. A *thin* market where there are few trades usually has high bid–ask spreads and can be extremely illiquid. In contrast, *thick* markets where there are thousands of investors trading by the minute tend to have higher reversibility and liquidity and, by extension, investors will have more confidence in this busier market as it is easier to sell (liquefy) assets.

## Complexity

Many financial securities have become extremely complex. However, complex securities tend to be just the bundling together of securities that are less complex. Key players on the financial markets, such as investment bankers, take a basic security and add various criteria and options that make it attractive to either the issuer or investor. Complexity has increased over the past three decades as more companies have looked to the financial markets either to issue or invest. Financial firms have reacted to this demand by creating evermore complex instruments.

## Riskiness

For all financial security purchases, the more unpredictable and variable the return is deemed to be, then the more risky is the initial investment. Begin by looking at financial securities for their riskiness: examine the chances of obtaining the promised cash flow and the impact that a change in interest rates will have on the return of the security – both principal amount and interest.

 **Assessment advice**

Make sure you can discuss all the characteristics that affect financial instruments and their return. Begin to link these characteristics to develop an understanding of how yields are determined. For example, securities with longer maturities will be affected by interest rate changes much more than those of shorter maturities. This is due to the greater uncertainty in the longer term.

## Risk and return

Remember that all financial securities will have some sort of combination of the above characteristics and that this combination will determine a security's price. Also remember that some of the above characteristics are *intrinsic* to the security – that is, they are determined by the issuer, for example the maturity or promised cash flow. Other characteristics are externally determined by the economy or the market on which the security is traded, for example the costs of trading or the market interest rate (in the case of a variable interest security).

When securities first come to the market, issuers will want to obtain as much capital (money) as they can in the most efficient way. In contrast, purchasers or investors will want to assess all the characteristics of the security to ensure that they make the correct purchase decision – in line with their incentives to invest. Investors are commonly referred to as **risk loving**, **risk neutral** and **risk averse**, and this will affect their investment decisions.

All financial securities have some sort of **risk–return trade-off**. Generally, the relationship holds that as the risk associated with a security increases, the return will increase to compensate for the risk, as shown in Figure 2.1. The *x*-axis indicates the risk of the security and the *y*-axis the return. The maroon line indicates the relationship between risk and return in the financial markets, showing that as return increases, the level of risk also increases.

> ### ✳ Assessment advice
>
> Don't be 'put off' by diagrams like Figure 2.1 – they are two-dimensional spaces indicating the relationships between two items. Use them in your answers to assessments. Here the diagram indicates that as return increases, so does risk. The maroon line establishes the relationship between the two items.

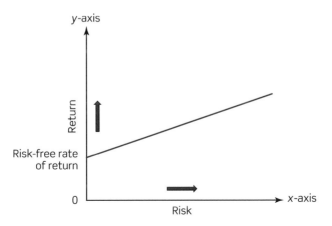

**Figure 2.1** As return on a security increases, so does its risk.

The point where the line touches the *y*-axis is known as the **risk-free rate of return** – this plays an important role in finance and you should familiarise yourself with this idea. It is the rate at which an investor can theoretically obtain a risk-free return. In practice, as we have established, all securities have a risk–return trade-off, however small the risk. The risk-free rate is commonly used in financial models and the rate used is that of the issuer with the least risk. As a result the risk-free rate of return is commonly associated with government-issued securities; in the UK and the United States the three-month Treasury Bill rate is used.

## Recap

All financial securities will sit somewhere within the space between risk (usually indicated by the *x*-axis) and return (usually the *y*-axis). All financial securities have a risk–return trade-off which will be dependent on the security's characteristics. The risk-free rate of return is where you can invest, obtain a return, but bear no risk. This is where the line in Figure 2.1 touches the *y*-axis. It is usually the Tbill rate.

## Test yourself

**Q1.** How is risk related to return?

**Q2.** Draw a diagram showing the risk–return trade-off which should also indicate the risk-free rate of return.

**Q3.** What 'rate' is commonly used to indicate the risk-free rate of return in the UK?

## Key definitions

**Financial security**

A form of IOU which usually provides a return in exchange for cash today.

**Return**

The amount of money made on a financial security, usually expressed as a percentage.

**Coupon**

The promised 'cash flow' or interest rate stated on a security when issued, usually paid twice a year.

**Risk**

The potential for an issuer of financial securities to have inadequate funds to meet their financial obligations can also be viewed as the variance in return on a financial asset and the potential for loss.

**Liquidity**

The ease with which a financial security can be exchanged for liquid assets, usually cash.

**Maturity**

The time it takes for a financial security to pay back in full.

**Inflation**

An increase in the price of goods and services in an economy over time.

**Investors**

Those individuals or companies that purchase financial securities.

## Nominal return, real return, expected return and actual return

There are various returns that may be quoted when discussing financial securities. The most important to distinguish between are: **nominal return; real return; expected return;** and actual return.

### Nominal return

The nominal return is the return before we take account of anything else regarding the security or its return. It does *not* take into account inflation or any associated expenses. For example, if you bought a fixed rate bond for £1,000 with a maturity of one year and an interest rate of 10% then at the end of the year you would receive £1,100 (this equals $1000 + (1000 \times 0.10)$). You may have also come across the term holding period return (HPR) which is more commonly used when looking at equities – it is also a nominal return. The HPR is calculated by taking the price of the equity at the end of the investment period plus any dividends received minus the initial price you paid for the equity, and dividing this figure by the initial price you paid:

$$\text{HPR} = \frac{\text{equity price at end of your holding period} + \text{dividends received} - \text{price paid for the equity}}{\text{price paid for the equity}}$$

## Real return

The real rate of return is the return having taken account of inflation (and any other associated expenses). Taking the above example, how much is the *real* return worth when you eventually receive both the money you lent to the company and any interest payments if the inflation rate during that year was 4%? You received your £1,000 back after one year plus £100 in interest – a total of £1,100 – but given that inflation was 4% then your £1,100 would be worth 4% less in purchasing power than at the start of the year, that is £1,057.69 (this equals £1,100 ÷ 1.04). In this case the real rate of return is 5.769% (this can be approximated by subtracting the 4% inflation from the 10% nominal interest rate to get 6%).

## Expected versus actual return

If we look further at the risk–return diagram, the *y*-axis is expressed as return but more accurately it represents the expected return for a given amount of risk. That is, if a financial security has risk then the return has an associated probability, or chance, of not happening – and this has to be taken into account when calculating the possible returns on a security.

### Recap

All investments have some future degree of risk and therefore all future returns are uncertain – as a result all returns are expected and not actual. The expected rate of return is the 'best guess' forecast. The actual return is the return that an investor actually receives at the end of the investment period and is regarded initially as either the nominal return or real return (if inflation is taken into account). You can only calculate the actual return after you have sold the security and received all your payments. As we will see, financial models provide us with a way of calculating the probability of receiving a return given the characteristics and past behaviour of the same or similar securities.

Given that the characteristics listed above will feature in all securities, it is the proportions of these characteristics that will combine to give the main features of an individual security – and this will help an investor determine its probability of failure or success.

## The basics of pricing financial securities

You will need to be familiar with the various pricing techniques used to calculate returns for investments in financial securities. Below is a run-through of the most commonly utilised ones; use it to check your learning.

## Simple interest return

You purchase a £1,000 two-year UK Treasury Bill (Tbill) that pays 8% on the last day of each year. You *do not* reinvest the return from the first year in the second year. The **simple interest** return equals:

PRINCIPLE + INTEREST ⟶ £1,000 + £1,000(0.08) ⟶ £1,000 + £80 ⟶ £1,080
OR

£1,000(1.08) ⟶ £1,080

If you then take the £80 earned in the first year and keep it at home until the end of year 2, this £80 does not provide you with any further return. In the second year the £1,000 remains invested as you bought a two-year Tbill and it again earns you £80, so the total simple interest return at the end of year 2 is:

PRINCIPLE + INTEREST IN YEAR 1 + INTEREST IN YEAR 2

⟶ £1,000 + £1,000(0.08) + £1,000(0.08) ⟶ £1,000 + £80 + £80 ⟶ £1,160

OR

£1,000 + £1,000(0.08)2 ⟶ £1,160

## Key definitions

**Nominal return**
The actual money received, usually expressed as a percentage.

**Real return**
The return having taken account of inflation and any other associated expenses.

**Expected return**
The amount one would expect to receive from an investment that has various known or expected rates of return. It is the average return given these known 'possible' returns.

## Compound interest return

**Compound interest** is an important concept that you will come across again and again. Ensure that you understand that, when compounding, the investor reinvests the annual return, in this case the 8%, and then the investor earns 8% on the 8% earned in the first year. You *earn interest on your interest* – that is, it is compounded. The first-year return will remain the same as the simple interest figure at £1,080 as you are yet to receive a return; however, once you have received this return, it is reinvested and adds to your final overall return, so that:

PRINCIPLE + INTEREST IN YEAR 1 + SIMPLE INTEREST IN YEAR 2 + INTEREST ON INTEREST FROM YEAR 1

$\longrightarrow$ £1,000 + £1,000(0.08) + £1,000(0.8) + £1,000(0.08)(0.08) (this is for the interest on the interest)

$\longrightarrow$ £1,000[ 1 + 2(0.08) + (0.08)$^2$]  $\longrightarrow$ £1,000[1 + 0.16 + 0.0064]

this is for the two lots of simple interest

$\longrightarrow$ £1,000[1.1664]  $\longrightarrow$ £1,166.4

OR

PRINCIPLE (1 + RATE OF INTEREST)$^n$ (where $n$ = the number of years the investment pays annual interest before maturing)

£1,000(1.08)$^2$  $\longrightarrow$ £1,000[1.1664]  $\longrightarrow$ £1,166.4

PLEASE NOTE WHY THIS WORKS AND WHY WE USE THE POWERS AT THE RIGHT HAND CORNER OF THE PARENTHESIS

## Present value

The present value relies on compounding and the notion that £1 today is worth more than £1 in one year's time. Why? Because you could have placed the £1 in an interest-bearing account and at the end of the year would have had more than £1. As a result, if somebody owes you £1 and pays you in one year's time, the £1 will not be worth as much as the £1 you gave that person one year ago (even before considering inflation). Thus from the examples above you know that if you gave this person £1,000 and charged them 8% interest then you would receive £1,000 × (1 × 0.08) = £1,080. If you lend for longer than one year then the returns will be compounded as in the above example. This means that your £1,000 today is worth £1,080 in one year's time and £1,166.4 in two years' time. £1,000 today is not worth £1,000 in a year's time.

## Test yourself

**Q1.** Explain the difference between the nominal return and real return.

**Q2.** What does compounding mean?

**Q3.** Define present value.

This concept also works in reverse – so that a future amount can be valued today – to obtain the current **present value**, so you can work out the present value of an investment if you are promised a future return (referred to as the future value). So, taking the example above, somebody may promise you £1,166.4 in two years' time. How much is it worth today assuming they promise to pay you 8% per year?

## Key definitions

**Simple interest**
The return from an investment for each time period considered, usually one year.

**Compound interest**
The return on an investment taking into account multiple periods and the interest received on the interest in these periods.

**Present value**
The value today of a future stream of cash flows, given a specified rate of return.

PRINCIPLE $(1 + \text{RATE OF INTEREST})^n$ (where $n$ = the number of years the investment pays annual interest before maturing)

$$£1,000(1.08)^2 \longrightarrow £1,000[1.1664] \longrightarrow £1,166.4$$

So, working backwards:

$$£1,000 \ (\text{PV}) = \frac{1,166.4 \ (\text{CF})}{(1 + 0.08)^2}$$

Again, most textbooks refer to the £1,000 as the Present Value (PV) and the future payments as the Cash Flow (CF). We then have:

$$\text{PV} = \frac{\text{CF}}{(1 + r)^n}$$

The relationship described above is the simple present value and tells you that £1,166.40 in two years' time is the value of £1,000 now if interest rates are 8%. However, having understood this concept it is extended to look at securities that pay back a cash flow at the end of each year with each of those (usually) yearly cash flows having a present value.

Therefore, to calculate the present value today of a stream of payments these payments must first be calculated using the formula above and then added together. This will then give you today's price of, say, a loan, given all the present values of the future cash flows that you will receive:

$$P = \frac{CF_1}{(1 + r)^1} + \frac{CF_2}{(1 + r)^2} + \frac{CF_3}{(1 + r)^3} + \cdots + \frac{CF_N}{(1 + r)^N}$$

where:

$P$ = price

$CF$ = cash flow

$N$ = number of cash flows (maturity of the bond, usually years)

$r$ = discount rate used

Do not be put off by the use of $N$ in the above equation – it is used only to signify that the cash flow can be of any length (or maturity). For example, for a security with a maturity of five years you include five cash flows (CF), so instead of $N$ you would put 5.

### Present value, securities and coupons

As discussed earlier (see Chapter 1) there are a number of different types of financial securities and they have slightly different ways of calculating the present value. The most common will calculate the present value of a coupon-bearing financial security such as a bond. To do this you must add all the present values of the cash flows from the coupon and then add in the present value of the final payment of the face value of the bond. A coupon is the cash flow paid once a year (or usually twice), so if you had a £1,000 face value bond paying an annual 8% coupon then each yearly payment would be £80 (or £40 paid twice). To calculate the present value:

$$P = \frac{C_1}{(1 + r)^1} + \frac{C_2}{(1 + r)^2} + \frac{C_3}{(1 + r)^3} + \cdots + \frac{C_N + F}{(1 + r)^N}$$

where:

$P$ = price

$C$ = coupon

$F$ = face value of bond – received when security matures

$N$ = number  of cash flows (maturity of the bond, usually years)

$r$ = discount rate used

## Asset properties, the discount rate, yield to maturity and the effect on value

The present value is the value today of a string of future payments and it is dependent on a number of factors included in the relationships shown in the boxes above. This is:

- the cash flow or coupon;
- the face value of the bond at maturity;
- the number of cash flows;
- the discount rate.

Given that the coupon, face value and number of cash flows will all be prede-termined, what equates the present value (*P*) of each cash flow to be received in the future with the securities' overall present value is known as the **yield to maturity (YTM)** or **discount rate (DR)**. The factors that affect the YTM have been widely discussed in finance but nobody can be totally sure of the 'cor-rect' rate to use; however, it will be related to the characteristics of financial securities discussed at the beginning of the chapter.

Thus, Fabozzi *et al.* (2010) believe it will be related to the:

- real rate of interest;
- inflation premium;
- default risk premium;
- maturity premium;
- liquidity premium;
- exchange rate premium.

## Recap

Remember, there are two significant features of security pricing, namely the YTM (or discount rate) and the present value:

- All the above bulleted factors are linked to the risk of the security and as such investors (those who purchase securities) will want additional compensation (expected return) as the risk of a security increases (as shown in Figure 2.1). As a result *r* (discount rate) will increase;
- The present value calculation with *r* (discount rate) being used in the denominator means that if the discount rate (YTM) increases then the current price of the security falls – and if the discount rate falls then the current price of the security rises. There is an *inverse relationship* between price and discount rate. Ensure that you understand why this is the case.

So, putting all this together, we get the relationship between the coupon (or interest rate) on the bond, which is calculated on the par value of the bond (say £1,000), and the discount rate (or YTM) that is used to find the present value of the bond. For example, assume a £1,000 par value bond has a maturity of three years and pays an annual interest of £80; the coupon is therefore 8%. The appropriate discount rate will be found by adding all the premiums that investors are asking for: the real rate of interest + inflation premium + default risk premium + maturity premium + liquidity premium + exchange rate premium. This may, for example, come to 10% when added together. Again, remember that this is a best guess figure used as an indicative rate – to best indicate these factors – in order to obtain a present value. In this case, the current price of the bond would be:

$$P = \frac{80}{(1.10)^1} + \frac{80}{(1.10)^2} + \frac{1,080}{(1.10)^3}$$

10% (0.10) discount rate

$P =$ £72.73 + £66.12 + £811.42

$P =$ £950.27

Now, to show the inverse relationship between the discount rate and the price of a bond assume that one of the factors affecting the discount rate changes due to updated information – for example, the inflation rate premium drops. This has the effect of reducing the discount rate from 10% to 9%.

$$P = \frac{80}{(1.09)^1} + \frac{80}{(1.09)^2} + \frac{1,080}{(1.09)^3}$$

$P =$ £73.39 + £67.33 + £833.96

$P =$ £974.68

Note that:

- the coupon rate of 8% stays the same;
- as the discount rate drops, the current price of the bond increases – there is an inverse relationship;
- information may change at any time so $r$, the discount rate, may be different in each time period.

---

### ✳ Assessment advice

You may be asked to distinguish between an interest rate and a return on a security. The interest rate referred to may be the coupon, but the return is the overall value that you receive when you sell the bond (or it matures). This can be thought of in terms of the holding period return so that the return at maturity = the coupon payments/purchase price of the bond + any capital gain, which is the maturity price minus the purchase price, divided by the purchase price.

## Key definitions

**Risk–return trade-off**

The principle that in most cases as risk increases so does (expected) returns.

**Risk appetite**

An investor's or company's 'appetite' for risk.

**Risk-averse investors**

Will only take on additional risk if they are compensated by additional expected returns.

**Risk-neutral investors**

Will concentrate upon expected returns rather than risk, investing in assets for their returns and tend to ignore risk.

**Risk-loving investors**

Will seek high returns but will bear greater risk for a relatively lower expected return.

**Risk-free rate of return**

The rate at which investors can receive a return with certainty. It is usually the Treasury Bill rate.

# Sensitivity

The sample on page 42 shows that the YTM (discount rate) changes to equate the current bond price with the required rate of return. This explains the inverse relationship – if investors demand a higher yield due to changing market conditions then the present value of each cash flow decreases in value and so does the current price (as the yield is the denominator in the present value formula). However, due to different securities having different characteristics any discount rate (YTM) change will have different effects on the current price. The price **sensitivity** of a security will be linked to the characteristics introduced throughout this chapter, represented in the present value calculations as maturity and coupon rate.

This is because the longer the maturity, the more the cash flows have to be discounted, and as you go further into the future the world becomes more risky and uncertain. In order to understand this concept look at the worked example of a three-year security on page 42 – as the discount rate decreased from 10% to 9% the price increased by £974.68 − £950.27 = £24.41. If we complete the same yield change, with the same assumptions, but change the maturity to 10 years, the change in price (sensitivity) to the change in yield is 935.81 − 877.08 = £58.73. Compare this to the price change for the three-year bond with exactly the same characteristics of £24.41.

---

### 10-year maturity bond with a YTM=10%

$$P = \frac{80}{(1.10)^1} + \frac{80}{(1.10)^2} + \frac{80}{(1.10)^3} + \frac{80}{(1.10)^4} + \frac{80}{(1.10)^5} + \frac{80}{(1.10)^6} + \frac{80}{(1.10)^7}$$

$$+ \frac{80}{(1.10)^8} + \frac{80}{(1.10)^9} + \frac{1,080}{(1.10)^{10}}$$

$P = 72.73 + 66.12 + 60.11 + 54.64$

$\qquad + 49.67 + 45.12 + 41.05 + 37.32 + 33.93 + 416.39$

$P = £877.08$

### 10-year maturity bond YTM drops from 10% to 9%:

$$P = \frac{80}{(1.09)^1} + \frac{80}{(1.09)^2} + \frac{80}{(1.09)^3} + \frac{80}{(1.09)^4} + \frac{80}{(1.09)^5} + \frac{80}{(1.09)^6} + \frac{80}{(1.09)^7}$$

$$+ \frac{80}{(1.09)^8} + \frac{80}{(1.09)^9} + \frac{1,080}{(1.09)^{10}}$$

$P = 73.39 + 67.33 + 61.77$

$\qquad + 56.67 + 52.00 + 47.70 + 43.76 + 40.15 + 36.83 + 456.20$

$P = £935.81$

Price change to change in yield = £935.81 − £877.08 = £58.73.

---

Again this is related to risk: the less you get back in each payment, the more risk is being held by the purchaser (investor) in the security. A clear example is a zero-coupon bond which does not pay any coupons with the interest rate being the difference between the purchase price and the par value at which the bond is issued. A zero-coupon bond only pays back on maturity, thus an investor in a five-year, zero-coupon bond has to wait in principle five years without the bond paying back any return – increasing risk. In contrast, with a five-year coupon bond the investor receives some interest each year.

Thus, the lower the coupon on a security (or no coupon), the greater the price change to a change in yield.

## Three-year maturity £1,000 bond with a YTM of 10% and a 4% coupon

$$P = \frac{40}{(1.10)^1} + \frac{40}{(1.10)^2} + \frac{1,040}{(1.10)^3}$$

$P = 36.36 + 33.06 + 781.37$

$P = 850.79$

### YTM drops by 1% - from 10% to 9% (ceteris paribus)

$$P = \frac{40}{(1.09)^1} + \frac{40}{(1.09)^2} + \frac{1,040}{(1.09)^3}$$

$P = 36.70 + 33.67 + 803.07$

$P = 873.44$

Price change to change in yield 4% COUPON = £873.44 − £850.79 = £22.65

Price change to change in yield 8% COUPON = £974.68 − £950.27 = £24.41

AND FOR A ZERO-COUPON BOND:

$$P = \frac{1,000}{(1.10)^3} = 751.31$$

### YTM drops by 1% - from 10% to 9% (*ceteris paribus*):

$$P = \frac{1,000}{(1.09)^3} = 772.18$$

Price change to change in yield ZERO COUPON = £772.18 − £751.31 = £20.87.

### Recap

Note that the price change for the bond with the higher coupon of 8% is greater - however - the % price change (sensitivity) is greater for the lower coupon bond:

4% coupon bond percentage price change = 22.65/850.79 = 2.66

8% coupon bond percentage price change = 24.41/950.27 = 2.57

zero-coupon bond percentage price change = 20.87/751.31 = 2.78

> ## Recap
>
> - The longer the maturity of a security, the greater the price sensitivity to a change in yield.
> - For securities which differ only in their coupon rate – the one with the lower coupon rate will have the greater price *sensitivity* to a change in the yield to maturity.
> - At lower yields to maturity, any changes in the yield will have a greater impact on the current price than at higher yields. This is a marginal effect – the change is greater from 4% to 5% than it is from 10% to 11%.

## Basis points

Each year students lose marks by placing the decimal point in the wrong place when asked a question regarding interest rates and interest rate changes, so remember:

    1 **basis point** = 0.0001 or 0.01%

100 basis points = 0.01 or 1%

and

    a change in interest rates from 5% to 6%   = 100 basis point change in interest rates

    a change in interest rates from 5% to 5.5% = 50 basis point change in interest rates

> ## Key definitions
>
> **Discount rate or yield to maturity**
>
> The rate which equates the present value of each cash flow to be received in the future with the securities' overall present value.
>
> **Sensitivity**
>
> How a security's price is affected by changes in the discount rate (or YTM).
>
> **Basis point**
>
> A term used to denote changes in interest rates. One basis point change is 1/100th of 1%, so a 1% change = 100 basis points, and 0.01% = 1 basis point.

## Test yourself

**Q1.** If you won on a lottery scratch card and had a choice of prizes of either £40,000 for life or a £1 million lump sum then, assuming no tax on both prizes and an interest rate of 5%, what would the prize be worth today if you chose the £40,000 and lived for another 30 years? Which prize would you choose? Why?

**Q2.** What would you expect to happen to a security's price as risk and maturity increase and liquidity decreases? Explain why these characteristics change the price of a security.

**Q3.** What is the difference between a security's convertibility, liquidity and reversibility?

**Q4.** What happens to a five-year coupon bond as the discount rate increases?

**Q5.** Compare the price sensitivity of a £1,000, five-year, 10% coupon bond currently yielding 15% with a £1,000, five-year, 5% coupon bond currently yielding 15%. What happens to price if the yields on both bonds drop by 5%?

**Q6.** If there is a change in interest rates from 5% to 9%, by how many basis points have interest rates moved?

## Examples & evidence

### Why the real interest rate matters: the case of India

Economic agents make their decisions not only on the basis of current economic conditions but also by taking into account future expectations about significant economic variables. For example, workers might bargain for increased salaries on the basis of expected increase in the inflation rate. Consumers may increase consumption on the basis of expected promotions.

Foreign Institutional Investors (FIIs) might flee the domestic market due to expected depreciation of the rupee. Making an expectation, at the economy level, depends on the education level of economic agents. In very primitive societies, generally static expectations work at large. Economic agents in these societies have static expectations irrespective of what is happening in these economies.

In developing economies, adaptive expectations work. Here, generally rational expectations play a role in shaping decisions of economic agents. They take into account not only current information but also likely events while making decisions. For entrepreneurs, the most significant factor determining decisions about investments is the real interest rate. Not only the current real interest rate, but also expectations about its behaviour in the future. In the last two monetary policy mid-term review meetings, the Reserve Bank of India (RBI) has signalled the beginning of a U-turn in its stance by reducing Cash Reserve Ratio (CRR) by 0.25% each time, and indicating a reduction in policy rates in the near future.

It would create a feel-good factor in the economy besides infusing additional Rs 34,000 core worth of liquidity in the system. The expansionary monetary policy would only affect nominal interest rate in the short-run. Investment in the economy would depend on the current and expected future real interest rates. The effect on the expected future real interest rate depends on two factors:

- Whether increase in money supply is resulting in economic agents revising expectations of the future nominal interest rate;
- Whether the increase in money supply leads economic agents to revise their expectations of the future inflation rate.

If, for example, the economic agents expect that the future nominal interest rates would be further lowered and inflation rate would be same or decrease less than the nominal interest rate, so that the net future real interest rate in the economy would be lesser than the current real interest rate, it would have a positive impact on spending (investment) not only in the medium- and long-term but even in the short-run as well.

Similarly, if the inflation rate is expected to increase in future as a result of increase in money supply so that the expected real interest rates decrease by more than the expected future nominal interest rate, it would also have positive impact on spending (investment) in the short, medium and long term. Now that the RBI has assumed a dovish stance, it would help economic agents to expect reduced future nominal interest rate and increased inflation rate in the medium- and long-term, implying reduced expected real interest rates in the future.

It should have a positive impact on production in the short-run as well. It implies that the impact of the current monetary policy stance would be decided by not only the current real interest rate and current level of production but also expected future real interest rate and expected future level of production. When expected real interest rate is down and expected level of income is higher in the economy, they would even increase the production in the short-run too.

*Source:* 'Economic Times', by Anshuman Gupta, University of Petroleum and Energy Studies, Dehradun.

## Questions

The Indian economy is growing at an impressive rate and this article argues that much rests on expectations and the real interest rate:

1.  Define the difference between the nominal and real interest rate.
2.  How is inflation linked to the real rate of interest?
3.  How will ignoring the real interest rate affect investment?
4.  How do changes in interest rates affect present value calculations?

Read Chapter 3 for more on this topic.

## Chapter summary – pulling it all together

By the end of this chapter you should be able to:

| | Confident ✓ | Not confident? |
|---|---|---|
| Define the common characteristics of securities | | Revise pages 30–32 |
| Understand that risk is linked to (expected) return | | Revise pages 32–33 |
| Define and discuss the differences between nominal returns, real return, expected return and actual return | | Revise pages 35–36 |
| Calculate simple interest on a security | | Revise pages 36–37 |
| Calculate compound interest on a security | | Revise pages 37–38 |
| Understand and explain the concept of present value and its relationship with the coupon, yield and maturity | | Revise pages 38–40 |

| | Confident ✓ | Not confident? |
|---|---|---|
| Understand and explain what affects the yield to maturity on a security | | Revise pages 40–43 |
| Understand that as yields on securities increase price decreases – there is an inverse relationship | | Revise pages 40–46 |
| Calculate the present value on a security | | Revise pages 40–46 |
| Understand sensitivity in the present value calculations | | Revise pages 43–46 |
| Define a basis point | | Revise page 46 |

Now try the sample question at the start of this chapter, using the answer guidelines below.

## Answer guidelines

### ✱ Assessment question

Define the key characteristics inherent in all securities. Critically examine why £1 today is not worth £1 in two years' time. Your answer should include a thorough examination of the use of present value calculations.

### Approaching the question

It is key to the understanding of finance in general and specific to this question that you understand the characteristics of securities. Make sure you begin by discussing the relationship between risk and (expected) return – this will then enable you to discuss what influences return: which are a security's characteristics; which make up its risk? Some of these characteristics are internal to the security, examples being the security's maturity, liquidity and unpredictability (or variability) – ensure you know the list of characteristics noted in this chapter. Other characteristics which will influence pricing are external to the security, such as the risk-free rate of return and/or inflation.

The second part of this question is examining your understanding of present value – this is also key in finance as it forms the foundation of many more calculations. Begin this section by discussing simple interest rates and returns and then show that you understand compounding and the effect it has on pricing. Now that you have indicated an understanding of the dynamics of interest rates, show how £1 today is worth less in one year's time given prevailing interest rates (provide an example); if interest rates were 10% then the £1 would be worth £1.10 in one year's time, so the present value of £1 in one year's time is $1/1.1 = 91$p. This example would then allow you to introduce the notion of present value today of £1 promised in a year's time. You should then continue fully to elucidate present value calculations.

## Important points to include:

- Detail the present value formula and explain the denominator and numerator.
- Ensure you discuss all the components of the present value formula, which are: the cash flow or coupon; the face value of the bond at maturity; the number of cash flows; the discount rate.
- Show that you understand the difference between the interest rate on a bond and its discount rate.
- Provide a critical explanation of the discount rate including the factors that influence the discount rate: real rate of interest; inflation premium; default risk premium; maturity premium; liquidity premium; and exchange rate premium (and link these to the first part of the question).
- Explain why there is an inverse relationship between price and discount rate.
- Elucidate sensitivity.
- Discuss any flaws in the present value method.

## Make your answer stand out

You will gain marks by showing a full understanding of the dynamics of asset pricing. Make sure that you provide clear, well-explained examples of the formulae involved in simple interest, compound interest and present value. Again, real-world examples and data of bond prices in the markets (and their movements) will show that you have engaged with the subject and will help increase your grade. Refer to key journals and key academics such as Tobin, Hirshleifer, Fama or Sharpe.

## Read to impress

### Textbooks

Here is a selection of books that introduce the above concepts in an understandable way, each offering a slightly different perspective. It is recommended you start with Fabozzi *et al.*:

Fabozzi, F., Modigliani, F. and Jones, F. (2010) *Foundations of Financial Markets and Institutions*. Pearson Education.

Mishkin, F.S. (2012) *The Economics of Money, Banking and Financial Markets*. Pearson Education.

Pilbeam, K. (2010) *Finance and Financial Markets*. Palgrave Macmillan.

Ritter, L.S., Silber, W.L. and Udell, G.F. (2008) *Money, Banking and Financial Markets*. Pearson Education.

It is also recommended that you try to get hold of Sharpe's seminal text *Investments* (or *Fundamentals of Investments*), though both have been out of print for some time:

Alexander, G.J., Sharpe, W. and Bailey, J. (2000) *Fundamentals of Investments*. Prentice Hall Finance Series.

Sharpe, W. (1981) *Investments*. Prentice Hall.

### Journal articles

Journal articles become very technical very quickly in the areas of risk, asset pricing and the discount rate. As a result, I recommend only a few articles for this chapter, although others, which build upon what you have learnt in this chapter, will be included in subsequent chapters:

Greenbaum, S. (1971) Liquidity and reversibility. *Southern Economic Journal*, Vol. 38 (1), pp. 83–5.

Hirshleifer, J. (1961) Risk, the discount rate and investment decisions. *American Economic Review*, Vol. 51 (2), Papers and Proceedings of the Seventy-Third Annual Meeting of the American Economic Association, pp. 112–20.

Ross, S.A. (1978) A simple approach to the valuation of risky streams. *Journal of Business*, Vol. 51 (3), pp. 453–75.

Ross, S.A. (1995) Uses, abuses, and alternatives to the net-present-value rule. *Financial Management*, Vol. 24 (3), pp. 96–102.

Tobin, J. (Undated) Properties of assets. Yale University.

## Periodicals

Check out the research published by central banks in Europe or the Federal Reserve Banks in the United States – these can provide a clear insight into key topics and advance your understanding:

European Central Bank (2000) Asset prices and banking stability. Banking Supervision Committee, ECB.

Cecchetti, S.G., Genberg, H., Lipsky, J. and Wadhwani, S. (2000) Asset prices and central bank policy. The Geneva Report on the World Economy No. 2, ICMB/CEPR.

## Data sources

Check out the websites of the following for data on financial market securities:

Bank of England

Bloomberg

Investors Chronicle

London Stock Exchange

Morningstar

Reuters

The City UK

The Financial Times

## Companion website

Go to the companion website at **www.pearsoned.co.uk/econexpress** to find more revision support online for this topic area.

## Notes

# 3 Interest rate dynamics

- Determination of interest rates

- Fisher's classical approach

- Interest rate dynamics

- Interest rate determination: The loanable funds theory
  - The supply of loanable funds
  - The demand for loanable funds

- Interest rate determination: Keynes's liquidity preference theory
  - The equilibrium rate of interest
  - Changes in the interest rate: Shifts in demand
  - Changes in the interest rate: Shifts in supply
  - Money supply changes and interest rate changes
  - Liquidity effect
  - Income effect
  - Price-level effect
  - Price expectations effect

- Risk, maturity and interest rates

- The term structure of interest rates:
  - Expectations theory;
  - Liquidity premium theory;
  - Preferred habitat theory; and
  - Market segmentation theory.

A printable version of this topic map is available from **www.pearsoned.co.uk/econexpress**

## Introduction

As financial systems develop, an ever-burgeoning number of securities are created and traded. Remember that companies are creating financial securities that are claims on future production and all securities will have a return which in some way will be linked to an interest rate. What we now look at are the dynamics of interest rates – how interest rates are determined and their term structure. This builds upon on a security's characteristics introduced earlier (see Chapter 2).

Interest rates play a vital role in the functioning of an economy. On a personal level, ask yourself:

- How much money do you want to spend?
- How much do you want to save?
- Why do you want to save at all?
- If you do save, how much 'return' do you want from saving?
- How much risk do you want to bear?

Further, these decisions can be extended to companies and their decisions to spend today or invest. For example, how much will it cost to borrow now and purchase a piece of machinery that will increase output today? As companies make these decisions they will affect economic output, economic growth and standards of living, and so interest rates become important to governments.

The rate of interest is a crucial economic variable which affects the sum of consumption, saving and investment in an economy. To understand whether investment ideas are wealth creating you will need to have a clear understanding of interest rates and the time value of money. This chapter will discuss the different theories of interest rates, the structure of interest rates and the theories that explain the term structure of interest rates. Before continuing, ask yourself: why do people choose to save and why do people choose to borrow?

 **Revision checklist**

*Make sure that you understand:*

- ❑ how the equilibrium interest rate is determined under Fisher's classical approach;
- ❑ the loanable funds theory of interest rate determination;
- ❑ the difference between nominal and real interest rates;
- ❑ how the equilibrium interest rate is determined under the liquidity preference theory;
- ❑ the effects of a change in the money supply on the interest rate;
- ❑ the three theories that explain the term structure of interest rates.

**Assessment advice**

This chapter covers interest rate dynamics. Make sure you understand how the interest rate is determined under the three different theories. This understanding can then be used throughout any exam questions that you undertake in finance. For example, you should know what factors cause shifts in the equilibrium rate of interest. You should also know how changes in money supply affect interest rates. Ensure that you understand the basics from the previous chapter – the characteristics of securities and how they are priced – and bring these into your understanding of interest rate movements. Your lecturer will be looking for an understanding of the basic Fisher model and for you to show understanding of the differences between the 'classic' theory, the loanable funds theory and the liquidity preference theory. Practise drawing the diagrams and think what moves the demand and supply schedules in each theory. Draw the diagrams as part of your answer. Read around the subject – especially Keynes and Friedman. It is always impressive to quote leading relevant names in an exam – it shows that you have prepared.

 **Assessment question**

Critically discuss how equilibrium interest rates are determined under the loanable funds theory and the liquidity preference theory.

Can you answer this question? Guidelines on answering the question are presented at the end of this chapter.

## Determination of interest rates

Like all prices, **interest rates** will be derived by the interaction of demand and supply, in this case the demand and supply of money in the economy. As interest (price) goes up, as is usual, demand for borrowing will decrease (*ceteris paribus*). This is because individuals either cannot afford or choose not to borrow at the higher rate. In addition, company investment in machinery and IT will not produce enough profit to justify the price of investment today.

As price affects demand for borrowing (and therefore investing) in the economy in both the short and long term, the level of interest rates will be a concern to governments in their conduct of macroeconomic policy, particularly monetary policy and future expectations about the conduct of economic policy.

The theory of interest rates usually begins with an explanation of Fisher's classical approach before explaining the two most influential theories of the determination of the *interest* rates:

● Fisher's loanable funds theory; and
● Keynes's liquidity preference theory of interest.

## Fisher's classical approach

**Irving Fisher's classical approach to interest rate determination** looks at an individual's desire to spend or save. This will be influenced by three factors:

● **Marginal rate of time preference**: this is the willingness to defer spending now for more future spending.
● **Levels of income**: the higher the income, the more individuals can usually save.
● **Rate of interest or price for deferring spending today**: usually a higher interest rate will entice more people to save.

The interaction of these factors will help determine total savings in the economy and therefore the funds available for people and companies to borrow (take out loans) as shown in Figure 3.1.

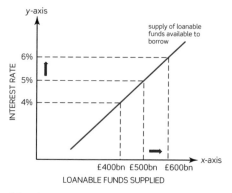

**Figure 3.1(a)** Supply of funds.

### ✱ Assessment advice

You must be aware of what Figure 3.1a shows and be ready to use it where relevant. *Ceteris paribus* it shows:

- a left to right upward-sloping supply curve – there is a *positive* relationship between interest rate and total savings;
- that as interest rates *increase* there will be an increase in saving – making *more* funds available to borrow;
- that as interest rates *decline* there will be a reduction in saving – making *less* funds available to borrow.

Be aware that, just as there is a variable supply of funds from those wishing to save, there will also be a variable demand for funds from those wishing to borrow. Companies will demand funds for projects that will provide a profit (over any costs). This will also be influenced by two factors:

- **Marginal productivity of capital**: this is the gain from investing in the next profitable project (marginal, meaning the gain (or loss) from an increase (or decrease) of the next bit of capital invested). As investment increases, profitable opportunities decline (they dry up).
- **Rate of interest**: in direct contrast to what incentivises the supply of funds, demand will increase as interest rates (or the costs of loans) fall. In essence falling interest rates will affect the marginal productivity of capital because, as interest rates fall, more projects become profitable, which increases the demand for funds. Conversely, if the interest rate is high, firms have to pay more interest for their borrowed funds and this will reduce the amount of profitable projects.

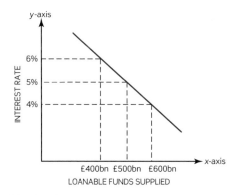

**Figure 3.1(b)** Demand for funds.

The equilibrium rate of interest (equilibrium meaning the state of rest with no tendency for change) is determined by the interaction of the supply and demand functions, which occurs at the intersection of the demand and supply curves. In Figure 3.1c the equilibrium level of savings in the economy is where the quantity of funds people want to save equals the quantity of funds borrowers demand.

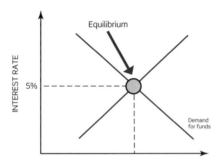

**Figure 3.1(c)** Equilibrium.

To gain a fuller understanding of Fisher's classical theory of interest rates you must begin to question the placement and movement of the demand and supply curves. Why are they where they are? What will move them? This will be down to the interaction of the factors influencing the demand and supply for funds and the level of, and change in, technology. Two examples are the following:

- If new technological advances make production cheaper, then firms will demand more funds at each and every interest rate because each investment becomes more attractive at each and every interest rate: the marginal productivity of capital increases at each and every interest rate (*ceteris paribus* – all other factors remaining the same).

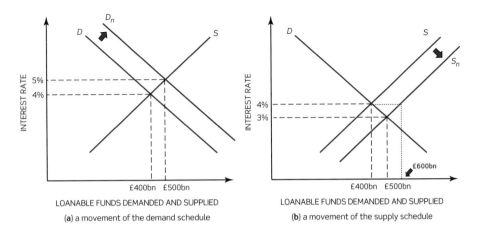

**Figure 3.2** Movement of (a) the demand schedule and (b) the supply schedule in Fisher's classical approach.

- If individuals desire more saving at each and every interest rate, that is there is a fall in the marginal rate of time preference, in this case more funds will be supplied at each and every interest rate.

These two scenarios are shown in Figure 3.2.

What is happening here? For those less familiar with economics let us take the shift of the supply schedule. As individuals now want to save more at each and every price (rate of interest), they are now willing to supply £600bn of funds. However, at the price of 4% only £400bn of funds are demanded. In order for the market to find equilibrium (where funds demanded equals funds supplied) the price needs to drop, so that demand increases and meets supply. This is achieved at 3% and £500bn of funds/investment. In essence competition between lenders to lend funds forces the price down.

You must note:

- As the demand and supply schedules move, so does the interest rate and so does the loanable funds demanded/supplied.
- As marginal productivity of capital increases, more projects become profitable. Firms will demand more funds in order to invest and this has the result of more demand at each and every interest rate. Equilibrium interest rates increase and with them loanable funds (as suppliers supply more funds at the higher rate).
- As society becomes more willing to save at each and every interest rate, the supply schedule moves out to the right. Equilibrium interest rates fall and more projects become profitable for firms, resulting in investment increasing (demand for loanable funds increases).

## Test yourself

**Q1.** Fisher's theory of interest rate determination states that an individual's desire to spend or save will be influenced by which three factors?

**Q2.** Under Fisher's theory, in a two-dimensional space with interest rate denoted on the y-axis and loanable funds supplied on the x-axis, which way will the supply of loanable funds curve slope?

**Q3.** What determines the equilibrium interest rate under Fisher's theory?

## Key definitions

**Interest rate**

The interest rate is the price that a borrower pays to the lender for the use of that money today. The amount of money lent is known as the principal and the price paid for that amount is expressed as a percentage of the principal, namely the interest rate, usually expressed as an annual rate.

**Fisher's classical approach to interest rate determination**

A theory based upon three factors: the marginal rate of time preference; levels of income; and the rate of interest or price for deferring spending today.

**Marginal rate of time preference**

The willingness to defer spending now for more future spending.

## Interest rate determination: the loanable funds theory

The **loanable funds theory** is an extension of Fisher's classical theory to take account of:

- the role of governments and their demand for funds and their ability to create cash;
- individuals and firms holding cash (and not lending or borrowing).

The theory contends that economic agents choose to hold their financial wealth either as interest-earning financial assets or as money – or some combination of the two.

### The supply of loanable funds under the loanable funds theory

The reserve of loanable funds on which interest is determined depends on a number of factors:

- the amount of savings, which includes purchases of financial securities, mortgage repayments, retained profits in businesses, funds for capital depreciation and government savings;

- holding money or saving (and making funds available);
- an increase in loans by financial institutions;
- levels of income;
- levels of confidence (for example, pessimism about the future may lead individuals to save more = a fall in the marginal rate of time preference).

As with the classical theory (*ceteris paribus*) a rise in interest rate will lead to an increase in all the above factors. So, the supply of loanable funds is a positive function of the interest rate – as interest rates rise so does the supply of funds. Hence the supply of loanable funds curve is upward sloping as shown in Figures 3.1a and c. In addition, all the factors above can interact to produce a shift of the supply curve, which may be to the right as in Figure 3.2b – but it may also be to the left.

## Test yourself

**Q1.** How would the above factors have to change to move the supply schedule upwards or downwards?

## The demand for loanable funds under the loanable funds theory

The demand for loanable funds increases with an increase in aggregate demand in the economy stimulated by increases in consumption, investment and/or government expenditure. The demand for loanable funds is also determined by a number of factors:

- investment demand from the private sector or the government sector, perhaps for capital projects like schools, housing or hospitals;
- borrowing for consumption, which increases with consumer confidence in the economy or growth in consumer income;
- money demand by firms and individuals who may want to increase their money holdings – this equals a change in their preferences;
- an increase in future expected income;
- increased probability of a fall in future interest rate;
- a rise generally of confidence in the economy.

Again, as in the classical theory, *ceteris paribus*, a rise in the interest rate will lead to a fall in all the above factors. The demand for loanable funds is therefore negatively related to interest rate: as the interest rate increases, demand falls. Hence the demand for loanable funds schedule is downward sloping as shown in Figures 3.1b and c. In addition, all the factors above can interact to produce a shift of the demand curve which may be upwards as in Figure 3.2a, but it may also be downwards.

## Test yourself

**Q1.** How would the above factors have to change to move the demand schedule upwards or downwards?

As you will have noticed, there are only subtle differences between Fisher's classical theory and the loanable funds theory (which brings in more factors). These are as follows.

The classical approach is based in a simple economy and assumes:

- individuals make two choices, save or consume;
- firms borrow unconsumed income by taking out loans to invest;
- a market for loans;
- projects for investment.

The loanable funds theory extends the classical approach and assumes:

- the introduction of government, which can create money and demand money;
- individuals may hold money.

## ✳ Assessment advice

When answering assessment questions on this topic you should know how to explain the difference between shifts upwards or downwards of the demand and supply curves and movements along the curves. In addition you must also be able to explain what factors move the curves up and down according to the loanable funds theory. Also, be aware of the differences between Fisher's classical approach and the loanable funds theory.

## Test yourself

**Q1.** The reserve of loanable funds on which interest is determined depends on a number of factors. List these factors.

**Q2.** What are the two main differences between Fisher's classical approach and the loanable funds approach to interest rate determination?

# Interest rate determination: Keynes's liquidity preference theory

The liquidity preference theory was developed by John Maynard Keynes. Again, like the loanable funds theory, it examines the interaction of demand and supply, in this case the supply of money and the economy's demand for money. Keynes believed that the **money supply** was fixed by the government.

Key features/assumptions:

- people hold either cash or bonds;
- cash = demand deposits – these are considered equivalent, are liquid and can be spent at no cost;
- demand deposits pay no interest;
- bonds are illiquid and generate interest;
- bonds are long term;
- bond prices vary inversely with the interest rate (and so have a risk element – see Chapter 2);
- bonds are issued by either governments or companies;
- cash is demanded for three reasons: transaction purposes, precaution against unforeseen circumstances and speculation about possible changes in interest rates;
- demand for money will be affected by interest rates – at low rates people will prefer to have the advantages of holding money rather than receive a low return from bonds (look at this another way: people will need tempting out of holding cash by receiving more cash in the future – as the total amount (principal plus interest) falls, so does the desire to save by purchasing bonds);
- the supply of money is entirely under the control of the central bank (Bank of England in the UK, the Fed in the United States) and is not affected by the rate of interest, so the supply of money is the same at all interest rates – this means it is a straight vertical line as shown in Figure 3.3;
- the equilibrium level of interest rate (IR), is determined by the intersection of the demand for and supply of money, as shown in Figure 3.3.

Implications of these assumptions, as argued by Keynes, are that since there is an inverse relationship between the price of bonds and interest rates (as interest rates increase, the price of bonds falls, see Chapter 2), when interest rates are low there is a chance that the next move of interest rates will be upwards, which would result in a fall in the price of bonds.

Conversely, when the interest rate is high people will hold bonds rather than cash as the cost of holding money will be high (they will miss out on high interest payments). In addition, when the interest rate is high a fall in interest rate may be more probable. A fall in the interest rate will increase the price of

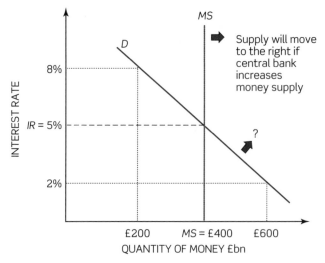

**Figure 3.3** Keynes's liquidity preference and the determination of interest rates.

bonds (making them more desirable for holders to maintain ownership of the bonds). Therefore, at a higher interest rate people tend to hold less money. Think of this as an opportunity cost issue: as interest rates on bonds increase, the opportunity cost of holding money increases.

As a result the demand for money curve, *D*, is a downward-sloping function of interest rate as shown in Figure 3.3. MS refers to money supply.

---

### ✱ Assessment advice

You should be able to explain what Figure 3.3 shows.

In essence it shows the opportunity cost of holding money (as opposed to bonds). The opportunity cost is the cost of forgoing the next best alternative choice. In the diagram, at an interest rate of 8% £200bn of cash are demanded. However, as the interest rate drops the opportunity cost of holding money reduces, so demand increases. That is, if you are holding cash when interest rates are 8% (if we assume interest rates are annual) then you are forgoing £8 in that year for every £100 you hold in cash. If interest rates were 2% you would be giving up only £2 for every £100. The opportunity cost is less, so demand increases. Equilibrium occurs where demand equals the money supply at 5%, which equals £400bn of cash demanded.

---

## The equilibrium rate of interest under Keynes's liquidity preference theory

As with any demand and supply analysis, equilibrium can change with shifts in demand or supply which move the curves.

## Changes in the interest rate: shifts in demand

Keynes identified two factors that, when they change, will move the demand curve:

- Level of incomes in the economy: as incomes rise people will demand more money as a store of value for future occurrences and will also begin to increase consumption and carry out more transactions using cash, so demand for money will increase. In this case demand will increase at each and every interest rate. The demand curve in Figure 3.3 moves to the right (answering the question mark).

- The price level for goods and services – inflation: Keynes believed that people will hold money for what it can purchase in real terms. So if inflation begins to rise the cash that people held last year will no longer purchase the same amount of goods, so they will increase their nominal money holdings to take account of this effect. Again, demand will increase at each and every interest rate. The demand curve in Figure 3.3 moves to the right (answering the question mark).

## Changes in interest rate: shifts in supply

The liquidity preference theory states that the supply of money is under the control of the central bank, meaning that a rightward shift in the supply schedule can only take place if the central bank increases the money supply. This is known as expansionary monetary policy and can be undertaken by central banks to reduce interest rates (*ceteris paribus*). The dynamics are shown in Figure 3.4.

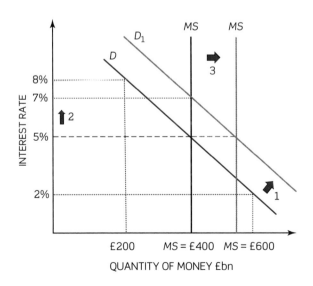

**Figure 3.4** Changes in the money supply and the interest rate.

Figure 3.4 shows:

The first change is the movement of the demand curve to the right from $D$ to $D_1$ (Point **1** in Figure 3.4). This results in a new equilibrium interest rate of 7% as there is no initial move of the money supply (**2**). At this stage more money is demanded but not supplied and as more people are chasing the same amount of money the price (or interest rate) of money increases to 7%. The central bank realises this and wants to return interest rates to 5%. It can achieve this by an expansion of the money supply to £600bn (**3**). As there is now more money in the economy, price (or interest rates) will drop as the initial increase in demand at 5% is accommodated.

To summarise:

- Demand curve $D$ moves to $D_1$.
- $D_1$ meets the $MS$ schedule at 7%.
- $MS$ is expanded by the central bank and interest rates return to equilibrium at 5%.

Note that:

- The interest rate is again at 5% but the money supply has expanded to £600bn.
- As the money supply expands, interest rates will fall (*ceteris paribus*).

## Money supply changes and interest rate changes under Keynes's liquidity preference theory

The main assumption that you may have gained from the above analysis is that as the money supply expands, interest rates fall: interest rates are negatively related to the money supply. However, this has been questioned by the economist Milton Friedman. He concurred that all things remaining the same (*ceteris paribus*) then interest rates would fall, but believed that after an expansion of the money supply, other factors altered.

In his work, Friedman, when analysing the liquidity preference theory, argued that changing the money supply had a number of effects on the level of interest rates. These are the:

- **liquidity effect**;
- **income effect**;
- **price-level effect**; and
- **price expectations effect**.

These effects may not occur simultaneously following a change in the money supply. Some effects are more immediate and one effect may cancel or overcome another. The final magnitude and direction of the impact of a change in money supply depend on the economy's level of output and employment.

## Liquidity effect

As central banks increase the money supply by whatever means (for example, buying bonds and so giving cash to the holders of bonds) then, *ceteris paribus*, when the money supply is increased and the schedule moves to the right interest rates will decline. Interest rates are negatively related to the money supply. This is shown in Figures 3.4 and 3.5.

### Recap

To understand the next effects, you need to consider the secondary effects of an increase in the money supply; so, as the money supply increases, how would it affect demand? If you are confused go back and re-read the factors that shift the demand schedule in the liquidity preference theory.

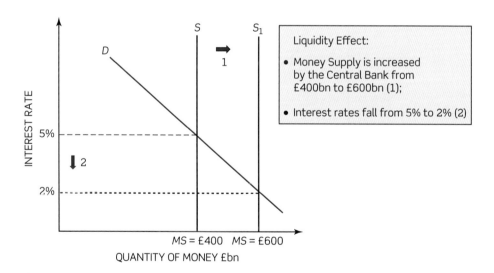

Figure 3.5 The liquidity effect of an expansion in the money supply.

## Income effect

When the central bank increases the money supply it as an expansionary effect and will raise incomes. Banks have more money to lend and the borrowed money will be spent on consumption and investment. More people will be employed and those that are in work may demand higher wages. As incomes rise we know from the liquidity preference theory that demand will increase at each and every interest rate. In this case the demand curve in Figure 3.3 moves to the right as shown in Figure 3.6.

The income effect of the money supply increase may or may not negate the liquidity effect of the money supply increase – the extent of the effect is unknown (as depicted by the question mark next to the 6%) as is the time it takes for this effect to take hold. So where the demand curve comes to rest is unknown, as is the level of interest rates. It will depend on the dynamics of the economy when the money supply changes. This includes such factors as levels of confidence or the means of production.

### Price-level effect

An increase in the money supply can increase the overall price level in an econ-omy and, as we know, as the price level begins to rise the cash that individuals held last year will no longer purchase the same amount of goods. In this case individuals will increase their nominal money holdings to take account of this effect. Demand will increase at each and every interest rate and the demand curve in Figures 3.3 and 3.6 moves to the right.

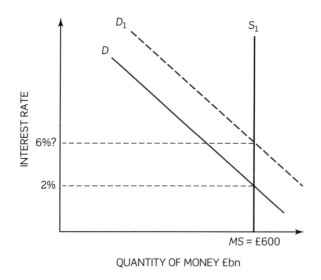

Figure 3.6 Interest rates will rise after an expansion of the money supply.

### Price expectations effect

This effect is linked to the state of the economy: as the money supply rises, if the economy has slack (surplus production that is not being used) then the expansion after the money supply rises may not lead to inflation. If the economy is at full productive capacity then the rise in money supply will garner expectations of a rise in prices in the near future. As expectations of inflation increase, people will demand more money, which in turn will move the demand curve rightwards and as we know this will move interest rates upwards as in Figures 3.3 and 3.6. So in a full-employment economy, an increase in money supply will lead to an increase in interest rate, similar to the income effect. Once again, how much this affects demand is unknown. The difference between this and the price-level effect is that the expectations effect will begin to dissipate once the price level has stopped rising, though the price-level effect will remain.

 **Assessment advice**

You should be able to explain the difference between the liquidity effect, income effect, price-level effect and price expectations effect.

## Test yourself

**Q1.** List four assumptions of the liquidity preference theory.

**Q2.** Keynes identified two factors that when they change will move the demand curve under the liquidity preference theory. What are they?

**Q3.** When analysing the liquidity preference theory Friedman argued that changing the money supply had a number of effects on the level of interest rates. List these effects.

## Key definitions

**Loanable funds theory of the determination of interest rates**

An extension of Fisher's classical theory to take account of the role of governments and their demand for funds and their ability to create cash; and individuals and firms holding cash (and not lending or borrowing). The theory contends that economic agents choose to hold their financial wealth either as interest-earning financial assets or as money – or a combination of the two.

**Money supply**

The stock of cash and other liquid instruments in an economy.

**Liquidity effect in the loanable funds theory**

As the money supply increases, then interest rates will decline. Interest rates are negatively related to the money supply.

**Income effect in the loanable funds theory**

Increases in the money supply have an expansionary effect on the economy and will raise incomes leading to an increase in interest rates.

**Price-level effect in the loanable funds theory**

An increase in the money supply will increase the overall price level in an economy and as the price level begins to rise, the cash that individuals held last year will no longer purchase the same amount of goods. Interest rates will rise.

**Price expectations effect in the loanable funds theory**

As expectations of inflation increase, people will demand more money, which in turn will move interest rates upwards.

## The term structure of interest rates

Securities with identical characteristics will have identical interest rates. However, academics have isolated the effect of maturity on securities with otherwise identical characteristics. Together these are known as the theories of the term structure of interest rates. There are generally four that you should be aware of:

- **expectations theory**;
- **liquidity preference theory**;
- **preferred habitat theory**; and
- **market segmentation theory**.

Before proceeding you will need to become familiar with the yield curve. A yield curve is a plot of the yields on bonds with different terms to maturity but the same risk, liquidity and tax characteristics. It explains the term structure of interest rates for particular types of bonds. It also examines how the yield behaves over time. Typically, the yield curves that are depicted are from the Treasury markets, as these are default free and active.

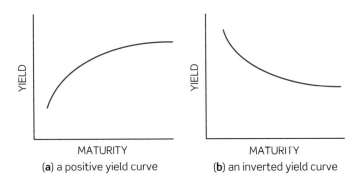

## Expectations theory

The market expectations theory suggests that long-term interest rates are determined by expectations about the path of future short-term (usually one-year) interest rates:

- The yield curve will be upward sloping when the market is expecting short-term interest rates to rise in the future.
- The yield curve will be downward sloping (inverse) when the market is expecting short-term interest rates to fall.
- There will also be the case of a flat yield curve, implying that the market expects the short-term interest rates to be fairly constant in the future.

### Recap

The expectations theory suggests that investors are totally indifferent between holding a short-term bond (one-year maturity) and a long-term bond (say of five years' maturity). They are perfect substitutes. So an investor will be equally content purchasing five one-year bonds one after another as holding one five-year bond for five years.

If we assume that the future path of short-term interest rates is known with certainty then the interest rate on an $n$-year bond ($n$ = the number of years to maturity) under the expectations theory is the arithmetic average of all the future known short-term interest rates. This can be shown as:

This is long-term interest rate with $n$ meaning the number of years to maturity – say 5 years

$$IR_n = \frac{r_0 + r_1 + r_2 + \ldots + r_{n-1}}{n}$$

These are the prevailing interest rates in each year – up until the final year

Assuming interest rates over the next five years for one-year bonds are expected to be 6%, 7%, 8%, 9% and 10%, then interest rates for a five-year bond will be:

$$IR_5 = \frac{r_0 + r_1 + r_2 + r_3 + r_4}{5} = \frac{6\% + 7\% + 8\% + 9\% + 10\%}{5} = 8\%$$

In this case the rising trend in short-term interest rates will produce an upward-sloping yield curve. Think of this as yearly 'pockets' of interest with each 'pocket' giving you a return in each year:

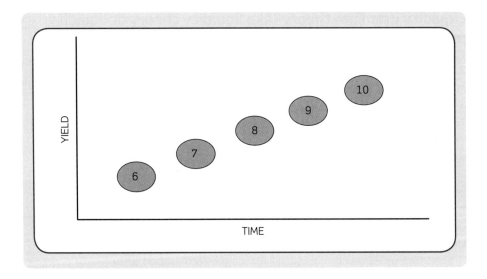

Now, looking at a change in expectations, assume that:

- The yield curve currently is flat.
- Due to the flat yield curve both short-term and long-term market interest rates are 8%.
- Price and interest rate are negatively related.
- Due to some economic news the market expects interest rates to rise in the future to 12%. What happens next?
- Long-term bondholders will be reluctant to hold (or purchase any more) long-term bonds at a lower interest rate than 12% (why?):
  - As it is expected that rates will increase, so the yield curve is expected to rise.
  - As the yield curve rises, the price of long-term bonds declines.
  - Those holding (or purchasing at the current price) will suffer a loss on the value they paid for the bonds.
- There will be a fall in the demand for long-term bonds as bondholders sell (long-term bonds) leading to a fall in price of the long-term bonds;
- The selling process will continue until the price of long-term bonds falls to a level where the interest rate on long-term bonds is also 12%.

However, remember that this theory does not account for risk in the future and if all spot rates were certain then we would know all future rates with certainty, which is not the case.

## Liquidity premium theory (aka liquidity theory or liquidity preference theory)

Given future uncertainty and that investors cannot predict future short-term interest rates, it is rational to expect that the longer the maturity period of a security, the higher the uncertainty associated with the interest rate forecasts. Again this fits in with what we have said about maturity – the longer the maturity, the higher the risk.

Taking into account the time to maturity of a security, the liquidity premium theory states that:

- risk-averse investors will prefer to hold shorter-term bonds than longer-term bonds;
- bonds of different maturities are substitutes but not perfect substitutes – investors must be compensated for longer-term uncertainty;
- bondholders will only hold longer-term bonds when they are compensated for the higher risk (by a 'liquidity' premium).

So the yield on longer-term bonds not only should indicate yearly market expectations of interest rates – as suggested by the expectations theory – but also should include a liquidity premium, which can also be thought of as a 'risk premium'.

---

### ✳ Assessment advice

Be aware of the fundamental idea behind the liquidity preference theory, which is that lenders of funds prefer to lend short, while borrowers normally prefer to borrow long. So borrowers are willing to pay a liquidity premium to lenders to encourage them to lend for longer periods. The size of the liquidity premium normally increases with the time to maturity. The interest rate on an $n$-year bond under the liquidity preference theory can be written as:

$$IR_n = \frac{r_0 + r_1 + r_2 + \cdots + r_{n-1}}{n} + L_{nt}$$

Here the term $L$ is the liquidity premium for an $n$-period bond at time $t$, so for a three-year bond with yearly interest of 3%, 4% and 5%, if the liquidity premium for holding a three-year bond was 0.25% then the interest rate on a three-year bond would be:

$$IR_3 = \frac{3\% + 4\% + 5\%}{3} + 0.25 = 4.25\%$$

# Preferred habitat theory

This is not to be confused with the liquidity premium theory, though it is similar:

- investors will desire a risk premium but the premium may not be solely based upon maturity;
- investors will have a preference for a certain maturity, say one-year bonds or four-year bonds, which is known as their 'preferred habitat';
- in line with liquidity premium theory, in order to tempt investors who 'prefer' two-year bonds to purchasing five-year bonds you will need to offer them a higher 'risk premium' or generally a higher return.

An example of this would be a commercial bank which has liabilities (mostly deposits) of varying maturity and assets (mainly loans) of varying maturities. At any one time a bank may demand, for operational purposes, to invest in a certain maturity of securities in order to manage its liquidity requirements.

# Market segmentation theory

The market segmentation theory of term structure views markets for different bonds as completely separate and segmented. This theory assumes that there are barriers to switching between short-, medium- and long-term investments. This is mainly due to impediments of the free flow of capital from one maturity spectrum to another. In other words, this theory assumes that bonds of different maturities are not substitutes.

Features of the theory:

- changes in interest rates in a particular segment of the market will have little influence on other segments of the market because investors do not shift funds between the various sectors;
- the yield curve is determined by separate supply and demand factors for bonds of different maturities;
- every investor will have a strong preference for bonds of one particular maturity and so they will be concerned with the expected returns only for bonds of the maturity they prefer.

This theory assumes that investors are risk averse, so they operate in their desired maturity spectrum. By splitting the bond market fragments into separate segments, the theory is consistent with the notion of market inefficiency in the pricing of bonds.

## Test yourself

**Q1.** Explain what a yield curve shows.

**Q2.** What affect will the liquidity premium have on yield curves?

**Q3.** Explain the difference between liquidity premium and the preferred habitat theory.

## Key definitions

### Expectations theory

A theory that suggests that long-term interest rates are determined by expectations about the path of future short-term (usually one-year) interest rates.

### Liquidity preference theory

A theory that contends that lenders of funds prefer to lend short, while borrowers normally prefer to borrow long. So borrowers are willing to pay a 'liquidity premium' to lenders to encourage them to lend for longer periods. The size of the liquidity premium normally increases with the time to maturity.

### Preferred habitat theory

A theory that contends that investors (lenders) will have a preference for certain time 'windows' or maturities.

### Market segmentation theory

This theory views markets for different bonds as completely separate and segmented, and assumes that there are barriers to switching between short-, medium- and long-term investments.

## Examples & evidence

Will the economy ever manage to do any better? Goldman Sachs economist Jan Hatzius reckons there's a chance it will turn a corner late next year, provided that Congress doesn't drive the country back into recession. In an interview with Business Insider's Joe Weisenthal, he describes his sectoral balances approach to business cycles:

'[E]very dollar of government deficits has to be offset with private sector surpluses purely from an accounting standpoint, because one sector's income is another sector's spending, so it all has to add up to zero. That's the starting point. It's a truism, basically. Where it goes from being a truism and an accounting identity to an economic relationship is once you recognize that cyclical impulses to the economy depend on desired changes in these sector's financial balances...'

'If the business sector is basically trying to reduce its financial surplus at a more rapid pace than the government is trying to reduce its deficit then you're getting a net positive impulse to spending which then translates into stronger, higher, more income, and ultimately feeds back into spending.'

Mr Hatzius is simplifying a bit here; in practice, the external balance may matter as well. But this is fairly straightforward macroeconomics. At any point in time different sectors of the economy have different levels of desired net saving. If desired net saving rises in one part of the economy (say, the household sector) and isn't offset by falling net saving in other sectors, then a net negative 'impulse' is the result. In other words, the economy experiences a demand shortfall.

Mr Hatzius goes on to note that by looking at trends in net saving behaviour, one can get a sense of how the economy may develop in coming years. He anticipates that net saving by the government will rise in early 2013 (deficits will fall), offsetting the slow, steady fall in net private saving associated with the end of deleveraging. That will net out to a generally weak economy. As 2013 progresses, however, he reckons the pace of fiscal consolidation may slow, and the economy may finally get 'over the hump' into a period of faster growth.

It's an interesting and useful analytical framework. But it leaves open a very big question: just what is governing trends in net saving behaviour across the economy? Consider the private sector. Some households have been severely credit constrained since early in the recession and have had no choice but to deleverage as rapidly as possible. They have been effectively interest-rate insensitive. But other indebted households have been strong enough financially to choose the rate at which they pay down debts. They're not interest-rate insensitive. Neither are the households and firms running surpluses. What Mr Hatzius is effectively saying is that interest rates have been too high, leading to too much saving in the economy and too little growth. And why would that be?

'[O]ne of the big lessons that we've taken away from the past few years is that the zero lower bound on nominal short-term rates is a really big deal because it does get quite a bit more difficult for central banks to provide stimulus once you've hit that zero bound.'

You all know where things go from here. The Fed can provide additional stimulus by pushing down long-term rates relative to their but-for level using asset purchases and forward guidance. But, crucially, it could continue to reduce short-term rates by raising inflation expectations. Mr Hatzius is aware of this and was an important early supporter of a move to shift Fed policy from a focus on inflation to a focus on nominal output, in part because of the importance of expectations. And he, rightly, suggests that the Fed is still some way away from such a shift, precisely because it would mean a different approach to inflation, with which too many central bankers are still too uncomfortable.

But he strays into interesting territory with this line:

'The last chapter hasn't been written yet. What you say is certainly possible. It would be a good outcome, it'd be nice to see. If we found that we haven't gotten that much traction yet with unconventional policy but **the real beauty of it will become apparent when there is a bit of natural velocity in the economy** and the Fed has, by that time, put in place a framework where they're committed not tightening policy for an extended period of time even in a more rapidly-improving economy and labor market. It's possible.'

The emphasis is mine (and note that Mr Hatzius isn't endorsing this outlook, but merely saying such a development would be welcome). I'll admit to occasionally indulging in this hope, as well: that forces within the economy will conspire to raise growth and inflation, and that the Fed—which isn't interested in deliberately raising inflation but which may feel comfortable tolerating a bit above target while unemployment is high—will stand pat, finally allowing expectations to jump and growth to take off. But like Mr Hatzius I suspect this is not how things will play out.

Economic actors are forward looking. If it seems reasonable that growth will accelerate in the future, perhaps for reasons reflected in Mr Hatzius' sectoral-balance analysis, and that when it does the Fed will tolerate more inflation, that should show up in current readings of inflation expectations. Those higher expectations in the present should be stimulative in the present, raising growth now. But that's not what we're observing. The economy is in an expectations trap, in which growth in the present is slow because growth in the future is expected to be slow. One can think of ways around this conclusion; perhaps expectations are low because markets are pricing in a meaningful probability of a bad fiscal cliff outcome, and a benign end to the fiscal drama will quickly raise expectations and launch America out of the trap. But perhaps not.

A change in the trajectory of recovery can only occur when markets expect growth to be faster in the future and adjust their behaviour in the present accordingly. The question is: what sort of change in economic conditions will generate such a shift? I'm sceptical that slow deleveraging can accomplish it; if so, that foreseeable healing ought to be priced into expectations now. Something else, not currently reflected in expectations, will be necessary. Surprisingly loose fiscal policy is one option. Surprisingly robust external demand is another. A third, however, is a surprise change in monetary policy. Maybe Washington's elected leaders will arrive at a benign fiscal deal and the way clear of the expectations trap will be open. If not, the Fed will have to decide whether it would rather sacrifice its sacred cows or accept current employment and growth trends as the best the economy can ever hope to do.

Source: *The Economist*, December 11, 2012.

This article brings to light some of the issues experienced after the financial crisis. Take time to consider how this article is related to the theories that you have read about in this chapter. Especially consider the author's question: Just what is governing trends in net saving behaviour across the economy?

## Chapter summary – pulling it all together

By the end of this chapter you should be able to:

| | Confident ✓ | Not confident? |
|---|---|---|
| Explain that there are two main theories of the level and structure of interest rates | | Revise pages 57–58 |
| Understand and explain how the marginal rate of time preference, levels of income, and the rate of interest affect saving in the Fisher approach | | Revise pages 58–59 |
| Understand and draw the demand and supply schedules relevant to the classical Fisher approach to interest rate equilibrium | | Revise page 59 |

| | Confident ✓ | Not confident? |
|---|---|---|
| Explain what factors may lead to a movement of the demand and supply schedules under the Fisher approach | | Revise pages 60–61 |
| Explain the differences between the Fisher approach and the loanable funds theory | | Revise pages 58–63 |
| Understand and explain what factors move the demand and supply schedules (and therefore interest rates) under the loanable funds theory | | Revise pages 63–64 |
| Discuss the differences between the loanable funds theory and the liquidity preference theory. | | Revise pages 62–66 |
| Explain the key assumptions of the liquidity preference theory | | Revise page 65 |
| Understand what shifts the demand schedule under the liquidity preference theory | | Revise pages 65–66 |
| Understand the immediate effects and the medium-term effects on interest rates of increasing the money supply | | Revise pages 66–72 |
| Understand and explain the difference between the expectations theory, liquidity preference theory, preferred habitat theory and segmented markets theory | | Revise pages 72–78 |
| Explain how the above theories affect the yield curve | | Revise page 73 |

Now try the sample question at the start of this chapter, using the answer guidelines below.

## Answer guidelines

### ✱ Assessment question

Critically discuss how equilibrium interest rates are determined under the loanable funds theory and the liquidity preference theory.

## Approaching the question

The determination of the interest rate is key to understanding the basic concepts of finance. So it is important that you start by defining the interest rate and discuss the key assumptions of the different approaches for determining the equilibrium interest rate. In the introduction make the reader of your exam paper know that you understand the difference between the classical approach, the loanable funds theory and the liquidity preference theory.

## Important points to include:

- Begin by defining interest rate.

- Discuss how the equilibrium interest rate is reached under Fisher's classical approach.

- Draw the diagram showing the demand and supply schedule and the equilibrium point.

- Introduce the loanable funds approach and explain how it differs to the classic approach to interest rate determination.

- Discuss the factors that affect the demand for and supply of loanable funds.

- Explain the factors that move the demand and supply schedules under the loanable funds approach.

- Introduce and explain the key assumptions of liquidity preference theory – how does it differ from the other approaches?

- Discuss the factors that lead to shifts in demand under the liquidity preference theory, referring back to how this may differ (or is similar) to the other theories.

- Explain the central bank's role in setting the money supply and how the money supply may affect the demand schedule (and therefore interest rates) in the short and medium term.

## Make your answer stand out

Your examiner will be looking for a full understanding of the theories – their assumptions and differences. Concentrate on what makes the demand and supply schedules move under each theory. Diagrams will be essential so practise them and use them in your answer. Once you have holistic knowledge of the theories, concentrate on the little things such as the difference between the price-level effect and the expected inflation effect. Again, real-world examples and data of interest rates in the markets (and their movement) will show that you have engaged with the subject and will help increase your grade.

## Read to impress

Here is a selection of books that introduce the above concepts in an understandable way, each offering a slightly different perspective. It is recommended to start with Fabozzi *et al.*

### Books

Fabozzi, F., Modigliani, F. and Jones, F. (2010) *Foundations of Financial Markets and Institutions*. Pearson Education.

Mishkin, F.S. (2012) *The Economics of Money, Banking and Financial Markets*. Pearson Education.

Ritter, L.S., Silber, W.L. and Udell, G.F. (2008) *Money, Banking and Financial Markets*. Pearson Education.

Pilbeam, K. (2010) *Finance and Financial Markets*. Palgrave Macmillan.

It is also recommended that you try to get hold of the work by John Maynard Keynes and Milton Friedman. Try:

Keynes, J.M. (1936) *The General Theory of Employment, Interest and Money*.

Friedman, M. (2011) *Milton Friedman: A concise guide to the ideas and influence of the free-market economist*. Harriman's Economic Essentials.

## Companion website

Go to the companion website at **www.pearsoned.co.uk/econexpress** to find more revision support online for this topic area.

# Notes

**Notes**

# 4

# Risky assets, diversification and the market model

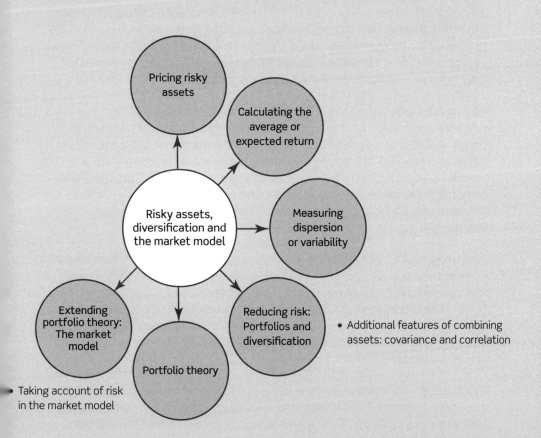

A printable version of this topic map is available from **www.pearsoned.co.uk/econexpress**

## Introduction

Earlier we looked at the characteristics of individual securities and introduced the concept of present value given the level of the interest rate and yield to maturity (see Chapter 2). We also introduced the concept of risk and return: because the future is uncertain the purchasing of any type of security will have some degree of risk – it is an expected return. This is because until you actually receive the promised return there will always be a chance that the issuer of the security defaults on payment and fails to pay you either the principal or interest on the security. Generally, individuals who invest in securities will want compensation for:

- forgoing spending today;
- risk.

Both of these factors will be linked to the attitude of each individual investor and in this chapter we will concentrate on returns given risk and how individuals deal with risk. Essentially this is linked with estimating the chances, known as probability, of a particular asset defaulting and assessing its nominal (or real if inflation is taken into account) **return probability**.

We begin by assuming that every security has a set of possible outcomes with each of these outcomes having a chance of happening. This is referred to as a **return distribution**. Investors calculate the return distribution to find the average (or mean) return over a time period and this provides the expected return. From this you can calculate the deviations away from the mean (or dispersion around the expected return), known as the variance. This is more commonly referred to as the standard deviation, which is the square root of the variance.

Combining assets with different return characteristics into a portfolio alters the return for a given level of risk. This is known as diversification (showing how, by combining securities with varying probabilities of happening, you can gain a more efficient return for the risk that you are bearing). Portfolio theory extends the notion of diversification. Concepts that you must become familiar with are: uncertainty; risk; probability; standard deviation; and portfolio. Take time to understand them.

This chapter will introduce and build upon these concepts and review the workings of portfolio theory, the capital assets pricing model and the arbitrage pricing theory. If at any time you lose your thread, review our earlier discussion (in Chapter 2) and the beginning of this chapter before attempting to move on to portfolio theory and the capital market theories. The chapter begins by introducing risk before taking a look at pricing risky securities.

## Recap

- All securities bear some sort of risk and provide some sort of return.
- The higher the perceived risk, the greater the (expected) return.
- Risk is not the same as uncertainty: risk is measurable; uncertainty is not.

 **Revision checklist**

*Make sure that you understand:*

- ❏ The characteristics of securities and can calculate the holding period return.
- ❏ The definition of probability.
- ❏ What is meant by an equities probability and frequency function.
- ❏ How to calculate the average or expected return on a security.
- ❏ The formula used to express expected return noting that $\Sigma$ means 'sum all'.
- ❏ The calculations used in measuring a securities dispersion or variance.
- ❏ That standard deviation is the most commonly referred to measure of risk and that it is the square root of the variance.
- ❏ How to calculate the variance and standard deviation for a security and portfolio.
- ❏ How to show that a portfolio reduces variance (and standard deviation) and therefore risk.
- ❏ The difference between risk averse, risk neutral and risk loving.
- ❏ What is meant by covariance and correlation.
- ❏ The dynamics of the market model and what is meant by systematic and unsystematic risk.

 **Assessment advice**

This topic tends to be more technical than some others covered in this text, so take your time to understand the basics, the foundations of which are that returns on assets are risky – they are not certain. Analysing returns over time enables the calculation of a distribution given market conditions. Remember that, given certain possible outcomes and their probability of happening, we can calculate the expected return. You will be familiar with some of the terms used, but they may be given different names. For example, the expected return is just the average return. Key to doing well in a question on pricing risky assets is knowing the relationships between possible return outcomes and the associated risk. It is essential that you understand how to present a frequency function and can 'write down' the formulae and explain them fully. The use of diagrams – especially the one representing the market model – will also gain you extra marks, as will knowing that the model was first introduced by William Sharpe in 1963.

 **Assessment question**

Analyse how holding a portfolio of assets helps reduce risk. Explain using the market model why, when holding a diversified portfolio, an investor is only exposed to systematic risk.

Can you answer this question? Guidelines on answering the question are presented at the end of this chapter.

## Pricing risky assets

All securities have a return which can be calculated with certainty after buying and then selling a security. This can be calculated as either the nominal return or the real return (the real return taking account of inflation). However, when purchasing (investing in) a security you will be uncertain of the final return because there will always be risk involved. The general exception to this case is government securities, which are accepted as being risk free (because governments rarely default on their debt obligations). So, a one-year government bond that costs £1,000 and promises a coupon of 4% is known with near 100% certainty that it will pay £40 at the end of the year. Government debt forms the basis by which to compare all other forms of risky investment. As investors know for certain that they can gain 4% without exposing themselves to risk, *ceteris paribus*, they will demand more than 4% for holding risky securities.

In a world where there is complete certainty the interest rate offered to potential investors to invest in a particular security will be linked to their desire to forgo spending which is linked to the characteristics of securities introduced earlier (see Chapter 2), for example liquidity, maturity or divisibility. The previous chapter hopefully gave you some understanding of the determination of interest rate levels. For example, due to their differing marginal rates of time preference, some individuals may only want to invest for short periods of time. Such individuals will be offered a lower rate of return (*ceteris paribus*) because they are forgoing current consumption for a shorter period of time. However, raising longer-term interest rates may change preferences and increase investment (saving) as those wishing to invest only in the short term find it difficult to resist the increased rate of return for long-term investments.

A starting point is to recap on the individual return on an investment introduced earlier. The most commonly used example is the HPR (Holding Period Return). The HPR is calculated by taking the price of the equities at the end of the investment period plus any dividends received minus the initial price you paid for the equities, and dividing this figure by the initial price you paid.

---

 **Assessment advice**

Be aware of how to calculate the holding period return. It forms the foundation of understanding returns of finance and will be tested and utilised across an array of assessment questions:

$$HPR = \frac{\text{equity price at end of your holding period} + \text{dividends received} - \text{price paid for the equity}}{\text{price paid for the equity}}$$

If equities in a company cost an investor £5,000 and they hold the equities for one year, receiving a dividend of £100 and then selling the shares for £5,200, the HPR would be:

$$HPR = \frac{5,200 + 100 - 5,000}{5,000} = 6\%$$

Also note that the same holds for any security:

$$HPR = \frac{\text{selling price of a security} - \text{purchase price} + \text{coupon (if appropriate)}}{\text{price paid for the security}}$$

---

The HPR can be calculated because we know the purchase price, the selling price and the dividend, but investing in the equity would have been risky and when initially choosing to purchase the equities there were any number of possible return outcomes. The listing of the probabilities for an equity is referred to as its probability distribution. The listing of all the possible valid outcomes for the equity alongside the subjective probabilities of the outcomes actually happening is known as the equity's frequency function. An example using the above information is given in Table 4.1.

**Table 4.1** An example of a frequency function for an equity.

| Possible return (%) | Subjective probability | Outcome |
|---|---|---|
| 2 | 0.1 | 1 |
| 4 | 0.2 | 2 |
| 6 | 0.5 | 3 |
| 8 | 0.2 | 4 |
| | **Must add to 1.0** | |

The equity has four possible outcomes, all with a given probability of happening:

- outcome 1 has a 10% chance of occurring and would provide a 2% return;
- outcome 2 has a 20% chance of occurring and would provide a 4% return;
- outcome 3 has a 50% chance of occurring and would provide a 6% return;
- outcome 4 has a 20% chance of occurring and would provide a 8% return.

## Recap

In this example there are only four possible outcomes so the probabilities must add up to 1. A probability of 1 means the event will happen with 100% certainty.

## Test yourself

**Q1.** What is the difference between nominal return and real return?

**Q2.** What is meant by the expected return?

**Q3.** Define probability. What is meant by a probability or frequency distribution for a financial security?

## Calculating the average or expected return

Before moving on to analyse a portfolio (a number of securities held together), consider the average or expected return given the above four possibilities. Averages are used in many subjects and are most commonly calculated by adding up a number of outcomes and dividing by the number of outcomes. For example, if you earned £20,000, £25,000 and then £30,000 over three years your average income over those three years would be £75,000 divided by 3 = £25,000. If we switch to possible returns on an investment as in Table 4.2, there are two ways of calculating the average return which are shown in Example 1 and Example 2. Given that it is extremely unlikely that the subjective probabilities would be the same, the method used in Example 2 is more commonly used.

**Table 4.2** Calculating the expected return for an equity.

|  | Example 1 | Example 2 |  |
| --- | --- | --- | --- |
| Possible return (%) | Subjective probability | Subjective probability | Outcome |
| 2 | 0.25 | 0.1 | 1 |
| 4 | 0.25 | 0.2 | 2 |
| 6 | 0.25 | 0.5 | 3 |
| 8 | 0.25 | 0.2 | 4 |
|  | **1.00** | **1.0** |  |

## Example 1

**All possible outcomes equally probable**

Since all probabilities are the same, the average or expected return is calculated by adding the possible returns together and dividing by the number of outcomes:

$$\text{Expected return} = \frac{2 + 4 + 6 + 8}{4} = 5\%$$

## Example 2

**All possible outcomes not equally probable (0.1, 0.2, 0.5 and 0.2)**

The more common method used to find the expected return given a frequency distribution is to multiply each return by the probability of that return happening and then add each result, which gives the weighted average of possible outcomes. This method should be used when the subjective probabilities are different as in the third column of Table 4.2:

$$\text{Expected return} = 0.1(2) + 0.2(4) + 0.5(6) + 0.2(8) = 5.6\%$$

### Recap

The expected return is higher in Example 2 because the return is more heavily weighted towards a return of 6%; that is, there is a 50% chance that the return will be 6%.

It is common to see the above relationships expressed as a formula. Familiarise yourself with this notation:

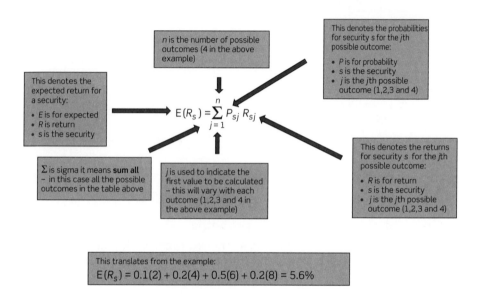

This denotes the expected return for a security:
- $E$ is for expected
- $R$ is return
- $s$ is the security

$n$ is the number of possible outcomes (4 in the above example)

This denotes the probabilities for security s for the $j$th possible outcome:
- $P$ is for probability
- $s$ is the security
- $j$ is the $j$th possible outcome (1,2,3 and 4)

$$E(R_s) = \sum_{j=1}^{n} P_{sj} R_{sj}$$

$\Sigma$ is sigma it means **sum all** – in this case all the possible outcomes in the table above

$j$ is used to indicate the first value to be calculated – this will vary with each outcome (1,2,3 and 4 in the above example)

This denotes the returns for security s for the $j$th possible outcome:
- $R$ is for return
- $s$ is the security
- $j$ is the $j$th possible outcome (1,2,3 and 4)

This translates from the example:
$$E(R_s) = 0.1(2) + 0.2(4) + 0.5(6) + 0.2(8) = 5.6\%$$

What this formula states is that for each possible outcome given in a frequency function for a security, the probability of that return happening ($P$) should be multiplied by its return ($R$) if that outcome occurs and each individual outcome added to each other ($\Sigma$, sigma).

### Test yourself

**Q1.** If a financial security has a return which has an estimated probability of 1 of happening, what does this signify?

**Q2.** How do you calculate an expected return on a security which has a number of possible outcomes that are not equally probable?

**Q3.** What does $\Sigma$ (sigma) signify?

## Key definitions

**Return probability**

The chances of a financial security realising a certain return.

**Return distribution**

A set of possible outcomes for a financial security with each of the outcomes having a chance of happening.

## Measuring dispersion or variance

Once the **expected or average return** has been calculated the next step is to measure how much the actual return differs from this expected value. Remember, risk is the chance of investing in a security and failing to gain the calculated expected return. The difference between the actual return and the expected return for a security (estimated over a period of time) is a measure of its dispersion or variability. An intuitive way to think about this is to examine the *actual* returns for a security and compare this with the *expected* return. Taking Table 4.2, Example 1, there was a 25% chance of achieving a return of 2%, 4%, 6% or 8%, and the expected return given the equal chance of achieving any of these returns was 5%.

What the average or expected return calculates is that over a period of time (say five years) it is 'expected' that the return provided will be 5%. However, in any one return period you may receive less than the expected return, that is 2% or 4% or, more, 6% or 8% (there is a 25% chance of this happening). One way of calculating the deviations from the mean would be to calculate the sum of the differences over time by taking the actual return and subtracting the expected return. In the above example this would be as follows.

### Recap

**How to calculate deviations from the mean**

Expected return from Example 1 = 5%; there were four return possibilities and the sum of the differences between the actual return and the expected return would be:

2% return: $2 - 5 = -3$

4% return: $4 - 5 = -1$

6% return: $6 - 5 = 1$

8% return: $8 - 5 = 3$

Sum of the differences: 0

As you can see, the problem with this method is that the negative and the positive returns cancel each other out and add up to zero, which tells us nothing about the variance or dispersion around the expected value. As a result, two solutions are discussed in the textbooks:

- ignore the minus signs and take absolute values;
- square all the differences, because all squared numbers are positive.

The second solution is most commonly used to measure the variance across all financial assets and portfolios and is the basis by which to calculate the **standard deviation**. The standard deviation is the square root of the variance. Consider the example used in the re-cap box on page 95.

**Table 4.3** Calculating the standard deviation for a security.

|  | Example 1 | Example 2 |  |
| --- | --- | --- | --- |
| Possible return (%) | Subjective probability | Subjective probability | Outcome |
| 2 | 0.25 | 0.1 | 1 |
| 4 | 0.25 | 0.2 | 2 |
| 6 | 0.25 | 0.5 | 3 |
| 8 | 0.25 | 0.2 | 4 |
|  | 1.00 | 1.0 |  |
|  |  |  |  |
| Mean (or expected) return | 5.0% | 5.6% |  |
| Variance | 5.0 | 3.4 |  |
| Standard deviation | 2.24 | 1.84 |  |

---

## Example 1

**All possible outcomes equally probable (all 0.25)**
Deviations of actual returns from the mean return:

2% return: $2 - 5 = -3$ with $-3$ squared $= (-3)^2 = 9$

4% return: $4 - 5 = -1$ with $-1$ squared $= (-1)^2 = 1$

6% return: $6 - 5 = 1$ with 1 squared $= (1) = 1$

8% return: $8 - 5 = 3$ with 3 squared $= (3)^2 = 9$

The average squared deviation (or variance $\sigma_s^2$) is (notice that these values are now all positive):

$$\frac{9 + 1 + 1 + 9}{4} = 5$$

The standard deviation ($\sigma_s$) is therefore $\sqrt{5} = 2.24$.

As a formula the above relationship would be:

$$\sigma_s^2 = \sum_{j=1}^{n} \frac{(R_{sj} - E(R_s))^2}{n}$$

## Recap

This formula in the above example says: 'sum all the squared deviations of the actual return from the expected return for all possible outcomes and divide by all possible outcomes' (all notation is the same as in the above formula for expected return).

## Example 2

**All possible outcomes not equally probable (0.1, 0.2, 0.5 and 0.2)**

If all possible outcomes vary then we follow the same method as we did for finding the expected return in that we multiply the square of the difference by its probability of happening and then add them together:

2% return: $(-3)^2 \times 0.1 = 0.9$

4% return: $(-1)^2 \times 0.2 = 0.2$

6% return: $(1)^2 \times 0.5 = 0.5$

8% return: $(3)^2 \times 0.2 = 1.8$

Variance $\sigma_s^2 = 3.40$

Standard deviation $\sigma_s = 1.84$ ($\sqrt{3.40}$)

The formula of the above relationship for the variance is:

$$\sigma_s^2 = \sum_{j=1}^{n} [P_{sj}(R_{sj} - E(R_s)^2]$$

## Recap

In the above, $\sigma_s^2$ is the variance and $\sigma_s$ is the standard deviation (the square root of the variance).

**Remember:**

$P$ is for probability

$R$ is for return

$s$ is security

$j$ is the $j$th possible outcome

$E$ is for expected

After calculating the variance or standard deviation it must be interpreted – it is essentially a risk measure of how much the security (or **portfolio**) may vary from its expected value.

## Recap

The larger the standard deviation, then the greater the dispersion of future returns from the expected return and therefore the greater the risk.

So in the above examples, Example 1, which has equal chances of returning any of the four possible outcomes, varies from its expected value more than Example 2, which has different probabilities of the four outcomes happening. In this case, the explanation can be found in the 50% chance of a 6% return, which reduces the variance on this security.

## Reducing risk: portfolios and diversification

The relationships that have been described above for an individual security also hold for calculating the expected return and variability of a portfolio of assets. If you are given the same information – that is, if there is a frequency function provided for the portfolio then the expected return on the portfolio and the variance can be calculated – just substitute the portfolio ($p$) for the security ($s$) in the formulae provided.

However, when calculating the frequency function and the variability for a portfolio of securities (a portfolio may comprise any number and types of assets) and comparing it with individual assets within the portfolio:

- the variance (indicating levels of risk) of the individual assets within the portfolio can be higher than for the entire portfolio;
- the average return for individual assets can be less than for the portfolio.

This contradicts what has been explained so far when discussing the risk return trade-off in that higher risk has been equated to higher expected returns. The answer to this is to be found in **diversification** – or what happens when you begin to combine individual assets into a portfolio. Diversification helps because the variance or standard deviation in expected returns associated with an individual asset held in a portfolio can be cancelled out, or reduced, by an alternative variance of another individual asset held as part of the portfolio. This effect means that the standard deviation for a portfolio of assets is less than an average asset within that portfolio. This is shown in Table 4.4.

## Recap

By combining two or more individual assets the combined variances interact with each other to reduce the overall variance, which essentially reduces risk (measured as variance) but maintains return. For further clarity check out the example shown in Table 4.4.

## Test yourself

**Q1.** What is meant by the terms variance and standard deviation with regards to a financial security?

**Q2.** Which formula do you use to calculate the standard deviation for a security when all possible outcomes are not equally probable?

**Q3.** What does a large standard deviation figure signify?

## Key definitions

**Average/expected return**

The amount expected from an investment that has various known or expected rates of return. It is the average return given these known 'possible' outcomes.

**Variance**

A measure of risk which equals the deviations away from the expected or average return (or dispersion around the expected return).

> **Standard deviation**
>
> A measure of risk equal to the square root of the variance.
>
> **Σ (sigma)**
>
> Notation used to mean 'sum all'.

**Table 4.4** Reducing risk by combining assets into a portfolio.

| Market conditions | Subjective probability | Company A asset Return (%) | Company B asset Return (%) |
|---|---|---|---|
| Good | 0.5 | 20 | −3 |
| Bad | 0.5 | 5 | 11 |
| | | | |
| Expected return | | 0.5(20) + 0.5(5) **12.5%** | 0.5(−3) + 0.5(11) **4%** |
| Variance | | 20 − 12.5 = (7.5)² × 0.5 = 28.125 5−12.5 = (−7.5)² × 0.5 = 28.125 **56.25** | −3 − 4 = (−7)² × 0.5 = 24.5 11−4 = (7)² × 0.5 = 24.5 **49** |
| Standard deviation | | $\sqrt{56.25}$ **7.5** | $\sqrt{49}$ **7** |

Before proceeding we will make some assumptions:

- When market conditions are good, company A pays 20% on its issued assets but company B provides a negative return of −3%.
- Expected returns using the formula provided earlier mean the expected return for company A is 12.5% and company B is 4%.
- Company A is known as an aggressive asset – making positive returns when the economy grows.
- Company B is countercyclical – it does better when the economy is in a downturn.

Assume that an investor has £1,000 and invests equally in the two assets:

| Market conditions | Subjective probability | Company A asset | Company B asset |
|---|---|---|---|
| | | Return | Return |
| Good | 0.5 | $0.2 \times £500 = £100$ | $-0.03 \times £500 = -£15$ |
| Bad | 0.5 | $0.05 \times £500 = £25$ | $0.11 \times £500 = £55$ |

The frequency function for the diversified portfolio with equal amounts invested in each asset:

| Market conditions | Subjective probability | Company A/B |
|---|---|---|
| | | Return (%) |
| Good | 0.5 | 8.5 |
| Bad | 0.5 | 8.0 |
| | | |
| Expected return | | $0.5(8.5) + 0.5(8.0)$<br>**8.25%** |
| Variance | | $8.5 - 8.25 = (0.25)^2 \times 0.5 = 0.03125$<br>$8-8.25 = (-0.25)^2 \times 0.5 = 0.03125$<br>**0.0625** |
| Standard deviation | | $\sqrt{0.0625}$<br>**0.25** |

Note that the first part of Table 4.4, shows that if:

- the investor places the £1,000 wholly into company A, the expected return is £125 (12.5%) with a standard deviation of 7.5;
- the investor places the £1,000 wholly into company B, the expected return is £40 (4%) with a standard deviation of 7.

The second part of Table 4.4, shows the effect of diversification, so that if the investor splits the £1,000 equally between company A and company B:

- in 'good' times the investor earns 8.5% or £85(£100 − £15);

- in 'bad' times the investor earns 8.0% or £80(£25 + £55).

The frequency function in the above example shows that:

- the expected return is 8.25%.
- risk or standard deviation is radically reduced (to 0.25) when compared with either of the individual assets held alone (7.5 and 7 respectively).

Overall this indicates that by splitting the £1,000 equally between two separate individual assets (diversifying) and creating a portfolio yields a slightly lower return in the 'good' times and a much higher (twice as much) return in the bad times. Importantly the risk return trade-off has drastically improved as combining these assets has almost eliminated risk.

Whether investors prefer to invest in company A, company B or the portfolio will come down to personal preference. Mostly you will come across reference to those investors that are risk averse, risk loving or risk neutral:

- **Risk-averse investors**: will only take on additional risk if they are compensated by additional expected returns.
- **Risk-neutral investors**: will concentrate upon expected returns rather than risk, investing in assets for their returns and tending to ignore risk.
- **Risk-loving investors**: will seek high returns but will bear greater risk for a relatively lower expected return.

Looking at the above example and generally assuming that the majority of investors are risk averse, then it would be rational to assume that an investor would:

- prefer to purchase the assets of company A rather than company B. Although company B is slightly less risky, company A has a much higher expected return;
- prefer the equally diversified portfolio to company B. The portfolio has higher expected return and lower risk;
- be less certain about whether to invest in company A or the portfolio. The portfolio has a much lower risk but a lower expected return, whereas investing in company A has a higher expected return but more variance (risk) in the return. This would depend on the individual's specific preferences and whether the extra 4.25% expected return compensates for the increased risk.

## Additional features of combining assets: covariance and correlation

The above example has highlighted the assertions that when individual asset returns are combined the effect is to change the risk–return trade-off, making it more efficient. That is, more expected return for an associated risk (as measured by the standard deviation). You must also be aware of an individual security's **covariance** and **correlation**.

In the above example the two assets had very different return characteristics, one doing well in good times, the other doing better in bad times. This helped show the effect of combining assets when we calculated the overall risk and return for the portfolio. Quite how the returns of individual assets are inter-related or how much their returns move up and down together is important in determining the overall risk–return profile of the portfolio. How assets are related to each other is known as the assets' covariance. In the above exam-ple, the individual assets were negatively correlated: given good times one of the assets of company A went up and those of company B went down; given bad times the situation was reversed. By combining these assets risk will be offset as the investor has covered or stabilised their returns in both good and bad times.

## Recap

- Combining assets that are independent, meaning that they have no covariance (in their risk–return trade-offs), will reduce risk (variability) making the expected return more certain. So combining assets that are not correlated has a greater effect on reducing variability (risk).
- Assets do not need to be completely independent to reduce a portfolio's variance.
- Negative covariance means that two assets move in opposite directions given economic conditions (in the example, good or bad conditions).
- Positive covariance implies they move in the same direction given conditions in the economy.
- The difference between covariance and correlation. Covariance can be thought of as related movement given economic conditions – how much do the returns of the assets move together? Correlation is an extremely similar concept and is regularly used as a substitute for covariance. The difference is mathematical – correlation is the calculated covariance of the assets in a portfolio divided by each of the asset's standard deviations added together.

Importantly, this effect of diversification will hold and will give an investor a more efficient risk–return trade-off as long as the assets that are com-bined are not perfectly correlated, which really means that they do not have exactly the same returns in good times and bad times. In the above example, the £1,000 were split equally between the two assets of company A and B but this does not have to the case, it could be any proportion, for exam-ple £100/£900. In all cases the effect on the portfolio returns will be the weighted average of each individual asset's returns placed into the portfolio (the weight referring to the proportion, so in the example 0.5 and 0.5; in the case of the £100/£900 split then 0.1 and 0.9).

## Test yourself

**Q1.** Define risk averse, risk loving and risk neutral.

**Q2.** What is meant by covariance and correlation with regards to a portfolio of financial securities?

## Key definitions

**Portfolio**

A collection of financial securities held together, usually by an individual or group.

**Diversification**

A combination of financial securities with different return characteristics held within a portfolio in order to benefit from a more efficient risk–return trade-off, such that, on average, it will yield higher returns and have lower risk than an individually held financial security.

**Covariance**

The related movement of two financial securities given economic conditions and a measure of how much the two financial securities change together. You are asking the question by how much do the returns of the securities move together?

**Correlation**

Very similar to covariance and regularly used as a substitute. The difference is mathematical – correlation is the calculated covariance of the assets in a portfolio divided by each of the assets standard deviations added together.

## Portfolio theory

The name **portfolio theory** is given to the bringing together of what has been discussed in this chapter and considers the returns on a portfolio given the returns on individual securities within the portfolio. The theory analyses the return on a portfolio of individual assets taking into account the weights given to each security in the portfolio (that is, how much money an individual invests in each security as a proportion of the total invested in the portfolio). It was first introduced by Markowitz in the 1950s. He introduced, like all economists, a number of assumptions:

- individuals will always prefer more wealth than less wealth;
- individuals are risk averse;
- returns on individual securities follow a **normal distribution**, allowing the use of the standard deviation as a risk measure;
- individuals cannot directly affect the probability distribution of an individual security;
- only existing securities are considered.

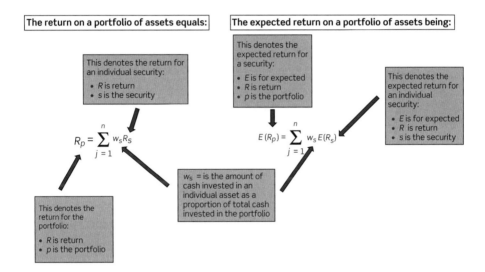

## Extending portfolio theory: the market model

After discussing the risk and return characteristics of individual shares and describing the variance and standard deviation, the textbooks and literature in this area advance to analyse the return on equities and how to predict or explain returns in more detail. Given that research has shown that a portfolio can essentially eliminate unsystematic risk, much of the work has analysed the relationship of individual assets and portfolios to movements in the market in order to assess and predict returns.

### Systematic versus unsystematic risk

If it was possible to bring together a number of individual assets that were entirely uncorrelated then the specific risk associated with a portfolio could be eliminated. This is not possible in reality because assets are affected by the system (or economy) in which they are issued. As was discussed in previous chapters, assets/securities are claims on future production and this production will be dependent in some way on external factors outside the control of individual companies and this production affects returns.

## Test yourself

**Q1.** List the key assumptions of portfolio theory.

**Q2.** Write down the equation used to calculate the expected return on a portfolio.

**Q3.** What is the difference between systematic and unsystematic risk?

Think of this as a game of table skittles where you throw a ball on a chain connected to a pole at some skittles placed on a table. If your aim in this game was to knock down only a few skittles by each throw of the ball, and if you knew the ball could only be thrown in a few different arcs, you would soon learn to place your skittles away from the arcing ball. You would move your skittles away from the specific risk associated with the game. However, if the table collapsed due to the floor (in this case the 'system') on which it was placed giving way, all your skittles would fall on the floor regardless of where you placed them. This event would affect all your skittles despite not being part of the game but part of the greater system on which the game had to stand.

In the same way you can add a myriad of uncorrelated assets to a portfolio and reduce specific (unsystematic) risk, but the portfolio will always be susceptible to systemic risk. Think of the collapse in the financial markets around the world in 2008: even if an investor was holding independently correlated assets issued in a number of different countries, the portfolio would most certainly have been affected by a reduced performance which was undiversifiable.

## Recap

- Unsystematic (specific portfolio or diversifiable) risk can be diversified and be mostly eliminated by investing in independent, uncorrelated assets.
- Unsystematic risk for a portfolio reduces as individual assets are added (up to a point, after a certain number of assets are added (research

suggests about 20) the benefits to the portfolio's standard deviation becomes less and less; in economics this is known as 'the law of diminishing returns').

- Systematic risk (also known as market risk or non-diversifiable) cannot be eliminated by any portfolio.
- All portfolios will suffer market risk as all assets are to some extent affected by market conditions.
- The variance on all portfolios, however well diversified, will depend on the market.

Refer to Figure 4.1.

Given what has been stated, the individual return on a security will have two elements:

Individual security return = systematic return + unsystematic return

Here, common notation is used in all the textbooks to form the formula:

$R = \beta R_m + a$

where $\beta R_m$ is the systematic return $\beta$ = (beta); $R_m$ = market return; and $a$ represents the unsystematic return which is independent of the market's performance (that bit of the return not explained by the market).

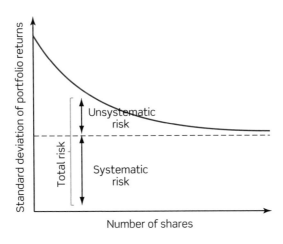

**Figure 4.1** Systematic (or market) risk versus unsystematic (or specific) risk.

**Assessment advice**

It is important to make sure you understand $\beta$ **(beta)** as it underpins the **market model**. It indicates how sensitive the individual security's return is to changes in the market, telling you how the return varies with movements in the market.

Interpreting $\beta$:

- if the $\beta$ value was 3 and if the return for the market was 5% then the systematic part of the return for the stock would be 15%;
- if the $\beta$ value was 2 and if the return for the market was 5% then the systematic part of the return for the stock would be 10%;
- if the $\beta$ value was 0.5 and if the return for the market was 5% then the systematic part of the return for the stock would be 2.5%;
- if the $\beta$ value was $-1$ and if the return for the market was 5% then the systematic part of the return for the stock would lose 5% – the security moves in the opposite direction to the market.

So generally:

- $\beta = 0$ means that the security will not provide a return that is market related – the return will be provided by the unsystematic part of the return (if any);
- $\beta$ between 0 and 1 will return less than the return on the market on the systematic portion of the return;
- $\beta = 1$ will return the same return as the market on the systematic portion of the return;
- $\beta$ greater than 1 implies that the return is more than the return on the market on the systematic part of the return;
- $\beta$ that is negative means returns will be in the opposite direction to the return on the market for the systematic portion of the return.

Interpreting $a$

- $a$ is independent of the market return;
- $a$ is the unsystematic portion of a securities return and will be unique to the company issuing the asset – for example, an increase in productivity from staff will increase performance, adding to the overall return on the security;
- $a$ is diversifiable in line with what has been stated in this chapter. As this part of the return is unique to the security, combining and diversifying many securities will inevitably reduce variance.

At this stage and to form the market model $\alpha$ is broken up into two components $\alpha$ and $e$ so that:

$a = \alpha + e$

where $\alpha$ **(alpha)** is the expected (or average) value of $a$, that is the expected value of the unsystematic return, and $e$ represents the uncertain part of $a$ and is random and thought of as being zero over time. This is because it is the 'pure' specific return for a particular company which is unexpected and as such random and unpredictable; over time these events will cancel each other out – that is, tend to zero (often referred to as the 'error' term).

Putting all this together we get Sharpe's (1963) **market model** (see Figure 4.2):

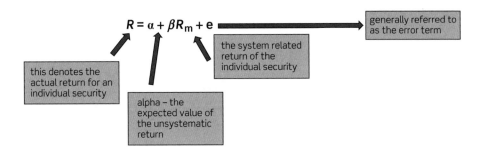

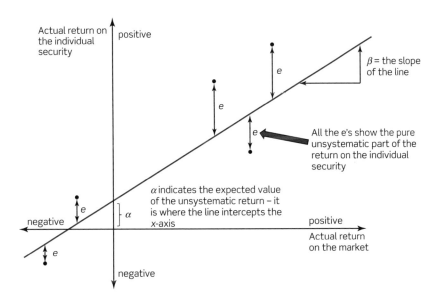

**Figure 4.2** A graphical representation of the market model.

What the market model and Figure 4.2 show and mean is as follows:

- all the black dots represent returns on an individual security over time;
- the maroon line is known as the line of best fit through the calculated returns (this is the regression line of best fit);
- given the line of best fit, any deviation from this line is the error of the regression and in the market model represents the pure unsystematic risk of the individual security $e$;
- $\beta$ is the slope of the line and its value informs us of the relationship between the security and the market (as above, if the slope of the line is 2 (that is, $\beta = 2$) if the return for the market was 5% then the systematic part of the return for the stock would be 10%);
- $\alpha$ represents a constant and is the expected value of the unsystematic return of the security – that is, if there was no movement in the market this would be the return from this individual security.

## Taking account of risk in the market model

Using Sharpe's market model leads to the definition of **systematic and unsystematic risk**, which is the standard deviations of what makes up the return – namely, the systematic and unsystematic returns (if this is confusing, recap on variance and standard deviation – understanding will come from understanding the expected return and standard deviation on a security described above).

Thus we have the systematic risk equal to $\beta$ multiplied by the standard deviation (risk) of the market return:

$$\text{systematic risk} = \beta\sigma_m$$

With the unsystematic return coming from the variance or in this case its extension, the standard deviation of the pure unsystematic return gives:

$$\text{unsystematic risk} = \sigma_e$$

And assuming that $\alpha$ is constant (stays the same over time), the individual security risk is given by:

$$\text{total risk on an individual security} = \beta\sigma_m + \sigma_e$$

This is usually extended to the portfolio by adding together the portfolio's systematic risk and the portfolio's unsystematic or specific risk. The portfolio's systematic risk is given by:

$$\text{systematic risk on a portfolio} = \beta_p\sigma_m$$

which is the $\beta$ value for the portfolio multiplied by the risk (standard deviation) of the market. The specific risk on a portfolio is given by the weighted standard deviations of the individual securities within the portfolio:

specific risk on a portfolio $= \sum_{j=1}^{n} w_s \sigma_{es}$

Putting this all together gives the total portfolio risk:

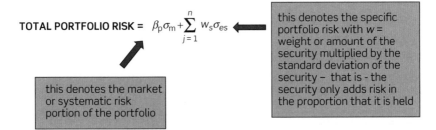

TOTAL PORTFOLIO RISK $= \beta_p \sigma_m + \sum_{j=1}^{n} w_s \sigma_{es}$

this denotes the specific portfolio risk with $w =$ weight or amount of the security multiplied by the standard deviation of the security – that is - the security only adds risk in the proportion that it is held

this denotes the market or systematic risk portion of the portfolio

It is also the case that the $\beta$ value for a portfolio is the average of the individual security $\beta$'s weighted by the amount of each individual security in the portfolio such that:

$$\beta_p = \sum_{j=1}^{n} w_s \beta_s$$

this denotes that the beta for the portfolio is the sum of all the individual beta's for the entire portfolio – with each beta being weighted by how much of that security is represented in the portfolio

## Test yourself

**Q1.** Which two elements combine to make up the individual return on a security?

**Q2.** What does $\beta R_m$ and $a$ signify when considering the individual return on a security?

**Q3.** If the $\beta$ value was 2 and if the return for the market was 5% then calculate the systematic part of the individual return.

**Q4.** In the market model alpha ($a$) is broken up into two components $\alpha$ and $e$. What do these signify?

**Q5.** What does the equation below signify? State the meaning of each of its component parts.

$$\beta_p \sigma_m = \sum_{j=1}^{n} w_s \sigma_{es}$$

At this point you may be thinking, so what? But the above relationships in the market model mean that:

- if all securities in the market were in the portfolio then $\beta$ would equal one;
- the unsystematic risk of a portfolio with diversification will tend towards zero (as explained in this chapter);
- individual security systematic risk is equal to the security's $\beta$ multiplied by market risk $\sigma_m$ (as indicated by the standard deviation);
- the portfolio systematic risk is the weighted average of all the individual security risks.

## Key definitions

**Portfolio theory**

The analysis of how investors can use diversification to construct a portfolio to minimise risk and maximise returns.

**Normal distribution**

Signifies that the different returns for a given security will be clustered around the expected return and will be symmetrically distributed above and below the expected return.

**Market model**

A model that states that the return for an individual security and by extension a portfolio will equal systematic return plus unsystematic or specific return of the (weighted) securities within the portfolio.

**Systematic risk of security**

The influence that outside or economic 'system' events have on the returns of a financial security.

**Unsystematic or specific risk of a security**

Risk events that only influence that particular financial security.

**$\beta$ (beta)**

A measure of how sensitive an individual security's return is to changes in the market or 'system', describing how the return varies with movements in the market.

**$\alpha$ (alpha)**

Represents a constant and is the expected value of the unsystematic return of the security. That is, if there was no movement in the market, this is the return from this individual security.

## Examples & evidence

DIVERSIFICATION is always cited as a good thing when investing. Spread your bets, and you will not be exposed to a sudden collapse in a single company, sector or economy. But for equity investors the task is getting harder and harder. International markets seem to be increasingly correlated.

In part, this may be down to the diversification process itself. Investors buy an exchange-traded fund based on the MSCI world index, or US mutual funds venture into more exciting emerging markets. Either way, a loss of confidence among such investors may cause a worldwide sell-off (as research shows: **http://www.economist.com/node/21528640**).

But it may also be that companies have diversified themselves. The table, from Orrin Sharp-Pierson at BNP Paribas, shows the proportion of corporate revenue that comes from various countries. So, for example, Canadian companies get 11.5% of their revenues from Europe; UK companies get 20% of their revenues from emerging markets.

**Corporate revenue exposure by area**

| % | Emerging markets | Developing Asia | Japan | Europe | North America | Implied revenue |
|---|---|---|---|---|---|---|
| GDP*, 2012 forecast | 11.1 | 7.0 | 0.9 | 2.5 | 2.5 | — |
| Canada | 9.2 | 0.6 | nil | 11.5 | 78.7 | 3.32 |
| Europe excl. Britain | 25.1 | 0.4 | 0.5 | 52.7 | 21.4 | 4.68 |
| Japan | 13.1 | 0.5 | 68.6 | 7.7 | 10.4 | 2.57 |
| Britain | 20.0 | 1.1 | nil | 46.2 | 32.7 | 4.28 |
| United States | 15.6 | 0.7 | 1.9 | 19.2 | 62.5 | 3.86 |
| Developing Asia | 36.8 | 35.4 | 1.7 | 13.3 | 12.8 | 7.24 |

Source: BNP Paribas                                                    *% change on previous year

So let us assume that revenues grow in line with GDP. Combine the mix of revenues, and GDP growth forecasts for 2012, and you can figure out how the revenues of national corporate sectors might grow. The result can be surprising. You might assume that the US economy will do better than the UK economy this year. But because of the UK's exposure to emerging markets, UK revenues will actually grow faster.

However, what is striking about the last column is how similar the numbers are; with the exception of non-Japan Asia, they are all in a range of 2.6–4.7%. Diversification does not get you very far.

There is a silver lining to this cloud, for investors at least. The ability of companies to diversify their sources of production means they can control their costs. That may explain why profit margins are so high. Of course, this does not seem quite such a wonderful thing if you are a worker in the West.

*Source:* Globalisation and diversification, *The Economist*, February 23, 2012, by Buttonwood.

## Question

Relate how this analysis may be linked to diversification and the market model. Putting real-world examples into your exam answer will help boost your grade. Think how what the author is saying relates to systematic and specific risk and portfolio theory.

## Chapter summary – pulling it all together

By the end of this chapter you should be able to:

| | Confident ✓ | Not confident? |
|---|---|---|
| Calculate the holding period return on a security | | Revise page 91 |
| Define and explain probability and understand probability and frequency functions | | Revise pages 90–92 |
| Calculate the expected return on a security | | Revise pages 92–95 |
| Understand and explain the notation used in expected return, portfolio theory and market model formulae | | Revise page 94 |
| Understand and calculate the variance and standard deviation for a security and portfolio – knowing the difference between variance and standard deviation | | Revise pages 95–98 |

| | Confident ✓ | Not confident? |
|---|---|---|
| Show how a diversified portfolio reduces variance | | Revise pages 98–102 |
| Define and explain the difference between risk-loving, risk-neutral and risk-averse investors | | Revise page 102 |
| Explain covariance and correlation within a portfolio | | Revise pages 102–104 |
| Show how the market model extends portfolio theory and how it explains systematic and unsystematic returns and risks | | Revise pages 104–112 |
| Provide and explain a diagram representing the market model | | Revise page 109 |

Now try the sample question at the start of this chapter, using the answer guidelines below.

## Answer guidelines

### ✳ Assessment question

Analyse how holding a portfolio of assets helps reduce risk. Explain using the market model why, when holding a diversified portfolio, an investor is only exposed to systematic risk.

Can you answer this essay-type question? Guidelines on answering the question are presented below.

## Approaching the question

Begin by introducing a single security and explain – using a frequency distribution – how holding a single security has 'risky' outcomes. Ensure that you fully explain your key terms – this is regularly ignored by students. Define variance and standard deviation and explain that these are terms used to calculate the dispersion around the expected return (stating that the expected return is the weighted average return given all possible outcomes). Once you have fully explained the risk on a single security, present a frequency distribution of two securities and combine them together in a 50/50 holding and show how this reduces variance (and standard deviation). To gain a higher grade introduce the concept of the 'risk-averse' investor.

The second part of the question is testing your knowledge of the market model. Begin by explaining that it was first introduced by William Sharpe in 1963. Define systematic and unsystematic risk and draw a diagram showing the difference between them. Explain that a security's return is made up of systematic and unsystematic returns – and begin to use the common formula notation and explain the notation fully. Begin to develop the model by explaining that the unsystematic return is broken down into alpha, the expected part of the unsystematic return, and an error term which is the 'pure' unsystematic return. At this point draw the market model diagram and place all the notation used in the formula on the diagram to show understanding. Once you have completed this, move on to analyse beta, explaining that the value of beta for a portfolio is the weighted values of beta for the individual securities and that the specific risk on a portfolio is given by the weighted standard deviations of the individual securities within the portfolio; again use the common notation. Complete your answer by referring to the question and summarising how after diversification an investor will only be exposed to systematic risk.

## Important points to include:

- Fully explain key terms such as risk, variance and standard deviation.
- Use the formula notation – write the formulae into your answer and explain them fully.
- Draw the appropriate diagrams and take your time to label them fully and correctly.
- Refer to the question repeatedly and remain 'on message'.
- Define unsystematic and systematic risk.
- Define what is meant by the market model.
- Write down the market model formula and label correctly using the common notation.
- Draw the market model diagram and label correctly.

## Make your answer stand out

This question is testing your knowledge and understanding of risk and why holding a variety of assets with different variances will reduce risk (for a given return). It is important that you explain your key terms and that all formulae are utilised and labelled correctly. Use of appropriately labelled diagrams will make your answer stand out. Once again, knowing and stating the research in this area will help your answer gain much higher marks – for example, in Keith Pilbeam's book he states research by Solnik where, after 20 shares, adding additional shares to a portfolio has only marginal benefits. Also, risk reduction via diversification cannot be reduced below 34.5%, that is an investor will be left with a significant portion of systematic risk despite diversification. Stating this research would achieve a higher grade. Further, if you introduced a variety of research in this area which is not from the textbooks, this would make your answer stand out in a crowd.

## Read to impress

### Textbooks

Here is a selection of books that introduce the above concepts in an understandable way, each offering a slightly different perspective. It is recommended to start with Fabozzi *et al.*:

Fabozzi, F., Modigliani, F. and Jones, F. (2010) *Foundations of Financial Markets and Institutions*. Pearson Education.

Pilbeam, K. (2010) *Finance and Financial Markets*. Palgrave Macmillan.

Ritter, L. S., Silber, W.L. and Udell, G. F. (2008) *Money, Banking and Financial Markets*. Pearson Education.

It is also recommended trying to get hold of William Sharpe's seminal text *Investments* (or *Fundamentals of Investments*) but both have been out of print for some time:

Sharpe, W. (1981) *Investments*. Prentice Hall.

Alexander, G.J., Sharpe, W. and Bailey, J. (2000) *Fundamentals of Investments*. Prentice Hall Finance Series.

### Journal articles

As has been stated, journal articles become very technical very quickly in the area of risk, asset pricing and the discount rate. I would recommend reading Sharpe's 1963 article introducing the market model:

Sharpe, W. (1963) A simplified model for portfolio analysis. *Management Science*, Vol. 9 (1), pp. 277–93.

## Periodicals

Check out the research published by central banks in Europe or the Federal Reserve Banks in the United States – these can provide a clear insight into key topics and advance your understanding:

European Central Bank (2000) Asset prices and banking stability. Banking Supervision Committee, ECB.

Cecchetti, S.G., Genberg, H., Lipsky, J. and Wadhwani, S. (2000) Asset prices and central bank policy. The Geneva Report on the World Economy, No. 2. ICMB/CEPR.

## Data sources

Check out the websites of the following for data on financial market securities:

Bank of England

Bloomberg

Investors Chronicle

London Stock Exchange

Morningstar

Reuters

The City UK

The Financial Times

## Companion website

Go to the companion website at **www.pearsoned.co.uk/econexpress** to find more revision support online for this topic area.

# Notes

**Notes**

# 5 The operation of the money markets

A printable version of this topic map is available from **www.pearsoned.co.uk/econexpress**

## Topic map

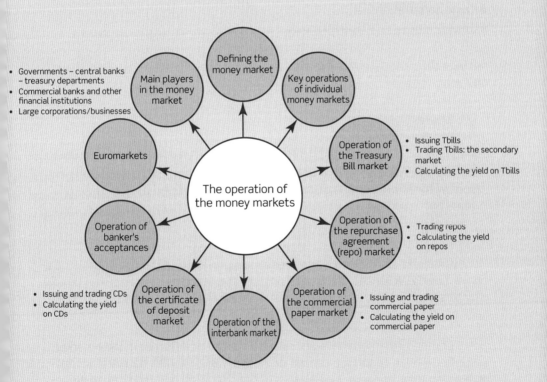

## Introduction

In previous chapters we looked at the rational for a financial system, the characteristics and pricing of financial assets, the dynamics of interest rates and how equilibrium rates are determined, and in the previous chapter we reviewed risky assets, the effects of diversification and the market model. This chapter moves back into the territory of the first chapter examining the structure of one of the key financial markets – the money market. Be aware that not all textbooks will have a chapter on money markets and may take each security traded in the money market and examine it separately; however, it is key to your understanding of financial institutions and markets that you understand the dynamics of the financial money markets.

The money market is a segment of the financial markets where:

- wealthy individuals,
- large financial institutions,
- large corporations, and
- governments and central banks

manage their short-term cash needs, short-term being defined as less than one year.

### Recap

Money markets allow those with short-term excesses of cash to invest for short periods of time and those with short-term cash obligations to borrow for short periods of time. Short-term is defined as less than one year.

Money markets are utilised when these main players find themselves in a position of having either too much cash or too little, but they are unsure as to how long this position may continue – meaning they may well require their money back or find themselves with more to invest.

Users of money markets have access to a variety of different money market securities. These securities consist of Treasury Bills (**Tbills**), bankers' acceptances, commercial paper, certificates of deposit (CDs) and repurchase agreements (repos). These were all introduced earlier (see Chapter 1; go back and recap on the basics of these instruments if you are unsure), but in this chapter we look at the operational dynamics of these different securities as they are traded on the money markets.

## Revision checklist

*Make sure that you understand:*

- ❑ How to define the various money markets, what money markets are used for and who uses them.
- ❑ The key features of money markets.
- ❑ The operation of each individual money market.
- ❑ How each market issues its securities and then trades them.
- ❑ How to calculate yields on all the main money market instruments.
- ❑ LIBOR and its worldwide significance.
- ❑ The operations of each of the main players on the money markets. Why do they use the money markets?

## Assessment advice

This chapter covers the different types of money markets and the key players in the money market. This understanding can then be used throughout any exam questions that you undertake in finance. For example, you should be able to explain the different money market securities and how they function. You should also to able to explain the key players in the money market. Ensure that you understand the basics from the previous chapters, the characteristics of securities and interest rate dynamics, and bring them within your understanding of money market securities. Key to scoring a high grade is to understand fully the actual operations of the money markets: How are the individual securities issued? How are they traded? How is the yield for each instrument calculated? The answers to these questions will help you come to terms with how the markets actually work and this will bring your answers to life. In addition, check out the central bank websites for up-to-date information on money market dynamics. This will make your answer stand out.

## Assessment question

Money markets play a key role in the financial system:

(a) Explain the different types of money markets and how they function. (70 marks)

(b) Who are the main players in the money markets and why do they choose to use the market? (30 marks)

Can you answer this question? Guidelines on answering the question are presented at the end of this chapter.

## Defining the money market

The money market is a market that trades short-term securities, it has an active secondary market which is extremely liquid, and all the main players have excellent credit ratings and money circulates rapidly.

This is because the main players in money markets, take for example large companies, will not receive payments for goods at exactly the same time when they need to pay for goods or services (or any other costs associated with running their business). Sometimes they will have too much cash and sometimes too little. If they have too much cash and do not invest the excess, they will be missing out on potential interest. If they have too little cash, they will need to borrow to pay their current creditors. Cash positions for all the main players on financial markets will be dynamic and change on a daily basis. The use of the money market allows them to manage their cash positions at the margin – gaining interest on excesses of cash and having rapid access to cash when required.

Key features of money markets:

- Securities traded in the money market are highly liquid and have a year or less to maturity (the majority being less than three months). Remember, a liquid security is one which can be readily bought and sold for cash.
- They are **wholesale markets** where the securities traded are sold in large denominations in excess of £1 million.
- Money market participants have a healthy **credit rating**, meaning that the traded securities are low in **default risk**, so money market securities can be viewed as risk free or having an extremely low risk of default.
- Transactions in the money market do not take place in any one particular location, traders arranging transactions over the phone and/or electronically.
- Money market securities have an active secondary market. A secondary market is where already issued securities are traded. The presence of an active secondary market makes money market securities extremely liquid (easily saleable), so much so that money market securities are commonly referred to as cash investments.

### Recap

Money markets exist to move cash to where it is required immediately and allow those who find themselves with short-term excesses of cash to invest immediately (but allowing them to convert back to cash immediately when required). The amount of securities (over a short period of time) is relatively fixed; it is the buying and selling of these securities again and again that allows the main players to manipulate their liquidity positions. This increases the efficiency of the economy and can lead to higher economic growth.

## Test yourself

**Q1.** Why would the main users of money markets need to manage their liquid assets?

**Q2.** List four key features of money markets.

## Key operations of individual money markets

A range of money market instruments are available to fulfil the varied needs of market participants and each security can be viewed as trading on its own delineated money market. The main money markets are the Treasury Bill market, commercial paper market, bankers' acceptances, certificates of deposit market, repurchase agreement market and Eurocurrency deposits. The main participants will trade on different money markets depending on their requirements.

## Operation of the Treasury Bill market

### Recap

Treasury Bills (Tbills) are short-term debt instruments issued by a country's government in order to help finance the country and/or manipulate the amount of cash in the economy. They are issued in the UK in minimum denominations of £5,000 at a discount to their face value for any period not exceeding one year. Although they are usually issued for three months (91 days), on occasion they have been issued for 28 days, 63 days and 182 days.

Key features:

- Pay a set amount at maturity.
- Have no interest payments.
- Sell at a discount, that is a price lower than you will receive at maturity (effectively, this becomes the interest rate). For example, you buy a 91-day Tbill for £4,700 which can be redeemed for £5,000.
- Most liquid of all financial securities.
- Most actively traded security on the money markets.
- Almost no risk as it would require the government to default (Tbills are often referred to as the risk-free rate of return).

- They are known as fixed income securities because the purchaser of the security knows the amount they will receive from the Tbill at the time of purchase. However, their price fluctuates in line with any change in market or current interest rates.
- Bought and sold mainly by banks.

### Issuing Tbills

The operations of the Tbill market will be similar for most western-style economies. Each week the Treasury department of a country (for example, the US Treasury) will announce the amount of new 13-week and 26-week Tbills that will be auctioned to the market that week. Active participants, for example securities dealers, financial institutions or even individuals, will submit bids to the central bank by a certain date/time. In the Unites States announcements are made on a Thursday and bids must be received by Monday, with those wishing to submit a bid submitting either a competitive or an uncompetitive bid.

### Competitive bid

All bidders place bids stating the amount of Tbills they want and the price they will pay. The central bank examines all bids, sets a price and fulfils all bids received at, or above, the set price. All winning bids pay the same price. The highest bidder receives their allocation first, then the next highest until that week's Tbill issue has been fully allocated. Bids are placed as a percentage of the face value of the Tbill, so for example a typical bid may be 99.55%.

### Uncompetitive bid

The bidders state the quantity of Tbills they want and agree to pay the price set by the central bank under the competitive bid. All uncompetitive bidders receive their allocations before the competitive bidders – they take preference. Uncompetitive bids are limited in value in the US market.

There are other ways of issuing Tbills, as follows.

### Tender issue

The central bank sets a minimum price and invites bids at or above this minimum price. Interested parties bid and when all bids are in the central banks calculate the price at which that week's allocation will be fully absorbed by the market. Those bidding above the minimum price receive all their stated allocation with any remaining Tbills allocated on a pro rata (proportional) basis to those bidding the actual minimum price.

### Direct placement

The central bank negotiates a price for a set amount of Tbills with a number of financial institutions. This may be used as part of overall monetary and/or economic policy.

## Recap

If financial institutions purchase Tbills it reduces the amount of cash that those financial institutions are holding because cash is transferred from the institutions to the central banks to pay for the Tbills.

### Public issue

The central bank offers Tbills at a fixed price.

In the UK Tbills are issued:

- by allotment to the highest bidder at a weekly (Friday) tender to a range of counterparties;
- in response to an invitation from the Debt Management Office to eligible counterparties;
- at any time to government departments (Bank of England website);
- to 'Treasury Bill Primary Participants', which totals 27 banks including those like Barclays and HSBC (counterparties are not publicly stated).

### Trading Tbills: the secondary market

The **secondary market** is essential and a key part of the Tbill money market, allowing those who have purchased Tbills to sell them quickly and those who wish to purchase Tbills to buy them quickly. Key players in this market are those designated by the central bank to 'make a market' in the buying and selling of issued Tbills. In the United States those designated are known as 'primary government securities dealers' and in the UK as 'Treasury Bill Primary Participants'. Make a market means they will actively buy and sell Tbills on a daily basis for their own account and for their customers who may wish to buy and/or sell Tbills.

These officially sanctioned participants must therefore offer continuous bid and ask prices on outstanding Tbill issues. 'Bid' refers to the price at which the **primary market** participants will purchase your Tbills and 'ask' is the price at which the primary participants will sell you Tbills. The secondary Tbill market is an over-the-counter (**OTC**) market and has no physical location since trades take place by telephone.

## Test yourself

**Q1.** Describe the various ways that Tbills may be issued.

**Q2.** What affect does selling Tbills have on the banking sector?

## Key definitions

**Short-term**

Used when referring to financial securities with a maturity of less than one year.

**Credit rating**

A 'rating' given to a company or financial security indicating ability to pay back the debt and chances of defaulting.

**Money markets**

Refers to markets that trade short-term securities.

**Wholesale markets**

Markets that are used by financial institutions, large companies and governments to transact in large quantities, most commonly hundreds of thousands of currency. These markets are not usually available to private individuals.

**Default risk**

The chance that a company or counterparty will not be able to pay back their debt.

**OTC**

Over The Counter, a term used to denote a type of market that has no physical location, where trading takes place electronically without a formal exchange.

**Tbill**

Treasury Bill, a short-term government issued security.

**Primary Market**

The market where financial securities are first issued.

**Secondary Market**

The market where financial securities, once issued, are traded.

## Calculating the yield on Tbills

Tbills are **issued at a discount** by governments. This means that they are sold at a price less than their par (or face) value, which is the price you will receive when the Tbills mature. The return is calculated as the difference between the price paid for the Tbills when purchased and the par value of the Tbill when it matures. For example, you may have paid £950 for a Tbill whose par value is £1,000.

The yield on Treasury bills is found by calculating the discount yield using the formula:

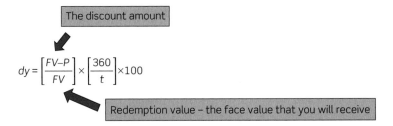

The discount amount

$$dy = \left[\frac{FV-P}{FV}\right] \times \left[\frac{360}{t}\right] \times 100$$

Redemption value – the face value that you will receive

where:

$dy$ = discount yield
$FV$ = face value paid to the Tbill holder at maturity
$P$ = purchase price of the Tbill
$t$ = is the number of days until maturity

Using the above example the discount yield would be:

$$dy = \left[\frac{1000 - 950}{1000}\right] \times \left[\frac{360}{182}\right] \times 100 = 9.89\%$$

The discount yield is not the actual return that the investor would receive, because in the above formula the redemption value of the bill has been used and not the purchase price of the bill. To convert the discount yield into the yield enjoyed by the purchaser of the Tbill, you need to change the denominator in the formula, thus:

$$ay = \left[\frac{FV - P}{P}\right] \times \left[\frac{365}{t}\right] \times 100$$

where:

$ay$ = the actual yield received by the investor

So the actual annualised yield on a six-month (182 days) £1,000 par Tbill that was bought for £950 will be:

$$ay = \left[\frac{1000 - 950}{950}\right] \times \left[\frac{365}{182}\right] \times 100 = 10.53\%$$

This states that if you purchase a Tbill today for £950 which has a face value of £1,000 and a maturity of six months then you will receive a yield of 10.53%, which is comparable with the bond equivalent yield.

The differences between the discount yield and the actual annualised yield are:

- Instead of using the purchase price as the denominator, the discount yield uses the face value, which is the price you receive when the Tbill matures.
- A 360-day year is used.

## Operation of the repurchase agreement market

A repurchase agreement (**repo**) is a transaction in which one party sells a financial asset to another party and agrees to repurchase an equivalent value of financial assets at some time in the near future. For example, a bank will sell Tbills to a company (providing liquidity to the bank) with an agreement (with the company) that the bank will 'repurchase' the Tbills at a slightly higher price sometime in the near future, say one week. The rise in price equals the interest rate charged by the company (lender) for borrowing the cash. The term **reverse repo** is also used: this is where one party buys Tbills from another party and agrees to sell them back at a future date. All repo transactions are both repo and reverse repo transactions because each transaction has a buyer and a seller – it just depends on which side of the transaction you are on. Determining whether it is a repo or reverse repo usually depends on who initiated the deal in the first instance.

In the UK the gilt repo market was introduced in January 1996 and quickly became a major tool with which the Bank of England could provide refinancing to the banking sector. Within three months of its introduction, over 50% of refinancing by the Bank was provided by the gilt repo and almost 50% of open market operations by the Bank were undertaken using the gilt repo. The value of gilt repos outstanding at banks and other financial institutions had expanded to an average of over £319 billion during 2009.

Key features:

- can be extremely short term, 1 to 14 days, and involve large denominations usually over £20 million;
- in contrast transaction can be for up to three months and tend to be lower denominations, usually over £5 million (this market is not as busy);
- the difference between the sell and buy-back price, providing the return, is known as the repo rate;
- very low risk because transactions are backed by Tbills.

---

### ✳ Assessment advice

Be aware of how repos are traded:
- It may be a direct transaction between two parties or involve a broker.
- If direct, money is transferred from the buyer of the Tbills' account to the seller's account.
- When the repo matures the money is transferred back to the buyer plus interest and the Tbills are returned to the seller.

- They are used by central banks as part of their overall monetary policy to make short-term adjustments in the money supply.
- Used by others to manage their short-term liquidity and speculate on interest rate changes.

## Calculating the yield on repos

Essentially the same as the equivalent bond yield above so that you attain the annualised yield between the selling price on the Tbills and the repurchase price. Assuming a 365-day year it would be:

$$\text{yield} = \left[\frac{R_p - P_s}{P_s}\right] \times \left[\frac{365}{t}\right] \times 100$$

where:

$R_p$ = the price at which the Tbills are to be repurchased (selling price plus interest)

$P_s$ = the price at which the Tbills are sold to the buyer

$t$ = days until the repo matures

So, if, in the UK, Barclays Plc. agrees to sell Tbills to Lloyds Plc. for £5 million (receiving £5 million worth of cash liquidity) and buy the Tbills back after two days for £5,001,010 then the yield on this repo deal attributable to Lloyds would be:

$$\text{yield} = \left[\frac{R_p - P_s}{P_s}\right] \times \left[\frac{365}{t}\right] \times 100$$

$$\text{yield} = \left[\frac{5,001,010 - 5,000,000}{5,000,000}\right] \times \left[\frac{365}{2}\right] \times 100 = 3.69\%$$

### Test yourself

**Q1.** What is meant by 'repo' and 'reverse repo'?

**Q2.** What short-term security is used in the process of lending and borrowing in the repo market?

**Q3.** How do you calculate the yield on a repo?

131

## Operation of the commercial paper market

**Commercial paper** is an unsecured, short-term debt issued by a corporation and having a maturity of between 1 and 270 days. Companies with excellent credit ratings issue commercial paper because it is cheaper than raising finance via a loan with an intermediary such as a bank. The commercial paper market thrives when the economy is strong and the number of failing companies is decreasing, reducing default risk. Potential purchasers of commercial paper will refer to a company's credit rating to assess the risk; typical credit rating agencies include Moody's or Fitch. Commercial paper is sold at a discount to its face value and like Tbills with discount yields being calculated based on a 360-day year.

Key features:

- Sold in varying denominations, for example £100,000; £500,000 and £1 million.
- Maturity is less than 270 days. In the United States this is because of regulations requiring companies offering debt with a maturity higher than 270 days to issue via the more costly corporate bond market.
- The higher the credit rating given by Moody's or Fitch to the company issuing commercial paper, the lower the rate of interest the issuing company will have to provide to incentivise people to purchase its commercial paper.
- Generally, the lower the difference (spread) between commercial paper interest rates and Tbill interest rates, the lower the default risk and the stronger the economy. As the spread between Tbill rates and commercial paper rates widens, it usually signifies the markets' view that default risk is rising (that is, companies are failing) which is usually an indication of an economy slowing down.
- If companies have a poor credit rating they can obtain a 'letter of credit' from a bank – this means that if the company fails, the bank that has written the letter of credit will pay off the commercial paper issue. The bank charges for this service and the company benefits from higher demand for its issue as well as a lower interest rate (piggybacking on the credit rating of the bank).

### Issuing and trading commercial paper

The key aspects are as follows:

- When sold directly to a buyer it is referred to as a direct placement, or when sold indirectly by dealers, it is known as dealer paper in the commercial paper market.
- It is issued in primary commercial paper. There is not an active secondary market with the dealer (usually an **investment bank**) buying back the issue if necessary.

- Investment banks are heavily involved in this market and will underwrite an entire issue: the investment bank will set the discount rate on the issue; use the bank's established reputation and contacts to sell the issue before it even comes to market; and manipulate the issue if necessary to ensure the whole issue is sold.
- Issuing directly to a buyer saves the fees of the investment bank but the issuing company must set its own discount rate and take the time to find a buyer, which will increase (search) costs.
- When issuing directly to the market, the issuer must decide how much they wish to issue and then post rates to buyers to assess demand. They will adjust rates in line with demand in order to clear the issue.

### Calculating the yield on commercial paper

Commercial paper yields are calculated in the same way as Tbills using the discount yield, which can then be converted to the actual annualised rate (bond rate equivalent). Ensure you recap on these formulae.

## Key definitions

**Issued at discount**

Issuing financial securities at less than their face value or price on maturity. The 'discount' is the difference between the price received for a financial security at maturity and its issue price.

**Repurchase agreement or repo**

A transaction in which one party *sells* a financial security to another party and agrees to repurchase an equivalent value of financial securities at some time in the near future.

**Reverse repo**

This is where one party *buys* financial securities from another party and agrees to sell equivalent financial securities back at a future date.

**Commercial paper**

An unsecured, short-term debt issued by a corporation and having a maturity of between 1 and 270 days

### Operation of the interbank market

The **interbank market** is one of the most significant of the money markets, mainly because it allows financial institutions to adjust their liquidity (cash holdings) immediately by borrowing and lending wholesale funds among themselves for periods ranging from overnight to 12 months. It is decentralised and there is no specific location or exchange. By using such borrowings, banks are able to hold less cash throughout the year on their balance sheet because they know that if they require additional cash, they can go to the interbank market. It also allows those banks that have found themselves with too much cash on a particular day (due perhaps to an increase in retail deposits) to gain interest on a short-term basis.

## Recap

Banks will utilise the markets to finance lending, to balance out fluctuations in their balance sheets, and to speculate on future movements in interest rates. Dealings in the interbank market are direct or through one of the many electronic brokering platforms, with Electronic Broking Services (EBS) and Thomson Reuters Dealing 3000 Xtra both providing these services.

There is a high degree of correlation between **LIBOR** (London Interbank Offer Rate) and the rate of interest in the Tbill market. If banks have a shortage of cash they will tend to sell Tbills to increase their cash holding, which will mean that the price of Tbills will fall but the Tbill rate will rise (recall the inverse relationship between price and interest rate). The shortage of cash in the banking sector means less cash available in the interbank market, which then increases the costs of unsecured lending and the LIBOR rate increases. In contrast, an increase in cash in the banking sector will lead banks to buy Tbills, the price of Tbills will increase and the Tbill interest rate will fall. The increase in cash in the interbank market will lower LIBOR.

Key features:

- The amounts involved are large, starting from £500,000, but £10–12 million is not untypical.
- The main players in this market are the large financial institutions.
- The rate at which a financial institution can borrow unsecured funds on the interbank market is known as LIBOR (London Interbank Offer Rate).
- LIBOR is a benchmark rate. It is an average of the lending rates of the 'contributor' bank.
- The British Banking Association (BBA) has a group of contributor banks which report their lending costs for that day between 11 a.m. and 11.10a.m.). The BBA asks the question:

*At what rate could you borrow funds, were you to do so by asking for and then accepting inter-bank offers in a reasonable market size just prior to 11 a.m.?*

- LIBOR is calculated for 10 currencies (for example, $LIBOR, £LIBOR and €LIBOR) for 15 different maturities from lending overnight to 12 months.
- The reported rates (all 150 of them: 10 multiplied by 15) are reported to Thomson Reuters who then discard the highest and lowest contributions (the top and bottom quartiles) and use the middle two quartiles to calculate the average. This is called a 'shaved mean' or 'trimmed mean'.

- Thus LIBOR represents the lowest reported average cost of unsecured funding in the London market.
- LIBOR is used as a reference rate for many financial instruments globally. For example, the Swiss National Bank uses LIBOR as a reference rate to determine monetary policy.
- LIBOR acts as a global reference rate (across its 10 quoted currencies) for over $360 trillion derivatives, loans and mortgages.

Recently the financial world has been shaken by reports that a number of British banks are involved in the LIBOR rate-rigging scandal. These banks have been found guilty of fixing LIBOR for their own benefit. Since LIBOR rates act as an international benchmark, this rigging can lead to a massive fraud affecting the entire financial system. Ensure you are aware of this scandal.

## Test yourself

**Q1.** Define commercial paper. What types of banks are heavily involved in this market?

**Q2.** What short-term security is used in the process of lending and borrowing in the repo market?

**Q3.** List the processes involved in the daily calculation of LIBOR.

## Operation of the certificates of deposit market

**Certificates of deposit (CDs)** are issued by banks and are similar to retail time deposits. However, unlike retail time deposits, in which individuals deposit cash with a bank for a period of time in return for interest, CDs are issued wholesale to market participants (again, usually banks or other financial institutions) and have a stated interest rate, maturity rate and amount. They are generally negotiable (meaning saleable) and have a thriving secondary market. The existence of the secondary market is important because it allows initial purchasers of CDs to sell them quickly and liquidate their position but also benefit from receiving a rate of interest.

## Recap

Banks benefit from the issuing of CDs because it increases flexibility in banks' balance sheet operations as they will not be as reliant on retail deposits. In addition, due to the CDs' liquidity (on the secondary market), banks can issue CDs with a lower interest rate (holders can always trade them if they want liquidity).

Most large CDs are held by banks, investment funds, institutional investors and money market funds. CDs can be issued in any major currency. Some term CDs pay floating interest rates, where the rate of interest varies from time to time in accordance with the changes in the base rate of interest. CDs may also be issued at a discount and without a coupon. The rate of interest is strongly related to the current market rate on sterling interbank deposits of a corresponding maturity.

Key features:

- CDs are usually issued for three months', six months' and 12 months' maturities.
- Negotiable CDs range from £100,000 to £10 million in value.
- CDs issued for maturities longer than a year are known as term CDs and can have maturities up to five years.
- CDs can be both negotiable and non-negotiable. A negotiable CD can be sold by the initial depositor in the open market before maturity.
- Non-negotiable CDs are held by the depositor until it matures.

Issuing and trading CDs

Key aspects are as follows:

- Banks which want to raise cash by selling CDs will publish the relevant interest rates for the maturities they are offering, for example 1 month, 6 months or 12 months.
- Negotiable CDs will be issued for common amounts, say £100,000.
- Larger CDs may gain a higher interest rate.
- CDs may be negotiated directly with the purchaser, to set the interest rate, maturity and amount.
- Interest rates on CDs are quoted using a 360-day year.
- Term CDs pay interest semi-annually.

## Calculating the yield on CDs

### Recap

Recap on the methods discussed earlier (see Chapter 2). If a bank issues a 6-month CD with a value of £100,000 and an annual interest rate of 3%, then if the purchaser held the CD until maturity they would receive 1.5% (3% annual interest but only issued for six months) of £100,000 which is £1,500:

Return = £100,000[1 + (0.03/2)] = £101,500 = £1,500

## Operation of bankers' acceptances

A **banker's acceptance** is a short-term financial instrument that increases certainty in the buying and selling of goods between two parties. Essentially the payment for the goods received by the purchaser is guaranteed by the bank – the bank has 'accepted' the risk that the purchaser of the goods will fail to pay. This reduces the financial risk of the seller of goods not receiving payment for the goods they have supplied. It is called a banker's acceptance because the bank 'accepts' and guarantees payment. It is commonly used to assist trade between two companies of different countries where a short-term draft written by a company to pay a certain sum of money in the future is guaranteed by the bank in case the purchaser defaults. Thus the exporter increases their certainty of payment from an importer of which they could not be certain of payment.

Issues and trading of bankers' acceptances:

- An exporter agrees to sell goods to an importer.
- The importer then attains a letter of credit from their domestic bank.
- The bank informs the exporter that when the goods have safely arrived the exporter can draw a time draft for the amount of the letter of credit with the importer's bank.
- The exporter then ships the goods and presents evidence of shipping to their own bank, which informs the importer's bank.
- The importer's bank stamps the draft 'accepted' and the draft becomes a banker's acceptance.
- Bankers' acceptances have an active secondary market. They pay low interest as the risk of default is low, requiring both the importer and the importer's bank to default.
- Like Tbills and commercial paper they can be traded at a discount from face value.

## Euromarkets

**Euromarkets** are where deposits and loans of a domestic country (such as short-term deposits or loans) are held in a foreign country. For example, Eurodollars are short-term deposits or loans made in dollars outside the United States. Similarly Eurosterling is pounds held and utilised in New York and Paris, and Euroeuros are euros held and utilised in the United States and the UK. Due to the stability of US dollars, many contracts around the world prefer payments in US dollars and so many companies and governments choose to hold dollars. Eurodollars can be held by anyone and importantly are not subject to the regulations which US-based financial institutions must comply with. The Euromarket began in the late 1950s/early 1960s due to countries such as Russia and China who had large reserves of US dollars from trading but did not want to hold these dollar reserves either in the United States or with US banks. They therefore started holding them with a French bank in Paris. In addition, UK banks were restricted in their sterling activities to foreign residents and so turned to dollars. Generally, the rise of the Euromarkets can be directly linked to an attempt to circumvent prevailing regulations.

Key features:

- The centres of Eurobanking are London, Paris, Luxembourg and Frankfurt.
- Offshore centres include Bahrain, the Bahamas and the Cayman Islands.
- Eurobanking is also undertaken in the United States.
- Regulation free – no reserve requirements for the Eurobanks.
- Main users are Eurobanks, other financial institutions, multinational corporations and central governments.
- The key interest rate is LIBOR.
- Eurobank assets and liabilities tend to be short term.

## Key definitions

**Investment bank**

A bank that offers many services to corporate clients, traditionally underwriting new share issues, acting as broker and trading on behalf of clients.

**Interbank market**

A market where (mainly) banks lend and borrow from each other for short periods of time, usually less than one week but more commonly overnight.

**LIBOR**

The London Interbank Offer Rate is the average rate that banks will lend to other banks on the London interbank market.

**Negotiable instrument**

A piece of paper or document promising to pay a fixed sum of money on demand or at a certain date. As it is a promise (or promissory note), it can be traded between counterparties.

**Certificate of deposit**

A short-term financial security mainly issued by large banks wholesale to other market participants. CDs have a stated interest rate, maturity rate and amount.

**Bankers' acceptance**

A short-term financial instrument that increases certainty in the buying and selling of goods between two companies because the payment for the goods received by the purchaser is guaranteed by the bank – the bank has 'accepted' the risk that the purchaser of the goods will fail to pay.

**Euromarkets**

Where deposits and loans of a domestic country (such as short-term deposits or loans) are held and utilised in a foreign country.

## Main players in the money market

Given that the money markets trade billions of pounds' worth of the securities mentioned above, it is worth describing who the main players are on the money markets in more detail. The main players are:

- governments and central banks (for example, the Bank of England or The Federal Reserve);
- large financial institutions;
- large corporations/businesses.

### Recap

Most players in the money market operate on both the demand and the supply sides of the market. For example, banks borrow in the money market by selling large commercial CDs. In contrast, they lend short-term funds to other banks by purchasing CDs issued by competing banks.

### *Governments – central banks – Treasury departments*

Key features:

- Governments raise money in the money market by issuing Tbills.
- Short-term issues allow governments to raise funds for immediately required expenditure until tax revenues are received. In the United States this is operated by the US Treasury, in the UK it is operated by the Debt Management Office whose role is set out as:

139

The DMO's cash management objective is to minimise the cost of offsetting the Government's net cash flows over time, while operating within a risk appetite approved by Ministers. In so doing, the DMO will seek to avoid actions or arrangements that would:

(a) undermine the efficient functioning of the Sterling money markets or

(b) conflict with the operational requirements of the Bank of England for monetary policy implementation.

The DMO conducts its cash management operations in accordance with the provisions contained in this Operational Notice and Information Memorandum, and it will act at all times in accordance with its published objectives and operate as required in order to achieve these objectives.

*(See Exchequer Cash Management in the United Kingdom issued by the UK Debt Management Office 2010,* **www.dmo.gov.uk/***)*

- The central bank also holds and issues Tbills to increase or decrease the money supply in the economy in line with current economic conditions and also uses repos and reverse repos to influence short-term interest rates and the money supply. In the United States this is operated by The Federal Reserve and in the UK by the Bank of England and HM Treasury (in addition to which the DMO may well assist).

## Commercial banks and other financial institutions

Key features:

- Commercial banks are the major issuers of negotiable CDs, bankers' acceptances and repurchase agreements.
- Commercial banks also hold a large percentage of Tbills, which helps them manage their liquidity as Tbills are near cash instruments (making a small return but quickly changeable to cash).
- Other financial institutions such as insurance companies also are heavily involved in the money markets – buying and selling all the main instruments to help smooth their own liquidity requirements.

### Large corporations/businesses

Businesses, mainly large corporations, use money market securities to invest their surplus funds and to raise funds in the short term. This is mainly via issuing commercial paper which trades billions of pounds in the UK and dollars in the United States. Large corporations which find themselves with excesses of liquidity (cash) will also purchase Tbills and all the other main securities traded on the money markets to make a small return in the short term.

## Examples & evidence

The average yearly size of the UK sterling money markets 2000–9 (£bn)

|  | Commercial paper | Treasury Bills | CDs | Interbank | Gilt repo |
|---|---|---|---|---|---|
| 2000 | 16 | 3 | 132 | 159 | 120 |
| 2001 | 20 | 4 | 138 | 178 | 132 |
| 2002 | 26 | 14 | 138 | 219 | 134 |
| 2003 | 35 | 18 | 140 | 263 | 153 |
| 2004 | N/A[1] | 19 | 138 | 298 | 208 |
| 2005 | N/A[1] | 20 | 142 | 383 | 229 |
| 2006 | N/A[1] | 19 | 149 | 519 | 286 |
| 2007 | N/A[1] | 16 | 157 | 492 | 319 |
| 2008 | N/A[1] | 26 | 162 | 203 | 293 |
| 2009 | N/A[1] | 49 | 132 | 237 | 319 |

[1] Data not available

### Question

The table shows the size of the main UK money markets. Why do you think the different money markets vary in size? What do you think led to their variations in value over the years? Consider the factors that led to the massive growth in the gilt repo market from 2000 to 2009.

## Chapter summary – pulling it all together

By the end of this chapter you should be able to:

| | Confident ✓ | Not confident? |
|---|---|---|
| Define what is meant by money market | | Revise pages 124–125 |
| Understand and explain the operations of the Treasury Bill market | | Revise pages 125–130 |
| Understand and explain the operations of the repo and commercial paper markets | | Revise pages 130–133 |
| Discuss the interbank market and how it operates | | Revise pages 133–135 |
| Understand and explain the operation of the CD Market | | Revise pages 135–136 |
| Explain bankers' acceptances and Euromarkets | | Revise pages 137–138 |
| Discuss the roles of the main players in the money market | | Revise pages 139–141 |

Now try the sample question at the start of this chapter, using the answer guidelines below.

## Answer guidelines

### ✳ Assessment question

Money markets play a key role in the financial system:

(a) Explain the different types of money markets and how they function. (70 marks)

(b) Who are the main players in the money markets and why do they choose to use the market? (30 marks)

## Approaching the question

Begin this question by explaining the general rational for a money market – what it does and how this is achieved. Show an understanding early in the question that you are aware of the importance of money markets to a well-functioning financial system. Explain liquidity and how all the main players in financial markets will require liquidity at times but will also have too much liquidity – explain how money markets solve these issues. After this concentrate on the question. Start by introducing all the main markets before explaining – one by one, how they operate and trade – including a discussion of the primary and secondary markets where applicable. Provide examples of each market. The second part of the question is worth fewer marks but you should continue to be robust in your answer. Explain who the main players are and how they utilise the markets. Contrast each of the main players and provide an analysed list of the benefits of using the money markets.

## Important points to include:

- Provide a definition of the money market and its role in a well-functioning financial system.
- Explain liquidity and how money markets help solve short-term liquidity requirements.
- Explain the benefits of using money markets if you have too much cash.
- Discuss each market separately and show an understanding of how they actually operate on a day-to-day basis.
- Include the primary markets and secondary markets.
- Explain the importance of LIBOR to the money market and the wider economy.
- Introduce each player and show how the money markets help them operate more efficiently.

## Make your answer stand out

Key to a high mark will be what extra you can bring to the question:

- What are the different yearly sizes of each money market? (Check out the UK Debt Management Office website for the size of the UK money markets).
- Put in an example of a primary market issue and an example of how the new issue would trade on the secondary market.
- Put in an example of calculating the yield on, for example, CDs or Tbills.
- Provide examples of how the main players utilise the markets and the monetary benefits (in terms of yields) that they may derive.

## Read to impress

### Textbooks

The most easily understandable book in this area is by Saunders and Cornett:

Saunders, A. and Cornett, M. (2012) *Financial Markets and Institutions*, 5th edition. McGraw-Hill.

Also try:

Pilbeam, K. (2010) *Finance and Financial Markets*. Palgrave Macmillan.

### Journal articles

Taylor, J.B. and Williams, J.C. (2008) A black swan in the money market. *National Bureau of Economic Research*, Working Paper 13943.

### Websites

To achieve a higher grade regularly check the websites of the central banks such as:

The Bank of England: **www.bankofengland.co.uk/Pages/home.aspx**

The European Central Bank: **www.ecb.int/home/html/index.en.html**

The Federal Reserve: **www.federalreserve.gov/**

These sites will have up-to-date data and information on the operation of the money markets that will enable you to show more understanding and make your answer stand out. Also check out:

Exchequer Cash Management in the United Kingdom issued by the UK Debt Management Office 2010(**www.dmo.gov.uk/**.)

Money Market Instruments (MMI) Blue Sky Taskforce Report issued by The Depository Trust and Clearing Corporation and The Securities Industry and Financial Markets Association (SIFMA) (**www.dtcc.com/downloads/leadership/whitepapers/MMI_White_Paper.pdf**.)

The Debt Management Office's Exchequer Cash Management Remit for 2012–13 issued by the UK Debt Management Office (**http://cdn.hm-treasury.gov.uk/dmo_exchequer_cmr_201213.pdf**.)

The LIBOR affair: Banksters (2012) How Britain's rate-fixing scandal might spread – and what to do about it. *The Economist*, July 7.

## Companion website

Go to the companion website at **www.pearsoned.co.uk/econexpress** to find more revision support online for this topic area.

# Notes

**Notes**

# 6

# The operation of the capital markets – the stock market

## Topic map

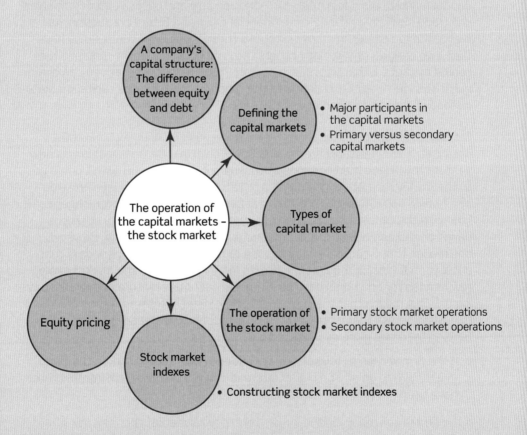

A company's capital structure: The difference between equity and debt

Defining the capital markets
- Major participants in the capital markets
- Primary versus secondary capital markets

The operation of the capital markets – the stock market

Types of capital market

Equity pricing

Stock market indexes
- Constructing stock market indexes

The operation of the stock market
- Primary stock market operations
- Secondary stock market operations

A printable version of this topic map is available from **www.pearsoned.co.uk/econexpress**

## Introduction

In the previous chapter we discussed the various money markets and their operation. This chapter concentrates upon the other major type of market, the capital market. It will introduce capital markets before analysing the characteristics and pricing of equities. The next chapter will look at the characteristics and pricing of the other major capital market instrument, namely bonds.

Capital markets are markets where long-term securities are traded, long term being defined as longer than a year; however, these securities will tend to have maturities much longer than a year. Mainly, capital market securities comprise:

- debt financing, mainly bonds; and
- equity financing, which is the issuing of stocks and shares.

Capital markets provide a market in which private and public sector companies can trade medium- and long-term financial claims on future production. As we mentioned earlier, in many textbooks these types of securities may have their own chapter and in many others they will come under the umbrella term capital markets. Either way, it is important from the outset that you can distinguish between equity and debt and the rationale for using the capital markets instead of the money markets.

For example, suppose that a firm wishes to expand by opening a new business unit; it will inevitably require additional cash in order to invest in this new venture. It will face many options as to where it sources this cash: it could go to the money markets; it could find a privately wealthy individual or individuals; it could use retained profit from past years; or it could look for longer-term financing through the capital markets. These would be individual decisions based on the operations of the firm and expected future income. However, one reason that a company may choose to finance for longer periods is that short-term financing requires the firm to keep returning to the market every few months for additional cash as its issued securities mature and require paying off. This means that the firm would be exposed to **interest rate risk** – in this case the risk that interest rates in the economy increase and the next funding becomes more expensive, thus:

- if the firm wishes to reissue the securities in the money market, the firm might have to do so at a higher interest rate if the short-term interest rates have risen.

If the firm raises money in the longer-term capital market then the risk of a rise in interest rates will disappear, since the securities can be issued for 20 years or more. This reduction in risk comes at a price as the interest cost of issuing longer-term securities is higher than for issuing short-term securities.

This is mainly due to the risk of the company failing or defaulting over the longer term and the changing nature of market interest rates. The future is uncertain and the longer-term future is more uncertain.

The chapter begins by discussing the differences between equity and debt. In practical terms this means a company choosing between issuing shares (**equity**) or **bonds** (debt). These types of security are issued onto the capital markets, which are discussed in general before analysing the stock market where equity (shares) are issued and traded. Primary and secondary stock markets are reviewed before looking at market indexes and the pricing of equities.

## Recap

- Longer maturity securities will be riskier than shorter-term securities and investors will expect a higher interest rate to compensate for this risk.
- Longer-term securities will be more volatile to changes in market interest rates, also increasing risk.

## → Revision checklist

*Make sure that you understand:*

- ☐ The difference between debt financing and equity financing for a company.
- ☐ Capital markets are long term, meaning that the securities that are issued are longer than one year.
- ☐ The benefits of a company issuing securities into the capital market rather than the money market.
- ☐ The features and differences of primary and secondary capital markets.
- ☐ The role of stock markets within an economy.
- ☐ Primary market operations in the stock market and the role of an investment bank in issuing equities into the primary market.
- ☐ Secondary market operations including the difference between brokers and market-makers.
- ☐ Quote-driven versus order-driven secondary markets.
- ☐ How and why market indexes are constructed.
- ☐ How to price equities using the dividend pricing approach.

---

### ✳ Assessment advice

Understanding the money markets goes hand in hand with understanding the capital markets so ensure that you understand both markets as this will enable you to contrast both of them when answering a question. Make sure that you also know the basics of capital markets: the main products and their maturities; the difference between brokers and market-makers; and the operation of the primary and secondary markets. The actual operation of the stock markets changes rapidly and the textbook your tutor may have used could well be out of date – to show you have up-to-date information check out the websites of the key markets. For example, the London Stock Exchange has an excellent site as well as the FTSE share indexes. Another tip is to get hold of textbooks used in the industry, such as the ones published by the Chartered Institute for Securities and Investment (CISI) as these tend to get updated regularly. When discussing the return on equities remember that the dividend used or any growth rate or **required rate of return** are 'judgement calls'.

---

### ✳ Assessment question

A well-developed capital market is essential for the proper functioning of an economy.

(a) Explain the difference between the primary and secondary capital markets. (40 marks)

(b) Discuss the steps involved in valuing equities, including any drawbacks to the methods utilised. (60 marks)

Can you answer this question? Guidelines on answering the question are presented at the end of this chapter.

---

## A company's capital structure: the difference between equity and debt

Both equity and debt are traded on the capital markets. There are key differences between these two forms of financing.

### Debt

In the capital markets debt instruments will mainly take the form of long-term bonds. Purchasers of long-term bonds have bought themselves a long-term financial instrument which provides them with a flow of cash interest payments at specific times in the future. Bonds will eventually pay off the principal amount sometime in the future. Purchasers of debt are classed as creditors or lenders and do not have ownership rights on the company. Most debt instruments have similar characteristics as discussed earlier (see Chapter 1), for example they will have a maturity date, a rate of interest and will carry risk. Debt instruments tend to be used by small-to medium-sized companies because debt is generally easier to obtain for such companies than equity and is a quicker process. Individuals or financial institutions that purchase company debt are known as creditors.

## Equity

Issuing equity involves investors buying ownership of a portion of the company, with each individual *share* representing individual ownership of a very small portion of the company. For example, if the company issues 1 million shares at £1 each, purchasing one share will give you a one-millionth share of the company. Individuals or financial institutions that purchase shares are known as shareholders.

### Recap

Equity does not:

- pay any interest;
- have a maturity date when the cash you have paid for the shares is paid back.

The incentive to purchase equity is to obtain:

- a legal share in the ownership of the company, which gives you the right to contribute to company strategy;
- a yearly dividend, shares that are known to produce a healthy dividend being known as 'income' stocks; or
- some benefit from a growth in the share price – these shares are known as 'growth' stocks.

## Dividend

The portion of a company's yearly earnings that is available to be distributed to shareholders on a per share basis is known as the dividend per share (DPS). The decision on whether to pay a **dividend** or not as well as the amount per share is made by the executive board responsible for the company.

## Comparing shares with bonds

Key features:

- Shares tend to be riskier than bonds because shareholders are a lower priority than bondholders if the company goes bankrupt. Shareholders only receive what is left after paying off bondholders.

- Returns to shareholders are not guaranteed as increases in share prices are not certain and firms may decide not to pay a dividend. For example, small, growing companies may not pay a dividend. Most bonds have a specified return that is paid biannually.

- Shareholders may benefit significantly if the firm performs well, both from a rise in share price and from the level of dividends. Bondholder returns will be linked to the initial specified coupon.

- Most shareholders have a right to vote in key company matters such as choosing company directors and issuing new shares. Bondholders do not have voting rights.

In addition, share prices may be more difficult to value than bonds because:

- investors know in advance the coupon payments they are going to receive each year from bonds but for shares the cash flow is uncertain and not guaranteed;

- there is a fixed maturity period which is known in advance by investors when they buy a bond but for shares there is no maturity date and the share never matures;

- it is difficult to determine the rate of return for equities into the future.

### Recap

Companies tend to have a combination of equity and debt, the mix being known as a company's capital structure. There is no correct mix between equity and debt for all companies and it may be difficult for firms to choose between raising capital by issuing equity or debt. However, companies that have access to both equity and debt markets should choose a capital structure in which it obtains capital at the lowest cost. This is because the value of a company on the financial markets can be viewed as the market value of its debt plus the market value of its equity. For example, suppose the total market value of a company's equity is £100 million and the total market value of the company's debt is £50 million. The combined value will be £150 million out of which £100/£150 or 66.7% of the firm's financing will be equity and the remaining £50/£150 million or 33.3% of the firm's financing will be debt. The company must choose the capital structure which has the lowest cost and maximises the value of the company.

## Defining the capital markets

The capital market is the market where companies obtain long-term finance. It has an active and liquid secondary market across most of the securities traded on its markets. Capital markets usually have a well-known trading location such as the London Stock Exchange (LSE) or the New York Stock Exchange (NYSE) or are traded over the counter (OTC) which has no physical location and trades are completed via the Internet or via telephone. The major participants in the capital market are the following.

### Governments

Governments issue long-term bonds to finance the national debt. In many countries, state and municipal governments issue bonds to finance different public projects, for example the construction of schools and roads. Governments cannot issue shares as they cannot transfer their ownership. Remember, shareholders are the owners of a company.

### Institutional investors

These include pension funds, unit trusts, investment trusts and insurance companies. These financial institutions purchase a portfolio of shares and benefit from a more efficient risk–return trade-off. They must manage their portfolios to maximise returns and, in the case of pension fund, provide their clients with a large lump sum in retirement. They are major players in capital markets.

### Individual investors

These purchase capital market securities as investments to earn a profit.

Capital markets, like money markets, are split into **primary markets** and **secondary markets**.

### The primary market

This is where firms initially sell their equity or debt with the proceeds from selling the issue going directly to the issuing firm (less costs of undertaking the sale). The main players on the primary markets are companies looking for long-term funding to increase their levels of capital or change their capital structure. Firms issuing securities for the first time are known as making an initial public offering (IPO).

### The secondary market

This is where previously issued securities are traded. An active secondary market is essential to attract investors to purchase securities issued on the primary market. If an active secondary market did not exist then those purchasing equity or debt would have nowhere to sell their securities if they required liquidity. This would mean that they would have to keep the purchased debt instruments until maturity, perhaps 20 years, and they would have nowhere to liquidate their equity holdings; that is, gain cash when required. This would significantly reduce the number of investors willing to purchase securities on the primary market. An active secondary market allows investors to sell their securities at any time. Capital market securities are traded in the secondary market through two types of exchanges: organised exchanges and OTC exchanges.

---

### Recap

Many finance textbooks will state that an active secondary market allows those parties that have issued securities into the primary market to assess the value of their security. This is because active trading in the secondary market requires the coming together of those demanding the security with those supplying the security, with the price of the security being determined by where demand and supply meet. This is fundamental to all secondary markets – prices are determined by those wanting to sell and those wishing to buy. Changes in a security's price will mean that either demand (those wanting to buy) has changed or supply (those wanting to sell) has changed.

Demand and supply will change when new information comes to the market and people assess the information. Not all investors will assess the information in the same way and, again, those investors assessing the information favourably (therefore demanding the security) will interact with those investors assessing the information unfavourably (therefore selling the security). This interaction will set the new price.

---

Key features:

- Allows securities issued on the primary market to be traded - providing liquidity.
- Provides pricing information for both shares and bonds.
- Reduces search and transaction costs.
- When trading securities on the secondary market, no cash goes to the initial issuing company but the cash goes to the party who owns the securities and is selling the securities.

- The price of a security in the secondary market is the consensus price that the security is selling for in the marketplace (the interaction of buyers and sellers).
- The price of a share is the value that the market places on a company's share.
- The price of a bond provides the implied interest rate and allows a company to assess the interest rate at which it could issue any new bonds into the primary market.
- Both the share price and the bond price are indications of how well the market believes the company is performing.

## Key definitions

**Bond**

A fixed interest financial security issued by large companies, financial institutions and governments whereby the investor (lender) gives money to the issuer (borrower) for a defined time period in return for a fixed rate of interest.

**Fixed income securities**

A type of security where the issuer promises to make fixed payments of a fixed amount during a fixed time scale until maturity.

**Equity**

A type of financial security that in return for cash provides part ownership of a company, with each individual share representing individual ownership of a very small portion of the company.

**Dividend**

The portion of a company's yearly earnings that is available to be distributed to shareholders on a per share basis.

**Interest rate risk**

The risk that unanticipated changes in interest rates will affect the price of debt or returns on investments.

**Primary market**

The market where financial securities are first issued.

**Secondary market**

The market where financial securities, once issued, are traded.

## Types of capital market

The two main types of capital market are:

- the stock market; and
- the bond market.

In this chapter we will concentrate upon the operation of the stock market. In the next chapter we will look into the workings of the bond market.

## The operation of the stock market

### Recap

The stock markets:

- allow those with excess funds to provide cash efficiently and cheaply to companies which then use the cash to invest in their company to drive profit;
- provide a system where companies, in exchange for cash, give investors ownership rights (shares) in the company as well as provide a cash flow known as a dividend;
- are split into two distinct markets, the primary market for issuing equity and the secondary market for trading equity.

The current trading level of the secondary market helps indicate a country's economic health, with the stock market's total capitalisation (which is the total value of all the companies stock traded in the exchange) being a good guide to future growth of the economy. This is because, generally, the volume of new issues will increase when companies believe the economy will grow, so they look to secure additional finance in order to invest and benefit from increased demand for their goods. These new issues are then traded on the secondary market. If investors believe a company will benefit from the healthy economy they will demand the company's shares, increasing the share price on the secondary market. As the number of companies issuing shares increases and trading on the secondary market increases, overall demand begins to increase and share prices begin to rise. If expectations are that the next move in share prices will be upwards then demand will again increase as investors seek to benefit from increasing share prices. This virtuous circle will lead to an increased total capitalisation of the stock market.

## Recap

Share price rises should be based on the key fundamental that the company issuing the shares will continue to perform well and produce increasing profits.

The stock market is dominated by the secondary market and is widely reported in the financial press – this is not only because share price movements are seen as predictors of economic performance, but also because many individuals as well as financial institutions purchase shares. This may be through purchasing shares directly or investing in some sort of mutual fund such as a pension.

## Primary stock market operations

Companies looking to raise financing via the stock market will need to issue new shares into the primary market. Companies can choose to issue **common stock** and/or preferred stock. Buyers of common stock (or shares) have bought shares with 'common' features, which means they are entitled to receive dividends (if any are given), voting rights and a share of the net asset value of the company after all other creditors have been paid off; when new shares are issued by the firm common stockholders have the right to buy those shares first.

In contrast, preferred stockholders receive a fixed dividend every year, which helps to stabilise the share price, so **preference shares** are relatively price stable.

Key features:

- Preference shares do not confer ownership of the firm.
- Preference shares do not normally carry voting rights. Individuals usually voting only when the firm has failed to pay the promised dividend.
- If the company is liquidated preference shareholders take priority over common stockholders but not bondholders.
- Preference shareholders are like bondholders in some respects as they receive a fixed dividend every year. However, interest on bonds is tax deductible but dividends are not, so from the firm's perspective issuing preferred stock is more expensive than issuing dividends.

## Issuing new shares

Originating a new share issue is most commonly undertaken using an investment bank. The investment bank acts as an intermediary between the issuing company and those purchasing the shares. In the case of issuing new shares the investment bank would:

- act as a consultant, advising on the share issue;

- advise on the new share issue characteristics, its issuance date and the net proceeds;
- supervise and co-ordinate the legal work required by regulations.

The investment bank and the issuing company will enter into one of two types of agreement:

**Firm commitment:** where the investment bank agrees to purchase the entire new issue and distribute it to both institutional and retail investors. The investment bank purchases the entire share issue for a set price, known as the net proceeds, and sells the issue to its client investors for a higher price, referred to as the gross proceeds. The difference between the net proceeds and the gross proceeds is the underwriting spread and is the difference between the price the bank receives from investors and the amount it pays to the issuing firm. The bank takes into account the risk of placing (selling) the issue and any other expenses.

**Best efforts agreement:** this is where the investment bank agrees to sell the shares but does not guarantee the price, charging a fee for its services.

In both types of agreement the investment bank will write the preliminary prospectus, print the stock certificates, and state the listing exchange. The bank will then begin to promote the issue around potential interested parties. Underwriting exposes the investment bank to the risk that it cannot resell the security on the markets and so it employs large sales staff who maintain relationships with institutional and high-net-worth investors. It is the initial feedback from contacting potential investors that allows investment banks to build up information and the issue of shares allows them to advise on the terms of the new issue. By maintaining a client list it may be that the investment bank is able to sell the entire new issue before it goes public, reducing the risk of a negative underwriting spread. If the new issue is too large for one investment bank then a syndicate may be formed, which benefits from an enlarged client list; in this scenario one investment bank takes the lead.

Once the shares have been issued and the cash received by the issuing company, and the underwriting spread has been distributed plus any additional fees to the investment bank, the bank may then act as a market-maker in the secondary market – buying and selling the shares. This is undertaken to reduce the risk of buyers of the new issue not being able to liquidate their shares. This concern would reduce demand in the first instance for the new issue. The shares now trade on the secondary markets.

## Test yourself

**Q1.** What is the difference between the primary and secondary capital markets?

**Q2.** Give a reason why a company's share price may rise.

**Q3.** What is meant by a best efforts agreement?

## Secondary market operations

The secondary market trading process has a number of key features with which you will need to become familiar to understand the operations of secondary markets. These are:

- the role of brokers;
- the role of market-makers;
- **quote-driven (dealer) markets**;
- **order-driven (auction) markets**.

### The role of brokers

In the operation of secondary market trading a **broker** is an intermediary or agent who matches buyers and sellers. They do not expose themselves to risk as they do not purchase, sell or hold financial securities and therefore do not suffer from shifts in price – they do not 'take a position' in the markets. Investors in shares utilise brokers for practical reasons who act purely as agents to purchase shares, find buyers for shares, obtain the best price and to execute buy and sell orders. For these services the broker receives a commission, which can also be viewed as a transaction cost of buying and selling shares on the market. Note that if the broker offers a client advice on share selection they will charge an additional fee.

> ### Recap
>
> You must be aware that the smallest allowable price change for a security is known as the tick size, which is commonly quoted as a fraction: 1/8th or 1/16th or as a number, USD 0.0625. Tick size may vary with price – with larger tick sizes at higher prices – and may vary across markets and geographic locations. Attempts are being made to standardise tick sizes across locations.

### The role of market-makers

**Market-makers** smooth the operation of secondary markets by holding an inventory of shares that can be traded when demand for, or supply of, a share changes abruptly. This may occur if a suddenly cash-rich investor demands a large amount of a particular share; the supply of the share may not be able to react 'immediately' even though the market consensus price is widely accepted as correct. If a market-maker did not exist then the price would temporarily spike until supply caught up with demand – at which point the price would drop back to the consensus or equilibrium price. If this happened continually then prices would be extremely volatile and uncertain and investors would eventually lose confidence in the market.

Market-makers reduce the effects of immediacy by holding a stockpile (or inventory) of shares and are willing to deplete or add to this stockpile as buy and sell orders come into the market. Market-makers are willing to 'make a market' on both sides of the deal:

- buying a financial asset at the 'bid' price; and
- selling at the 'ask' price.

By doing this they reduce market price volatility. In addition, market-makers provide reliable price information to the market and act as auctioneers, ensuring that the particular exchange rules are followed and trades are fair. Market-makers become specialists in certain stocks and are central to quote-driven markets. Note that market-makers will bear risk and this will be reflected in their buy and sell spread.

## Quote-driven (dealer) markets

These markets are so called because quotes of bid (buy) and ask (sell) prices are posted to the market on a continuous basis. Market-makers are central to quote-driven markets and are the individuals who act as dealers in a selection of shares of their choosing – they provide the quotes at which they will buy and sell chosen shares. As discussed above, market-makers stand ready to bid (buy) a share in which they trade at any time at their advertised price and 'ask' (sell) at any time at their advertised rate. The difference between the two prices is known as the spread and creates the profit for the market-maker. Dealers will compete with each other in their buy and sell prices for an individual share with spreads becoming closer for more hotly contested and liquid shares – that is, ones that many dealers are willing to trade and are easily sellable. OTC markets are quote-driven markets.

### Recap

The term 'inside market' is commonly used in quote-driven markets. It is the highest bid/ask spread across all the market-makers trading a specific share.

## Order-driven (auction) markets

These types of markets are usually extremely liquid with many trades taking place per hour – meaning that there is greater price certainty. Traders in these markets usually congregate in one location, originally physically on the exchange but today mainly electronically. In a pure order-driven market trades clear without the need for brokers or market-makers because participants' buy and sell prices converge to mutually agreeable prices and are executed. This has become easier with the use of technology as buy and sell prices are logged and cleared quickly when they 'cross'.

Order-driven markets can be either:

- continuous, where trades are executed at any time throughout the day as buy and sell prices meet; or
- periodic, also known as a call auction, where buy and sell orders are accumulated and executed at a certain time of the day.

Buying and selling orders come in two types:

- A market order: where an order is placed with a broker to transact at the best market price for the share available at the time of execution whether buying (looking for the lowest price) or selling (looking for the highest price).
- A limit order: an order to transact only when the share reaches a particular price (the limit). If the current price is nowhere near the limit price the market-maker will log the limit price for future reference and transact when the price is met.

Two of the most well-known secondary capital markets are the LSE and the NYSE. Both these exchanges operate their main market on a hybrid of the auction (or order-driven) continuous market structure. In the recent past each stock that was traded on the NYSE was assigned a specialist (who acts as the market-maker) with each stock only having one specialist. The specialist was located at a booth or post where they received buy and sell orders either physically – via a broker – or electronically. The specialist market-maker conducted the auction, taking into account the buy and sell orders to determine the execution price, and matches (or clears) the orders. The specialists also acted as market-makers (elements of the quote-driven market) to help reduce volatility and hold the limit order log book transacting when the market price reaches the limit. More recently, the NYSE introduced an automated system to execute trades, for example the NYSE Super Display Book (SDBK) system. This has led to the specialist system diminishing.

In a similar way the LSE uses the Stock Exchange Electronic Trading Service (SETS), which allows buy and sell orders to be electronically submitted and matched (also known as crossed) taking into account both market and limit orders. Under this system brokers assume responsibility for entering buy and sell orders to the electronic order book; market-makers are not used.

## Stock market indexes

All leading economies have stock markets that you will be aware of such as the NYSE, the LSE or the Tokyo Stock Exchange. All the main exchanges will have thriving capital markets which will trade a myriad of capital market instruments. They will also have market indexes associated with them such as the Dow Jones Industrial Average (in the United States) or the FTSE 100 in the UK.

**Stock market indexes** help to monitor the movement of a group of secondary market equities traded on a capital market, providing a guide to how equities have traded on a particular day. Indexes usually correspond to a portion of the market and can be defined by the size of the company as determined by the market capitalisation or by the sector that the company mainly operates within, such as oil and gas, technology or financial.

## Recap

- Many stock market indexes rise and fall in similar way most of the time, mainly in line with general economic expectations. Remember, equity prices move up or down when investors receive information which they translate into buy, sell or hold actions.

- Sometimes different indexes may show different patterns. This difference is mainly due to the difference in their construction, with a group of specific equities moving for specific reasons; that is, information which is mainly relevant to those specific stocks.

## Test yourself

**Q1.** What is the difference between a broker and a market-maker?

**Q2.** What is meant by the 'tick' size?

**Q3.** The term 'inside market' is commonly used in quote-driven markets. What does it refer to?

**Q4.** What is the difference between a quote-driven and order-driven stock market?

## Constructing stock market indexes

Indexes are constructed because those active in the financial markets thrive on information. An index allows investors regularly to assess and make trading decisions on trends within the entire capital market or constructed segments of the market. An index can be all encompassing, reflecting the entire market of equities traded on that exchange, or are a weighted average – weighted towards certain equities. In addition the weighting technique may vary between each index. In London the weighting technique tends to be market capitalisation weighted, meaning that larger companies carry a larger per cent weighting.

Examples of indexes used in the UK include:

- **FTSE All-share**: Information from the FTSE All-Share Fact Sheet (**www.ftse.com**):

    the FTSE All-Share is a market-capitalisation weighted index representing the performance of all eligible companies listed on the

London Stock Exchange's main market, which pass screening for size and liquidity... The FTSE All-Share Index covers 630 constituents with a combined value of nearly £1.8 trillion – approximately 98% of the UK's market capitalisation. The FTSE All-Share Index is considered to be the best performance measure of the overall London equity. FTSE All-Share Index constituents are traded on the London Stock Exchange's SETS and SETSmm trading systems.

- **FTSE 100**: Information from the FTSE All-Share Fact Sheet (**www.ftse.com**):

  The FTSE 100 is a market-capitalisation weighted index of UK-listed blue chip companies. The index is part of the FTSE UK Series and is designed to measure the performance of the 100 largest companies traded on the London Stock Exchange that pass screening for size and liquidity. FTSE 100 constituents are all traded on the London Stock Exchange's SETS trading system.

- **FTSE techMARK Focus:** This is an example of an index which focuses upon one sector, again from (**www.ftse.com**):

  The FTSE techMARK Index Series reflects the performance of the innovative technology stocks listed on the London Stock Exchange's techMARK. The industries... give investors exposure to stocks actively involved in technologies shaping markets of the future.

The main market index is the FTSE techMARK All-Share which includes all companies within the London Stock Exchange's techMARK sector.

These indexes (and others) are owed by the FTSE Group, which is a joint venture between the Financial Times and LSE.

## Key definitions

**Common stock or shares**

Same as equity providing holders with certain 'rights' such as entitlement to dividends, voting rights, and a share of the net asset value of the company after all other creditors have been paid off.

**Preference shares**

Similar to bonds in that preferred stockholders receive a *fixed* return in the form of a dividend every year which takes precedence over common stockholders but does not confer ownership of the company.

**Broker**

An entity that brings individuals together to enact trades. Brokers do not hold risk.

**Market-maker**

Similar to a broker but they smooth the operation of secondary markets by holding an inventory of shares that can be traded when demand for, or supply of, a share changes abruptly. Unlike a broker they bear risk.

**Quote-driven market**

So called because quotes of bid (buy) and ask (sell) prices are posted to the market on a continuous basis.

**Order-driven market**

A type of market where buy and sell orders are posted to a central location and are subsequently matched. The market price is derived from the interaction of these demand and supply orders.

**Stock market indexes**

A stock market index is a group of financial securities that are grouped together to measure a certain portion of a financial market.

## Equity pricing

One of the most common approaches to equity pricing is the dividend pricing approach. In this approach the price of the equity is the present value of its future cash flows as explained earlier (see Chapter 2). The future cash flows are from:

- dividends; and
- the profit that you earn from any rise in the equity price if you decide to sell the stock at a future date (the difference between what you bought the equity for and the price when you sell it).

The dividend pricing approach takes all the dividends that you may receive in future years plus the final possible selling price of the shares and divides this by the discount rate. In this way it is like pricing any other financial security. However, note that predicting the level (if any) of the dividend, the rise in the share price or the discount rate to be used is uncertain and will be a 'best guess'.

Taking an equity that you hold for two years such that you receive two dividend payments and a final price for the equity when you sell, the price of the security today can be calculated in the same way as for any security.

The price of the equity today will be the sum of all the future dividends plus the final selling price of the equity, all discounted by an appropriate discount rate. For an equity that will be held for two years the formula to calculate the current share price is:

$$P = \frac{D_1}{(1 + r)^1} + \frac{D_2}{(1 + r)^2} + \frac{P_2}{(1 + r)^2}$$

where:

$P$ = price of the equity today

$D$ = dividend payment in that year (1 signifying the first year)

$P_2$ = the price of the equity when sold at the end of year 2

$r$ = discount rate used

and the formula to calculate any length of holding period is:

$$P = \frac{D_1}{(1 + r)^1} + \frac{D_2}{(1 + r)^2} + \frac{D_3}{(1 + r)^3} + \frac{D_4}{(1 + r)^4} + \cdots + \frac{D_n}{(1 + r)^n} + \frac{P_n}{(1 + r)^n}$$

where:

$n$ = number of cash flows (to selling the equity – usually years)

### Recap

This is exactly the same formula as used previously for calculating the price of a bond (see Chapter 2) but in this case the dividends are the interest payments and the selling price of the share is the face value received from the bond.

The major flaw with the dividend pricing approach is that predicting dividends and the final selling price of the equity will be uncertain. Models attempt to take this into account by adapting a slightly different method depending upon the assumptions:

- the dividend has **zero growth rate**;
- the dividend grows at a **constant rate**;
- the dividend grows at a **non-constant rate**.

## Zero growth

If the dividend has a zero growth rate so that exactly the same amount of dividend is paid every year then $D_1 = D_2 = D_3$ etc. Assuming that the dividend is exactly the same each time simplifies the model to:

$$P = \frac{D_1}{(1 + r)^1} + \frac{D_2}{(1 + r)^2} + \frac{D_3}{(1 + r)^3} + \frac{D_4}{(1 + r)^4} + \cdots + \frac{D_n}{(1 + r)^n} + \frac{P_n}{(1 + r)^n}$$

The dividend is the same amount each year, every year. So the present value or price of the equity is the same as the present value of a security but in this case with a cash flow equal to the dividend $D$ each year. The price of the equity in this case can be written as:

$$P = \frac{D}{R}$$

where:

$R$ = the required return on the investment

**Example**

What is the current price of a stock of Blades plc if it pays a dividend of £8 per share every year and the required rate of return is 20%?
The present price of the stock is therefore $P = 8/0.20 = £40$ per equity.

### Constant growth or Gordon growth model

Gordon (1962) developed a model where he could calculate the current price if, instead of assuming the same dividend each year, it was assumed that the dividend grew at a *constant* rate every year, which was given the letter $g$. So if this year's dividend was $D_0$ then next year's dividend $D_1$ would be last year's dividend plus a bit extra for growth (again this would be the best guess figure).

For year 1 this would be calculated as:

$$D_1 = D_0(1 + g)$$

The dividend in year 2 would be:

$$D_2 = D_0(1 + g)^2 \text{ and}$$
$$D_3 = D_0(1 + g)^3 \text{ etc.}$$

If you follow this through, for any equity, of any length to maturity, assuming a constant growth in dividend then the present value or price of equity can be calculated using:

$$P = \frac{D_0(1 + g)}{(1 + r)^1} + \frac{D_0(1 + g)^2}{(1 + r)^2} + \frac{D_0(1 + g)^3}{(1 + r)^3} + \frac{D_0(1 + g)^4}{(1 + r)^4} + \cdots$$

$$+ \frac{D_n(1 + g)^n}{(1 + r)^n} + \frac{P_n}{(1 + r)^n}$$

where:

$g$ = the constant growth rate of the dividend

This can be simplified to:

$$P = \frac{D_0(1 + g)}{(r - g)}$$

and because we know that $D_1 = D_0(1 + g)$ we get:

$$P = \frac{D_1}{(r - g)}$$

### Recap

This model dictates that $r$, the required rate of return, be greater than $g$ to avoid the chance of a negative share price.

### Example

Blades plc will pay a dividend of £6 per share next year and the dividend grows every year by 8%. If the required rate of return is 20 % what is Blades plc's price per stock today?

Next year's dividend $D_1$ is £6, the required return $r$ is 20% (0.20) and the growth rate of the dividend $g$ is 8% (0.08). So the present price of Blades plc's equity is:

$$P = \frac{D_1}{r - g} = \frac{6}{0.20 - 0.08} = £50$$

## Non-constant growth model

The problem with all dividend pricing models is the uncertainty of dividends into the future. The above models calculate equity prices assuming either the same dividend or the same growth of dividend; however, dividends may vary year on year.

Again certain assumptions have to be made before we proceed. Assume a company does not currently pay any dividend but will begin in six years. Also assume the firm will begin to pay a dividend of £6 per equity in six years' time which will grow steadily every year by 10%. The required rate of return is 20%.

In this example we first calculate the price of the stock in year 5, which is $P_5$. We know that:

$$P = \frac{D_n}{(r - g)}$$

So:

$$P_5 = \frac{D_6}{(r - g)} = \frac{6}{0.20 - 0.10} = £60$$

The price of the stock in year 5 is £60, which is the future value of the stock. So in order to determine the current price of the stock we need to discount this future value by the required rate of return, which is 20%. So the current price of the stock would be:

$$P_0 = \frac{P_5}{(1 + r)^5} = \frac{60}{(1 + 0.20)^5} = £24.11$$

It may not be the case that the dividend is zero in the initial years and it may vary through time – for example, if Blades plc paid an annual dividend of £1.25 per share in the current year but investors believed that the company will increase its dividend by 20% every year over the next four years. However, after four years they believe the dividend will only grow at 4% annually. If investors' required rate of return on Blades equity is 16% then:

The assumption here is that the dividend will grow at a high rate of $g_1$ for the next few years and then it will grow at a modest rate of $g$ for ever. The relevant formula to calculate the present value of stock in this scenario is:

$$P = \frac{D_0(1 + g_1)}{(1 + r)} + \frac{D_0(1 + g_1)^2}{(1 + r)^2} + \frac{D_0(1 + g_1)^3}{(1 + r)^3} + \cdots + \frac{D_n(1 + g)^n}{(r - g)} \times \frac{1}{(1 + r)^n}$$

So:

$D_0 = £1.25$

$D_n = $ the dividend in year 4 ($n = 4$)

$r = 16\%(0.16)$

$g_1 = 20\%(0.20)$

$g = 4\%(0.04)$

Substituting these values into the above equation gives:

$$P_0 = \frac{1.25(1 + 0.20)}{(1 + 0.16)} + \frac{1.25(1 + 0.20)^2}{(1 + 0.16)^2} + \frac{1.25(1 + 0.20)^3}{(1 + 0.16)^3} + \frac{1.25(1 + 0.20)^4}{(1 + 0.16)^4}$$
$$+ \frac{1.25(1 + 0.20)^4(1 + 0.04)^4}{(0.16 - 0.04)} \times \frac{1}{(1 + 0.16)^4}$$

$$P = \frac{1.50}{1.16} + \frac{1.80}{1.16^2} + \frac{2.16}{1.16^3} + \frac{2.592}{1.16^4} + \frac{1}{1.16^4} \times \frac{2.696}{0.16 - 0.04} = 17.85$$

So in this case the price of the share is **£17.85**.

## Calculating the required rate of return r

*The required rate of return will equal the risk-free rate of return (usually Tbills) plus the expected* inflation rate plus any risk premium that the investor places on the risk of purchasing the equity.

We can also use the above relationships to calculate *r* because we know that:

$$P = \frac{D_0(1 + g)}{(r - g)}$$

Rearranging this for *r* gives:

$$r = \frac{D_0(1 + g)}{P} + g$$

### Recap

Remember that the dividend (and any change in the dividend) and the required rate of return are best guesses (or subjective) of each investor attempting to calculate the present value of the equity. Different investors may assume different levels of *r* or *D*.

### Key definitions

**Required rate of return**

The minimum acceptable rate of return for a given level of risk; it will equal the risk-free rate of return (usually Treasury Bills) plus the expected inflation rate plus any risk premium that the investor places on the risk of purchasing the equity.

**Zero growth model**

A model used to price equities which assumes that there is zero growth in dividends.

**Constant growth model**

A model of equity pricing where it is assumed that the dividend grows at a *constant* rate every year.

**Non-constant growth model**

A model of equity pricing where dividends are assumed to change over time in a non-constant or irregular way.

## Test yourself

**Q1.** What is the main purpose of stock market indexes?

**Q2.** When using the constant growth model, $r$, the required rate of return, should be greater than $g$. Why?

**Q3.** Write down the relevant formula for the non-constant growth model.

**Q4.** Why may different analysts obtain different results when using these models?

## Examples & evidence

FOLLOWING the world's stockmarkets recently has been a bit like watching an act of levitation. They are serenely calm, they rise gently, and it takes faith not to worry they'll come down with a bump. This week, markets hit record highs, as measured by Morgan Stanley Capital International's broadest global index. But they did so without the stomach-churning lurches that usually characterise over-exuberance. Volatility, which measures how much asset prices fluctuate in either direction, is abnormally low. And yet, a return to the ground looks overdue.

For instance, on only eight days this year has the S&P 500 index moved by more than 1%, compared with 12 times a month in the wake of the dotcom bust, and 11 times a month during the great sell-off in the 1970s (see chart). Meanwhile, the Chicago Board Options Exchange's Volatility Index (VIX), which measures the share movements implied in stock index

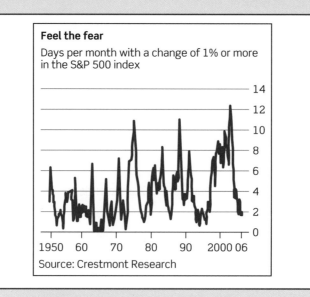

**Feel the fear**

Days per month with a change of 1% or more in the S&P 500 index

Source: Crestmont Research

options, is at record lows. It predicts that the S&P 500 will move by less than 1%, up or down, over the next month.

VIX is alternatively known as the "fear gauge", and all the signs are of an abnormally low level of anxiety among investors. There are plenty of reasons why they might feel unafraid. The world has enjoyed a long period of low inflationary growth, boringly predictable monetary policy and strong corporate earnings. Despite gently rising interest rates, there is still plenty of surplus cash to invest.

To stockmarket bears, however, low volatility is a warning sign: too much stability may, paradoxically, be destabilising. Ed Easterling of Crestmont Holdings, a Dallas investment firm, calls it "the calm before the storm". He worries that speculators may have become overly complacent. "The current state of volatility is an indicator of potentially sharp stockmarket decline," he says.

Episodes of extremely low volatility rarely last long, says Mr Easterling, and are usually followed by periods of exceptionally jumpy prices. There is, indeed, evidence that an increase in volatility often means a sell-off in markets.

Already, sentiment may be changing—like the corners of a picnic blanket, volatility is beginning to lift in the breeze. Currency and government-bond markets, for instance, which were placid last year, are showing signs of life, analysts say, pointing to the weaker dollar and rising American bond yields. This may reflect a growing perception of risk, as the Federal Reserve nears the top of its tightening cycle and people scratch their heads over where interest rates are heading next.

Within American stockmarkets, there has also been a "creeping" divergence in recent weeks between the performance of shares in strong sectors, such as energy, compared with weak ones, according to Robin Carpenter, of Carpenter Analytical Services, which tracks 1,000 stocks. That may explain why hedge funds, many of which seek to arbitrage pairs of assets, have performed well: volatility creates anomalies for them to exploit.

More frequent market gyrations do not have to mean prices will fall, however. During the dotcom boom, volatility rose to quadruple the level it is now. Large one-day jumps in the Dow and other indices were regular features on the nightly news.

Chris Watling of Longview Economics, a London consultancy, says that stockmarket volatility reflects risk in the corporate sector—and has a historical correlation with corporate bond spreads, which assess the same thing. It is fair to assume risks are starting to rise. An era of corporate prudence—of restructuring balance sheets and generating cash—is giving way to a more swashbuckling appetite for acquisitions and growth. But earnings continue to grow, price/earnings multiples are attractive, and American equities remain cheap relative to bonds, Mr Watling says.

In his view, low volatility is a reflection not of complacency, but of a long period of healing in corporate America and elsewhere, which puts it in good shape to enter the next—and riskier—phase of economic growth. Fair point, but complacency is obvious only when it is too late. Nabokov put it best: "Complacency is a state of mind that exists only in retrospective: it has to be shattered before being ascertained."

*Source*: The fear gauge: Share prices are breaking records. Are investors too complacent? *The Economist*, May 11, 2006.

## Question

This article appeared before the financial meltdown of 2008. Begin to use your knowledge obtained from all the previous chapters. You should be able to begin to realise what makes share prices move up or down and the role of perceived risk. Also note the effect of future expectations on the markets and on corporate finance.

## Chapter summary – pulling it all together

By the end of this chapter you should be able to:

| | Confident ✓ | Not confident? |
|---|---|---|
| Fully explain the difference between equity and debt financing for a company | | Revise pages 150–153 |
| Discuss the main participants of the capital markets and distinguish between the role of primary and secondary capital markets | | Revise pages 153–155 |
| Discuss the role played by the stock market in aiding to raise finance for companies and investment opportunities for investors | | Revise pages 156–157 |

| | Confident ✓ | Not confident? |
|---|---|---|
| Contrast the role of brokers with market-makers and quote-driven markets with order-driven markets | | Revise pages 157–158 |
| Show an understanding of how the primary stock market operates including the process of issuing new shares into the market | | Revise pages 159–160 |
| Discuss different stock market indexes and their construction | | Revise pages 161–164 |
| Understand the pricing of equities using the dividend pricing approach and the limitations of these models | | Revise pages 164–169 |

Now try the sample question at the start of this chapter, using the answer guidelines below.

## Answer guidelines

### ✳ Assessment question

A well-developed capital market is essential for the proper functioning of an economy.

(a) Explain the difference between the primary and secondary capital markets. (40 marks)

(b) Discuss the steps involved in valuing equities, including any drawbacks to the methods utilised. (60 marks)

### Approaching the question

Start your answer with a clear introduction explaining the role of capital markets and contrasting the capital markets with the money markets. Show that you understand the main characteristics of the instruments traded on these markets and differences between them. Begin answering part (a) with a brief explanation of both markets before proceeding to a more full answer. When discussing primary markets ensure that you analyse the process of bringing an issue of equities or bonds to the market including the role of the investment bank. Secondary market operations should then be fully explored explaining the role of brokers, market-makers and the different types of market trading systems. Complete this section by contrasting both markets and explaining that primary markets require the secondary markets in order to function efficiently. The second part of the answer should start with the fundamentals of pricing securities and then you should show that you are aware that the process of pricing equities is based upon these fundamentals. Introduce the dividend pricing approach and explain the different iterations of the model. Explain the benefits of this model and the drawbacks.

## Important points to include:

- Key definitions of the markets.

- A definition of a new issue and IPO (Initial Public Offering).

- The role of investment banks in the primary market.

- Contrasting brokers with market-makers and quote-driven and order-driven markets.

- The dividend pricing method to value equities.

- Any other methods that you think applicable, such as financial ratio analysis.

## Make your answer stand out

The markets and their processes change regularly. To gain a higher grade find the most up-to-date information by utilising key websites. The FTSE and LSE websites have already been mentioned, but also check the Bank of England website or key players in the financial markets, such as the major financial services companies. For example, Morgan Stanley produces research articles many of which are free, and large accountancy firms such as Ernst and Young produce briefing documents. Also try the big consultancy firms such as McKinsey. The more contemporary your information, the more likely you are to gain a higher grade. However, remember to introduce the information in a logical manner.

# Read to impress

## Books

There are many textbooks covering the topics in this chapter. Any book with finance or investment in the title will give some coverage. Once again, try a few and settle on the one that makes sense to you.

Bodie, Z., Kane, A. and Marcus, A. (2012) *Essential of Investments*. McGraw-Hill.

Fabozzi, F. Modigliani, F. and Jones, F. (2010) *Foundations of Financial Markets and Institutions*. Pearson Education.

Pilbeam, K. (2010) *Finance and Financial Markets*. Palgrave Macmillan.

For a more practical guide try:

Chartered Institute for Securities and Investment (2010) *Study Text: Global Operations Management*. BPP Learning.

To understand further the actual operation of these markets, try reading the many interesting books written by those who have worked in or analysed the industry. These are not textbooks but will provide you with greater understanding. Start with these:

Mackay, Charles (1995 edition) *Extraordinary Popular Delusions and the Madness of Crowds*. Wordsworth Reference.

Malkiel, Burton G. (2012 edition) *A Random Walk Down Wall Street: The Time-Tested Strategy for Successful Investing*. Norton.

Smith, Adam (1968) *The Money Game*. Random House.

## Journal articles

Gordon, Myron (1962) The Investment, Financing, and Valuation of the Corporation. Homewood, IL: R.D. Irwin.

Nasseh, A. and Strauss, J. (2004) Stock prices and dividend discount model: did their relation break down in the 1990s? *Quarterly Review of Economics and Finance*, Vol. 44 (2), pp. 191–207.

## Websites

To achieve a higher grade regularly check the websites of key players. Here is a starter list:

Ernst & Young: **http://www.ey.com/UK/en/home**

FTSE: **http://www.ftse.com/**

London Stock Exchange: **http://www.londonstockexchange.com/home/homepage.htm**

McKinsey & Company: **http://www.mckinsey.com/**

Morgan Stanley: **www.morganstanley.com**

The Bank of England: **http://www.bankofengland.co.uk/Pages/home. aspx**

The European Central Bank: **http://www.ecb.int/home/html/index. en.html**

The Federal Reserve: **http://www.federalreserve.gov/**

These sites will have up-to-date data and information on the operation of the capital markets that will enable you to show more understanding and make your answer stand out.

## Companion website

Go to the companion website at **www.pearsoned.co.uk/econexpress** to find more revision support online for this topic area.

## Notes

# 7 The bond market

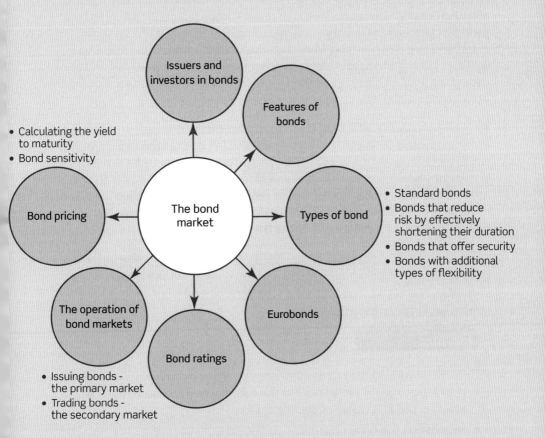

## Introduction

This chapter focuses on the issuing of long-term debt instruments, commonly referred to as bonds, and will review the operations of the bond market where bonds are issued and traded. The bond market is classified as a type of capital market (where securities issued have a maturity of more than a year).

A **bond** is a long-term form of debt instrument issued by companies or governments. As we examined in the previous chapter, companies issue bonds to fund their long-term investment plans, commonly referred to as **capital expenditure**. In such cases they require additional funds above that which they currently have at their disposal. For example, a company may issue bonds to fund the building of a new manufacturing plant, purchase a fleet of new vans or invest in brand-new IT infrastructure. This type of spending will cost thousands or millions of pounds and will take a number of years for the company to receive the full benefits of such investment. A key feature of any efficient financial system is to provide inter-temporal (between time periods) transfers of liquidity allowing companies to receive funds today, invest and begin benefitting from that investment immediately. Without a well-functioning financial system companies may well have to wait and save enough of their own funds in order to invest in new infrastructure, slowing the growth potential of the company and ultimately the economy.

As noted previously, all future company performance is uncertain and will carry an amount of risk that the company will fail, or that the new project which requires investment will fail or not perform as expected. Thus investing in company bonds will be risky and investors will expect to be paid an appropriate interest rate to the level of risk as well as being compensated for inflation. If the terms of the bond are not met and the issuer defaults, then the investors have a claim on the assets of the bond issuer.

The bond market is the place where bonds of all types are issued into the primary market and traded on the secondary market. As with equities, the secondary market for bonds provides a means whereby bondholders that require liquidity can sell their bonds.

### Recap

The issuer of bonds:

- promises to pay a set amount in the future when the bond matures, which is the face value of the bond; plus
- interest on the bond referred to as the coupon, or coupon interest. This is paid per bond issued and is the coupon rate multiplied by the face value of the bond.

**Revision checklist**

*Make sure that you understand:*

- ☐ The definition of a bond including the principal amount (face value) and the coupon (coupon interest).
- ☐ The main issuers and investors in bonds.
- ☐ How to calculate the simple coupon interest amount.
- ☐ A bond indenture and key features that may appear in the indenture.
- ☐ The different types of bonds issued into the market.
- ☐ The Eurobond market.
- ☐ Bonds ratings – including the ratings of the three leading rating agencies: Moody's, Fitch, and Standard and Poor's.
- ☐ Primary and secondary market operations in bonds and how the UK government issues gilts.
- ☐ How to calculate the price of a bond.
- ☐ How to calculate yield to maturity (YTM) using Microsoft Excel.
- ☐ Sensitivity and how changes in the variables of the present value formula affect the price of the security.

 **Assessment advice**

Make sure that you understand the key components of a bond including the face value, maturity, coupon rate and risk. Understand how these factors will affect the value of the bond. You will gain additional marks by bringing different topics together, so ensure that you have understood the key characteristics of assets and bring this understanding to your answers. It is good to show awareness of the practical side of bonds, such as the bond indenture and the possible features that may be written into the indenture. Again, link these together as many of the features change the risk characteristics of bonds and therefore their price. Key to a high grade in answering any question on bonds will be to fully understand bond pricing, yield to maturity (YTM) and bond sensitivity. Make sure you practise as many past exam paper questions on bonds as you can; there are only so many types of questions your lecturer can ask and most likely these have appeared in the past.

---

### ✳ Assessment question

(a) Outline the basic characteristics and features of a bond. (30 marks)

(b) Describe the different types of bonds that can be issued into the capital markets, including how their characteristics differ from a standard bond. (40 marks)

(c) Describe the components of the equation below. (30 marks)

$$P = \sum_{t=1}^{n} \frac{C}{(1 + r)^t} + \frac{F}{(1 + r)^n}$$

Can you answer this question? Guidelines on answering the question are presented at the end of this chapter.

---

## Issuers and investors in bonds

Bonds are mainly issued by:

- governments,
- local governments and
- companies,

all of which issue many different types of bonds onto the markets in order to gain long-term funding.

Government bonds and local government bonds tend to carry lower risk and therefore lower returns than company bonds and are issued to finance various public projects. Tax incentives may be provided to encourage investors to purchase them. Government bonds are traded by licensed bodies; in the UK they are traded on the London Stock Exchange by authorised gilt-edged market-makers (**GEMMs**).

Company bonds, usually referred to as corporate bonds, are bonds issued by firms to raise long-term funds. These bonds have 10–20 years' maturity and the issuer is obliged to pay specified coupon payments at particular dates and also pay the face value of the bond upon maturity.

Bonds are purchased by:

- individuals;
- businesses;
- governments (including local governments);
- foreign investors.

Corporate bonds are mainly purchased by financial institutions, which invest in bonds as part of their portfolios that they offer to the public. For example, being held as part of a pension fund or mutual trust.

## Features of bonds

### The basics that you will came across when dealing with bonds:

#### Principal amount/face value/par value

This is the face amount that is printed on the bond. The bond may trade at more or less than the principal amount, which will depend on the characteristics of the bond (see Chapters 1 and 2) such as the interest rate and risk. At maturity it is the principal amount or face value of the bond that the holder will receive.

#### Coupon rate

This is the annual coupon that the bondholder receives on specified dates until the bond matures, expressed as a percentage of the bond's face value (or par value or principal amount). For example, if a bond has

- a coupon rate of 7%,
- a face or par value of £1000 and
- a maturity period of 20 years,

the twice yearly coupon will be 0.07(7%) × £1000 = £70 every year until the bond matures.

In most cases the coupon will be paid semi-annually or twice a year, so the bondholder will receive £35 every six months.

The bondholder will receive £1000 if they hold the bond to maturity.

#### Maturity

This is the specified date when the face value (or principal amount or par value) of the bond is paid to the bondholder.

#### Bond indenture

Bond indenture is the written contract between the bondholder and the issuer of the bond specifying the bondholder's rights and privileges and the obligation of the issuer. The face value, coupon rate and maturity date are all specified as part of the indenture. In addition certain features may appear in the indenture to safeguard the rights of the bondholder. These may include:

- Restrictive covenant: This provision protects bondholders by limiting the dividends that the issuing company can pay out to shareholders, meaning that firms retain cash to pay interest to bondholders.

- Subordination of further debt: The inclusion of a subordination clause limits additional borrowings by firms. Under the subordination clause the current bondholders get priority over subsequent bondholders.
- Early-payment protection: Some bonds have a provision that allows for early repayment – which is beneficial to the bond issuer. This is because if interest rates drop significantly the bond issuer will obtain a lower interest rate on their debt if they paid off the current bondholders and issued bonds at the new lower rate. A company could undertake a new bond issue at the lower rate and use this money to redeem a more expensive bond issue from the past. Protection against early repayment can be written into the indenture:
  - Refunding protection: This stops an issuer from using bonds issued at a cheaper rate to redeem a bond issue before it matures. For example, if interest rates drop from 5% to 1% a company could issue 1% bonds and use the money raised to pay off the 5% bonds;
  - Call protection: This prevents a company paying off a bond issue before maturity for any reason.

  Bondholders will seek early-payment protection because if their bonds are paid off in full they will find it difficult to reinvest at similar risk/maturity levels without accepting the new, lower, market rate.
- Security: Some companies offer some sort of security in case of default. This will make the bonds more marketable. Bonds are generally issued with only the credit rating of the issuer taken into consideration, so if you are a blue-chip company (those with the very highest reputation and lowest risk of defaulting) this may be enough to entice investors even at low interest rates. For other, less reputable companies, offering security may help them lower the interest rate they would normally have to offer.
- Warrants: A warrant grants the bondholder the right to purchase equity (or any specified security) at a pre-specified price from the bond issuer usually within a specific time period. It is essentially a call option which can be exercised by the bondholder. If the bondholder decides to exercise the option and pay cash, they keep their initial holdings of bonds. Warrants make the bond issue more marketable.

## Recap

A call option gives the buyer the right, but not the obligation, to buy (call) a security (or any financial asset) at a pre-agreed price during a set time period or on a specific date.

## Test yourself

**Q1.** Who issues bonds into the capital markets?

**Q2.** What are GEMMs?

**Q3.** What is the principal amount of a bond?

**Q4.** Describe three common features that may appear in a bond indenture.

## Key definitions

**Bond**

A fixed interest financial security issued by large companies, financial institutions and governments whereby the investor (lender) gives money to the issuer (borrower) for a defined time period in return for a fixed rate of interest.

**Capital expenditure**

Refers to spending which has the potential to create future benefits for a company and usually involves raising money to purchase fixed assets or to invest more money in an existing fixed asset.

**Fixed asset**

A long-term physical asset used to operate a part of the business, for example machinery or real estate.

**GEMMs (Gilt-Edged Market-Makers)**

These are the licensed and authorised bodies that trade in UK government bonds on the London Stock Exchange.

**Bond indenture**

A written contract between the bondholder and the issuer of the bond specifying the bondholder's rights and privileges and any obligations of the issuer.

## Types of bonds

There are many different types of bonds which all tend to be based upon basic characteristics, each having a coupon, a maturity date and a level of risk. The standard basic bond that is issued for a set number of years and offers a semi-annual coupon may often be referred to as a 'plain vanilla' bond. Over the years bonds have developed additional features which are written into the indenture document – these are often referred to as 'exotics' or exotic bonds. It is usually these defining features that give the bond its name. They can be classified into a few categories:

- Standard bonds.
- Bonds that reduce risk by effectively shortening their duration (the time it takes to pay off the bond in full).
- Bonds that offer security.
- Bonds with additional types of flexibility:

## Standard bonds

### Term bonds

Bonds that are issued and mature within a set number of years are known as term bonds. Term bonds that are issued for a set number of years, say 10, can be paid off early if this is stated in the indenture. If this is the case the bond would normally be referred to as a callable or redeemable bond.

The 'call' forces the bondholder to sell the bond back to the issuing company. The interest rates on callable bonds are higher than ordinary term bonds to compensate the bondholder for the risk of early repayment and to make the bond more attractive to a potential bondholder.

### Bullet bonds

These are bonds that pay off in full on the maturity date but are not redeemable before this date. They are non-callable, pay regular coupons and pay the holder a single payment of principal amount or face value on maturity. Bullet bonds are term bonds with no provision for early payment.

### Zero-coupon bonds

Unlike the above bonds zero-coupon bonds do not pay any interest or coupon. As investors do not receive any yearly or biannual payments zero-coupon bonds tend to trade at a deep discount from their face value. This allows those holding the bonds at maturity a higher profit as the bonds are redeemed at their full face value. The deep discount on zero-coupon bonds is compensation for risk.

## Bonds that reduce risk by effectively shortening their duration (the time it takes to pay off the bond in full)

### Serial bonds

These are bonds that pay off some of the principal amount at set times before the bond matures. For example, some of the principal amount on a 10-year serial bond could be paid off after 6 years, 8 years and then finally paid off in full after 10 years. It reduces the chance of default as the holder is receiving funds throughout the term of the bond, which reduces what is known as the bond's duration.

### Sinking fund bond

A slightly different bond to a serial bond in that funds are placed (sunk) into an account held by the trustee, on a regular basis. This allows the issuer to accumulate cash plus interest earned on the cash to help pay the principal in full at maturity. This reduces risk and so may be issued by companies with lower credit ratings to improve the risk rating on the bond and therefore the interest rate. This type of bond also reduces the duration and the chances of default.

## Bonds that offer security

### Mortgage bonds

These are bonds that pledge property in case of default, so that purchasers have the right to be paid off by the sale of the property if the issuer defaults. The mortgage bond indenture would grant purchases of these bonds a 'lien' against the property. A lien is the legal right to sell the property if the bond issuer defaults.

### Collateral bonds

These are bonds that use financial assets other than property as collateral or security in case the issuing company defaults. It is the assets of the issuing company that the bondholder is entitled to receive if the issuer defaults on the bond. This could be, for example, a company's equity or bondholdings. The bondholder's rights to the collateral will be written into the bond indenture.

### Debenture bonds

These are bonds that are not secured by physical assets such as property or collateral. Debenture bondholders have a right to any assets not used to secure other forms of debt. Generally such bonds are sold on the high creditworthiness and reputation of the issuer and so tend to be issued by blue-chip companies and governments. The bondholder's rights to assets not currently securing other debt will be written in the bond indenture.

Some debenture bonds are known as subordinated debenture bonds (meaning of lesser order or importance) and as such will mean holders will rank lower than secured and debentured bondholders. This means that if the issuer defaults they will be paid off after secured and debenture holders have received payment.

## Guaranteed bonds

These are bonds that are 'guaranteed' by a third party if the issuer defaults.

# Bonds with additional types of flexibility

## Convertible bonds

These bonds provide holders with the option or right to convert their bonds into a predetermined number of shares of common stock. The conversion value is the number of shares for which each bond can be exchanged. A convertibility option generally makes the initial bond issue more attractive to bondholders as they will benefit if the future price of the company's shares increase.

### Recap

**Mechanics of a convertible bond**

If a convertible bond is issued with:

- a par value of £1,000,
- an option to convert the bond into 200 shares of the company's stock at any time and
- the current price of the stock is £3,

then if the bondholder converted immediately they would be holding shares with a current market value of $200 \times £3 = £600$. In most cases the bondholder will 'convert' their shares only when it is profitable to do so – in this example, when the share price rises above £5.

Note that bondholders may decide not to convert because they have a preference for holding debt rather than equity. In addition, if the bond issue was also callable then bondholders might convert at lower rates than £5 if they thought the issue was going to be 'called' and they would suffer from a lower market interest rate on bonds. They may also shift into equity at a price lower than £5 if their preferences changed and they now preferred holding equity.

## Floating rate bonds

These are bonds whose coupon/interest payments are tied or 'float' with some measure of current market rates. For example, the coupon might be adjusted to the change in the current Tbill rate, but it does not get adjusted to changes in the financial condition of the firm. Floating rate bonds have advantages for both buyers and sellers. For sellers the bonds may allow for closer matching of their liabilities and assets, especially in banks because they can purchase and issue floating rate instruments. In addition, as market rates change there will be less incentive to redeem the issue and go back to the marketplace, which would increase transaction costs. For buyers it provides greater flexibility against risk because, as market rates increase, so do their returns, which avoids having to sell to repurchase a higher yielding bond.

### Putable bonds

These bonds give the right to the bondholder to sell the bond back to the issuer at specified dates before maturity with the repurchase price set at the time of issue, but which is usually par value. This is beneficial to the bond-holder because, if market interest rates begin to increase, they can sell the bond back and find higher returns for the same risk/reward trade-off.

## Test yourself

**Q1.** What is meant by a 'vanilla' bond?

**Q2.** List the categories by which bonds may be classified.

**Q3.** If you bought a bond for £1,000 with an option to convert into 500 shares at any time in the future, at what price per share would you begin to think about converting your bond?

## Eurobonds

A Eurocurrency is a currency held and traded outside its native country. A **Eurobond** is an international bond that is issued and traded in a currency which is not the currency of the country where it is issued. So, in the UK, issues of bonds denominated in dollars are known as Eurodollar bonds. They have a few key features:

- they are underwritten by an international syndicate;
- they are offered to investors globally at the time of issue;
- they are not subject to regulations of the denominated currencies country;
- they pay annual coupons;
- they can be issued in any of the types listed above.

## Bond ratings

Given that one of the key characteristics of bonds is their probability of default (which is the risk associated with not getting your money back), information regarding the riskiness of a bond issue (and the financial position of the underlying company) will be in high demand among those investing in bonds. It is expensive for every single individual to collect such information by performing their own analysis. This role is undertaken by the credit rating agencies who specialise in the **bond rating** of each issue. The main agencies are:

- Moody's
- Standard and Poors (S&P)
- Fitch.

The systems of rating a bond issue are slightly different for each of these agencies but it can be argued that they are broadly similar. Some key features include:

- High grade equals low credit risk.
- **Triple A** (Aaa at Moodys; AAA at the others) is the highest rating a company/government can achieve.
- The next highest grade is Aa1 (Moody's) or AA+ at S&P and Fitch.
- Moody's break down its ratings by using numbers 1 to 3, Aa1 being a higher grade than Aa3.
- S&P and Fitch use + and − signs so AA+ is a higher grade than AA or AA−.
- Triple A's are termed as prime and are close to 100% certain not to default.
- Double A's are high quality.
- Single A's are termed upper medium grade.
- Triple B's are termed lower medium grade.
- Ratings that include Aaa to Bbb3 or BBB− are known as investment grade bonds.
- Ratings outside grades Aaa to Bbb3 or BBB− are known as junk bonds.
- Double B's are low grade and speculative and single B's high risk.
- C' and D's are extremely risky and have an extremely high chance of default.

Factors influencing the credit rating given to a bond will be linked to the issuing company's:

- general operations;
- outlook for the sector(s) in which it operates;
- position within the sector or sectors in which it operates;
- financial strength – the rating agency will undertake a full financial ratio analysis considering such factors as liquidity, profitability and level of debt;
- levels of collateral it offers as security.

## Key definitions

**Eurobond**

An international bond that is issued and traded in a currency which is not the currency of the country where it is issued.

**Bond rating**

Same as credit rating, a 'rating' given to a company or financial security indicating ability to pay back the debt and chances of defaulting.

**Triple A**

The highest rating a company/government can achieve.

The rating agency will also look at the type of bond being issued, and any provisions in the indenture which limit managerial power could be deemed beneficial to investors. For example, restrictions on taking on board additional debt. It is also important to note that the credit rating agency is paid by the issuing firm to rate its bond issue. This may cause a conflict of interest.

## Recap

Bond markets are mainly classified into three different types: Treasury bond markets, in the UK known as gilts; local government bonds; and corporate bonds.

## The operation of bond markets

### Issuing new bonds – the primary market

Issuing new corporate bonds is similar to the way that equities are issued with a new bond issue most commonly being undertaken using an investment bank.

As discussed earlier (see Chapter 6), the investment bank acts as an intermediary between the issuing company and those purchasing the bonds. In the case of issuing a new share issue the investment bank would:

- act as a consultant – advising on the bond issue;
- advise on the new bond issue's characteristics, its issuance date and the net proceeds and any other criteria to set out in the indenture;
- supervise and co-ordinate the legal work required by regulations.

The investment bank and the issuing company will enter into one of two types of agreement, as follows.

## Firm commitment

This is where the investment bank agrees to purchase the entire new issue of bonds and distribute it to both institutional and retail investors. The investment bank purchases the entire bond issue for a set price known as the net proceeds and sells them to its client investors for a higher price referred to as the gross proceeds. The risk here is that market interest rates suddenly change, affecting the price of the bond, or new information comes to market concerning the issuing company.

## Best efforts agreement

This is where the investment bank agrees to sell the bonds but does not guarantee the price, charging a fee for its services.

# Issuing gilts in the UK (see *UK Government Securities: A Guide to 'Gilts'*)

Gilts can be issued using: the 'tap' method, where gilts are issued gradually in order not to flood the market and depress the price; the 'tender' method, where institutions are invited to tender for a given issue; and the 'auction' method, where bonds are sold to the highest bidders among the 20 or so gilt-edged market-makers (GEMMs).

In the UK gilts are mainly issued by auction.

The UK government uses two different auction formats to issue gilts:

- Conventional gilts are issued through a multiple price auction which is also referred to as a bid price basis; that is, successful bidders pay the price that they bid, with non-competitive bids allocated at the average accepted price.
- Index-linked gilts are auctioned on a uniform price basis, this means a single price winner basis; that is, all successful bidders pay the lowest accepted price, with non-competitive bids also allocated at this lowest accepted price.

Competitive bids at auctions must be directed via the UK's primary dealers, the GEMMs, who have direct electronic bidding links to the Debt Management Office (DMO). Alternatively, individuals can bid directly by completing an application form (providing they are members of an 'Approved Group' of investors, as recognised by the DMO).

Bidders can choose to bid competitively or non-competitively.

- Competitive bids must be for one amount and at one price expressed as a multiple of £0.01 per £100 nominal, and for at least £500,000 nominal. Successful competitive bidders are allotted stock at the price they bid. There is no minimum price.
- Non-competitive bids are allotted in full at the weighted average of the successful competitive bid prices. GEMMs can each make a single

non-competitive bid of up to 0.5% of the nominal amount of stock on offer. Other bidders can make a single non-competitive bid of up to £ 500,000 nominal (subject to a minimum £1,000 nominal).

(From *GILTS: An Investors Guide*)

## Trading bonds – the secondary market

Bonds are traded in the fixed income market, which is an over-the-counter (OTC) market. Traditionally most trades were conducted over the telephone by brokerdealers. A brokerdealer is someone who acts as a broker for some transactions but also as a dealer for other transactions. As a broker they execute transactions on behalf of clients and as a dealer they trade on their own account. Today, however, the majority of bond trading will take place using technology via an electronic bond trading system.

### Test yourself

**Q1.** List the main features of a Eurobond.

**Q2.** When the main rating agencies are rating a bond, what ratings can be given to indicate investment grade bonds?

**Q3.** What is meant by an uncompetitive bid when bidding for UK gilts?

### Bond pricing

As in our earlier example (see Chapter 2), the most common way of calculating a bond price is to use the present value method. Future cash flows comprise two elements: one is the fixed coupon payments which the bondholders receive at specified time periods; and the second is the face value of the bond upon its maturity. So the price of the bond is the present value of these future coupons and the face value of the bond.

### Recap

Clean versus dirty bond prices:

- The **clean bond price** is the price of the bond excluding any accrued interest.
- The **dirty bond price** is the clean price plus any accrued interest that the holder of the bond would receive.
- The margin between the dirty price and clean price will increase as the coupon payment becomes due – that is, the dirty price will rise as investors are aware that they will be due an interest payment soon. Only bondholders holding the bond on the day the coupon is due are paid the coupon.

- The day the coupon is paid the dirty price equals the clean price and the mechanism begins again with the dirty price rising day by day.
- The clean price is usually used to compare yields.

## Recap

**WHAT YOU SHOULD KNOW**

Don't be put off by the use of 'n' – it is just used to signify that the cash flow can be of any length (or maturity). For example, for a security with a maturity of five years you include 5 cash flows (CFs) – so instead of n you would put 5.

This method adds all the present values of the cash flows from the coupon and then adds in the present value of the final payment of the face value of the bond. A coupon is the cash flow, paid once a year (or maybe twice). So if you had a £1,000 face value bond paying an annual 8% yearly coupon then each yearly payment would be £80 (each biannual payment would be £40).

Suppose the bondholder receives coupons $C_1, C_2, C_3, \ldots$ up to $C_n$ for a bond with $n$ periods until maturity. The face value or par value of the bond is denoted as $F$. So the price of the bond can be calculated as follows:

### Calculating the price of a bond

$$P = \frac{C_1}{(1 + r)^1} + \frac{C_2}{(1 + r)^2} + \frac{C_3}{(1 + r)^3} + \cdots + \frac{C_n + F}{(1 + r)^n}$$

where:

$P$ = price

$C$ = coupon

$F$ = face value of bond – received when security matures

$n$ = number of cash flows (maturity of the bond, usually years)

$r$ = yield to maturity or the discount rate used

This is the same as:

$$P = \sum_{t=1}^{n} \frac{C}{(1 + r)^t} + \frac{F}{(1 + r)^n}$$

where:

$n$ = maturity of the bond (say 15 for a bond that matures in 15 years)

$t$ = the time period under consideration, for example year 1, 2, 3 up to 15 for a 15-year bond

From the equation above you should note that the present value of a bond:

- will be more if the coupon payment is higher;
- will be more for bonds with longer maturity;
- will be less if the interest rate is higher.

To clarify, assume that a five-year bond has a par value of £1,000 and makes semi-annual coupon payments of 8% and has **a discount rate or YTM** of 7%.

 **Assessment advice**

Be aware that when a coupon pays semi-annually, you divide the interest rate by half (divide by 2) and double the time period. The YTM is 7% so divide it by 2 and double the time period from 5 to 10. Then you discount the coupon payments for 10 periods (10 periods of interest). You do the same for the coupon interest; in this case it is 8% which is £80 (£1,000 × 0.08); you need to divide this by 2 as it is also paid semi-annually, so each coupon payment is £40. Using these figures the price of the bond is calculated as follows.

## An example of calculating the price of a bond

In this case:

$$P = \frac{40}{\left(1 + \dfrac{0.07}{2}\right)} + \frac{40}{\left(1 + \dfrac{0.07}{2}\right)^2} + \frac{40}{\left(1 + \dfrac{0.07}{2}\right)^3} + \cdots$$

$$+ \frac{1,040}{\left(1 + \dfrac{0.07}{2}\right)^{10}} = 1,041.58$$

so the price of the bond is £1,041.58.

Now think what would happen if we assumed a different discount rate or YTM. If you recalculate assuming a 9% YTM but everything else remains the same, you would obtain a new price:

$$P = \frac{40}{\left(1 + \dfrac{0.09}{2}\right)} + \frac{40}{\left(1 + \dfrac{0.09}{2}\right)^2} + \frac{40}{\left(1 + \dfrac{0.09}{2}\right)^3} + \cdots$$

$$+ \frac{1,040}{\left(1 + \dfrac{0.09}{2}\right)^{10}} = 960.44$$

so the price of the bond is £960.44.

This shows that:

- when the coupon rate is higher than the YTM, the bond sells at a premium;
- when the coupon rate is lower than the YTM, the bond sells at a discount;
- there is an inverse relationship between bond prices and interest rates: as interest rates go up bond prices go down and vice versa.

## Calculating the yield to maturity

So the bond price today is equal to the value of a string of future payments and is dependent on the factors included in the relationships shown above. These are:

- the cash flow or coupon;
- the face value of the bond at maturity;
- the number of cash flows;
- the discount rate or YTM.

### Recap

The yield to maturity is the discount rate that makes the present value of a bond's payments equal its price. In the above relationships it is expressed as *r*.

Given that the coupon, face value and number of cash flows will all be pre-determined, what equates the present value (*P*) of each cash flow to be received in the future with the securities' overall present value is known as the *yield to maturity (YTM)* or *discount rate (DR)*.

The factors that affect the YTM have been widely discussed in finance, yet nobody can be 100% sure of the 'correct' rate to use. The YTM is a best guess figure used as an indicative rate.

Thus, Fabozzi *et al.* (2010) believe it will be related to:

- the real rate of interest;
- the inflation premium;
- the default risk premium;
- the maturity premium;
- the liquidity premium;
- the exchange rate premium.

**Assessment advice**

You should note two significant features of security pricing, the YTM (or discount rate) and the present value:

- That all the above bulleted factors are linked to the risk of the security and as such investors (those who purchase securities) will want additional compensation (expected return) as the risk of a security increases. As a result, $r$ will increase.
- That in the present value calculation – $r$ being used in the denominator means that if the discount rate (YTM) increases then the current price of the security falls — if the discount rate falls then the current price of the security rises. Thus there is an *inverse relationship between price and discount rate* (as shown in the above example). Ensure that you understand why this is the case.

## Test yourself

**Q1.** What is meant by the clean price and dirty price when referring to bonds?

**Q2.** What does the use of the term $N$ signify when calculating the price of bond?

**Q3.** Define yield to maturity.

The appropriate discount rate will be found by adding all the premiums that investors are asking for: the real rate of interest + inflation premium + default risk premium + maturity premium + liquidity premium + exchange rate premium; this may come to 10%, for example, when added together. The YTM is calculated on the assumption that future coupon payments can be reinvested at this rate of return. It is sometimes necessary to calculate the YTM when you have been given only the bond price, maturity and coupon rate. Here we show the same example as that used earlier (in Chapter 2) but without the YTM given.

Assume a £1,000 par value bond has a maturity of three years and pays an annual interest of £80 – the coupon is therefore 8% and the bond is currently selling for £950.27. In this you must solve for $r$ or the YTM.

## An example of YTM

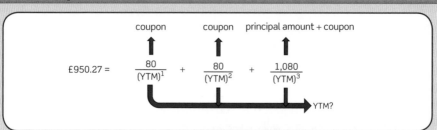

You know from the earlier example (in Chapter 2) that the relevant YTM which makes the present value of a bond's payments equal its price is 10%. This is not easy to calculate but could be done via estimation until you obtain the YTM figure that provides the answer £950.27. However, you can use the YIELD function in Excel or a financial calculator to work out the YTM given the above information.

In Excel you need to go to Formulas and then to Financial, then select YIELD. You will be asked for the following information:

Settlement:  The security's settlement date. This is the date after the issue date when the security is traded to the buyer

Maturity:  The security's maturity date. This is the date when the security expires

Rate:  The security's annual coupon rate

Pr:  The security's price per $100 face value

Redemption:  The security's redemption value per $100 face value

Frequency:  The number of coupon payments per year. For annual payments, frequency $= 1$; for semi-annual, frequency $= 2$; for quarterly, frequency $= 4$

## Bond sensitivity

The yield to maturity (discount rate) changes to equate the current bond price with the required rate of return. This explains the inverse relationship: if investors demand a higher yield due to changing market conditions then the present value of each cash flow decreases in value and so does the current price (as the yield is the denominator in the present value formula). However, since different bonds have different characteristics any discount rate (YTM) change will have different effects on the current price. The **bond sensitivity** *price* will be linked to the characteristics discussed earlier (see Chapters 1 and 2 and above), represented in the present value calculations as maturity and coupon rate. Also note the effect of yield changes at the lower end of yields.

**Recap**

The longer the maturity of a bond, the greater the price sensitivity to a change in yield. This is because the longer the maturity, the more the cash flows have to be discounted and, as you go further into the future, the world becomes more risky and uncertain.

In order to understand this concept look at the worked example of a three-year security below. As expected, when the discount rate decreases from 10% to 9% the price increases by £974.68 − £950.27 = £24.41.

## An example of sensitivity

Here:

$$P = \frac{80}{(1.10)^1} + \frac{80}{(1.10)^2} + \frac{1,080}{(1.10)^3}$$

$$= £72.73 + £66.12 + £811.42$$

$$= £950.27$$

Now, to show the inverse relationship between the discount rate and the price of a bond, assume that one of the factors affecting the discount rate changes due to updated information, for example the inflation rate premium drops. This has the effect of reducing the discount rate from 10% to 9%.

$$P = \frac{80}{(1.09)^1} + \frac{80}{(1.09)^2} + \frac{1,080}{(1.09)^3}$$

$$= £73.39 + £67.33 + £833.96$$

$$= £974.68$$

If we complete the same yield change, with the same assumptions, but change the maturity to 10 years, the change in price (sensitivity) to the change in yield is 935.81 − 877.08 = £58.73. Compare this to the price change for the three-year bond with exactly the same characteristics of £24.41.

For a 10-year maturity bond with YTM = 10%:

$$P = \frac{80}{(1.10)^1} + \frac{80}{(1.10)^2} + \frac{80}{(1.10)^3} + \frac{80}{(1.10)^4} + \frac{80}{(1.10)^5} + \frac{80}{(1.10)^6} + \frac{80}{(1.10)^7}$$

$$+ \frac{80}{(1.10)^8} + \frac{80}{(1.10)^9} + \frac{1,080}{(1.10)^{10}}$$

$$= 72.73 + 66.12 + 60.11 + 54.64 + 49.67 + 45.12 + 41.05$$

$$+ 37.32 + 33.93 + 416.30$$

$$= £877.08$$

For a 10-year maturity bond where YTM drops from 10% to 9%:

$$P = \frac{80}{(1.09)^1} + \frac{80}{(1.09)^2} + \frac{80}{(1.09)^3} + \frac{80}{(1.09)^4} + \frac{80}{(1.09)^5} + \frac{80}{(1.09)^6} + \frac{80}{(1.09)^7}$$

$$+ \frac{80}{(1.09)^8} + \frac{80}{(1.09)^9} + \frac{1,080}{(1.09)^{10}}$$

$$= 73.40 + 67.33 + 61.77 + 56.67 + 52.00 + 47.70$$

$$+ 43.76 + 40.15 + 36.83 + 456.20$$

$$= £935.81$$

Price change to change in yield £935.81 − £877.08 = £58.73.

## Recap

For bonds which differ only in their coupon rate (all other characteristics are exactly the same) the one with the lower coupon rate will have the greater price *sensitivity* to a change in the yield to maturity.

Again this is related to risk: the less you get back in each payment, the more risk is being held by the purchaser (investor) in the security. A clear example is a zero-coupon bond which does not pay any coupons with the interest rate being the difference between the purchase price and the par value at which the bond is issued. A zero-coupon bond only pays back on maturity, thus an investor in a five-year, zero-coupon bond in principle has to wait five years without the bond paying back any return – increasing risk. In contrast the investor with a five-year coupon bond is receiving some interest each year. Thus, the lower the coupon on a security (or no coupon), the greater the price change to a change in yield.

Thus, for a three-year maturity £1,000 bond with a YTM of 10% and a 4% coupon:

$$P = \frac{40}{(1.10)^1} + \frac{40}{(1.10)^2} + \frac{1,040}{(1.10)^3}$$

$$= 36.36 + 33.06 + 781.37$$

$$= £850.79$$

YTM drops by 1%, from 10% to 9% (*ceteris paribus*):

$$P = \frac{40}{(1.09)^1} + \frac{40}{(1.09)^2} + \frac{1,040}{(1.09)^3}$$

$$= 36.70 + 33.67 + 803.07$$

$$= £873.44$$

Price change to change in yield
4% COUPON = £873.44 − £850.79 = £22.65
Price change to change in yield
8% COUPON = £974.68 − £950.27 = £24.41
And for a zero-coupon bond:

$$P = \frac{1,000}{(1.10)^3} = £751.31$$

YTM drops by 1%, from 10% to 9% (*ceteris paribus*):

$$P = \frac{1,000}{(1.09)^3} = £772.18$$

Price change to change in yield ZERO-COUPON £772.18 − £751.31 = £20.87.

**NOTE:**

Notice that the price change for the bond with the higher coupon of 8% is greater –however, the % price change (sensitivity) is greater for the lower coupon bond:

4% COUPON BOND percentage price change = 22.65/850.79 = 2.66

8% COUPON BOND percentage price change = 24.41/950.27 = 2.57

ZERO-COUPON BOND percentage price change = 20.87/751.31 = 2.78

---

## ✳ Assessment advice

Be aware that at lower yields to maturity any changes in the yield will have a greater impact on the current price than at higher yields. This is a marginal effect − the change is greater from 4% to 5% than it is from 10% to 11%.

## Test yourself

**Q1.** What effect does the maturity of a bond have on price sensitivity as yields change?

**Q2.** For bonds with exactly the same characteristics, the one with the lower coupon rate will have the _____ price sensitivity to a change in the yield to maturity. Fill in the missing gap.

## Key definitions

**Clean bond price**

Is the price of the bond excluding any interest that has accrued.

**Dirty bond price**

The clean price plus any accrued interest that the holder of the bond would receive.

**Cash flow on a bond**

The regular payments on a bond as specified by the coupon.

**Bond sensitivity**

How a bond's current price is affected by changes in underlying factors.

## Examples & evidence

As France faces another downgrade to its government bonds, investors in ETFs tracking AAA-rated eurozone government debt may find their investment universe has shrunk.

This week the rating agency Moody's announced it had downgraded French government bonds from the top-quality AAA rating to the one-notch lower rating, Aa1, with a negative outlook. Moody's decision followed in the steps of S&P, which stripped French government bonds of their prized AAA qualification in January.

As of this writing, Fitch is the only rating agency still classing French government bonds under the AAA umbrella. However, Fitch's rating outlook for France was moved from stable to negative back in December 2011. There is a distinct risk that Paris might be in for a "full-house" of sovereign rating downgrades.

With two downgrades already in the bag, investors in exchange-traded-funds (ETFs) that track indices measuring the performance of the euro-zone AAA-rated government bond market are probably wondering whether they will soon be invested in "de facto" German government bond ETFs. Indeed, a rational investor would assume that French government bonds can no longer be part of those indices. If so, the statistical void left by France would have to be redistributed amongst the remaining AAA bond markets, with Germany as the overwhelmingly dominant force against the much smaller Dutch, Austrian and Finnish elements.

While it is fair to infer that investors in AAA-rated government bond ETFs are essentially seeking security, it would be wrong to assume they would be happy putting their money in pseudo-German-only investment vehicles. For a start, seeking safety does not necessarily mean forfeiting all possibility of yield, which is what one would do by going German in the current environment. In fact, investors in the AAA-rated vehicles have enjoyed a bit of yield pick-up courtesy of exposure to non-German (i.e. mainly French) government bonds. But besides that, a considerable swathe of investors simply refuse to see France as anything else than top quality, irrespective of what the rating agencies say.

What should you do at this point if you are invested in a eurozone AAA-rated government bond ETF and you still want exposure to France? Well, for most the answer would be "keep your money where it is". Over the years that I have been with Morningstar, one of the key messages I have always stressed to ETF investors is the importance of understanding the index an ETF is tracking. And this is one of those situations where knowing your index inside out would prevent you from making the wrong decision.

In our Morningstar ETF database, we find a total of eight ETFs tracking AAA-rated eurozone government bond indices, which are displayed in the table below. These ETFs are marketed by Lyxor, db X-trackers and Amundi. Each provider has opted to reference their ETFs to a particular index family: EuroMTS Eurozone AAA Macro Weighted Government indices for Lyxor; iBoxx EUR Sovereign Eurozone AAA indices for db X-trackers; and EuroMTS Eurozone Highest-Rated Government Bond indices for Amundi.

| Name | Ticker | TER | Replication | Domicile |
|------|--------|-----|-------------|----------|
| Amundi ETF GovBdHghst RtdEuroMTSInGr 1-3 | AA13 | 0.14 | Synthetic | France |
| Amundi ETF GovtBdHghstRt-dEuroMTSInvstGr | AM3A | 0.14 | Synthetic | France |

| Name | Ticker | TER | Replication | Domicile |
|------|--------|-----|-------------|----------|
| db x-trackers II iBoxx EUR SovErznAAA 1C | XBAT | 0.15 | Synthetic | Lux. |
| db x-trackers II iBoxx EURSvErzAAA1-3 1C | X13A | 0.15 | Synthetic | Lux. |
| Lyxor ETF EuroMTSAAAAMacroWeightedGovtBd | MAA | 0.17 | Synthetic | France |
| Lyxor ETF EuroMTS AAAMcroWghtdGovt1-3Y C | MA13 | 0.17 | Synthetic | France |
| Lyxor ETF EuroMTS AAAMcroWghtdGovt3-5Y C | MA35 | 0.17 | Synthetic | France |
| Lyxor ETF EuroMTS AAAMcroWghtdGovt5-7Y C | MA57 | 0.17 | Synthetic | France |

According to the rules governing EuroMTS indices tracked by the Lyxor and Amundi ETFs, eligible countries must have "no less than two AAA ratings" from the three main rating agencies (e.g. S&P, Moody's and Fitch). In principle, this would mean that France would be out. However, another rule clearly specifies that these particular indices must be comprised of a minimum of five issuing countries and where a credit rating downgrade for an eligible issuer would lead to the number of eligible countries falling below such minimum, then the issuer in question would remain in the index until a new issuer becomes eligible to replace it. In short, France will remain in the AAA-rated EuroMTS indices as: a) otherwise the number of issuing countries would be below the minimum and b) it is highly unlikely to foresee any of the remaining eurozone countries being upgraded to AAA. Morningstar has confirmed with EuroMTS that this is correct.

If you are invested in the db x-trackers AAA-rated eurozone government bond ETFs, then the situation may be different. Eligible bonds for the iBoxx indices these ETFs track must have an "average iBoxx rating" of AAA, which is calculated as the average of the ratings from the three main rating agencies. Before the Moody's downgrade, France still made it as AAA. However, as Markit has also confirmed with Morningstar, the average iBoxx rating for French bonds has now been scaled down to AA. This implies that French bonds would be stripped out of the iBoxx AAA-rated Eurozone government bond indices at the next rebalancing (i.e. at the end of the month). If so, the db X-trackers Eurozone AAA-rated government bond ETFs would become de facto German government bond ETFs, unless of course db X-trackers decides to change the index to the iBoxx EUR Sovereigns AAA-AA (yes, there is such an index!) in which case, you'd still get exposure to France, but would also gain exposure to Belgium.

Investing using ETFs is a straightforward way of gaining exposure to a large array of asset classes. However, you still have to do your research. Chief in this is understanding the index an ETF tracks. Morningstar's collection of ETF due diligence reports has specific sections dedicated to unravel all the main aspects of index construction and they can help you in your investment decision process.

*Source*: Jose Garcia-Zarate (2012) Slim Pickings for AAA-Rated Government Bonds, Morningstar, 23 November.

## Question

Ensure that you can follow this article. In the years since the financial crisis of 2008, many countries have found it difficult to maintain their AAA ratings. This can make it more expensive for them to raise new finance. What are your thoughts? How does this article link to bond pricing? Also note the importance of up-to-date industry analysis. Morningstar is an excellent source of up-to-date information.

## Chapter summary – pulling it all together

By the end of this chapter you should be able to:

| | Confident ✓ | Not confident? |
|---|---|---|
| Fully explain the features of a bond including: principal amount; coupon rate; and maturity | | Revise pages 181–182 |
| Discuss what is meant by the bond indenture and the key features that may appear in a bond indenture | | Revise pages 182–183 |
| Explain the different types of bonds that are issued into the capital markets including their distinguishing features | | Revise pages 184–187 |
| Explain a Eurobond | | Revise page 187 |
| Discuss the bond rating system and any differences between the systems used by the three main rating agencies | | Revise pages 187–189 |

| | Confident ✓ | Not confident? |
|---|---|---|
| Discuss the operation of the primary and secondary markets for bonds–including the issue of UK gilts into the primary market | | Revise pages 189–192 |
| Understand and calculate the price of a bond including the yield to maturity and sensitivity | | Revise pages 192–200 |

Now try the sample question at the start of this chapter, using the answer guidelines below.

## Answer guidelines

### ✳ Assessment question

(a) Outline the basic characteristics and features of a bond. (30 marks)

(b) Describe the different types of bonds that can be issued into the capital markets, including how their characteristics differ from a standard bond. (40 marks)

(c ) Describe the components of the equation below: (30 marks)

$$P = \sum_{t=1}^{n} \frac{C}{(1 + r)^t} + \frac{F}{(1 + r)^n}$$

### Approaching the question

This question requires you to show understanding of bond characteristics and the components that allow you to calculate a bond's price. Make sure that you fully understand the basics of bonds and write these down clearly and concisely. This will include describing what is meant by the principal amount (or face value), the coupon, maturity and rate of interest. More marks will be gained for relating this to risk and return for a bond. Link part (a) with (b) by describing the bond indenture and introduce the terminology, vanilla bond and exotic bond. Part (b) should select a variety of different bonds, contrasting their characteristics with a standard 'vanilla' bond. Examples, using data, will increase your grade. Part (c) is more straightforward: ensure that you understand the equation and describe each component separately. Again, use of an example utilising the equation will score highly.

## Important points to include:

- Clearly state the basic features of a bond like coupon, face value, time to maturity and interest rate.

- Describe the bond indenture.

- Explain the difference between a plain 'vanilla' bond and an 'exotic' bond.

- Choose a variety of 'exotics' and describe each one, using examples where appropriate.

- Disaggregate the equation into its component parts and explain each variable. Again, examples using data will score highly.

## Make your answer stand out

This answer requires clear explanations and links between the various bonds to highlight the differences. Incorporation of real-world examples will show that you have engaged with the subject and increase your grade.

## Read to impress

### Books

Understanding the principles of bond pricing is about building up your knowledge of the basic principles. Pilbeam is strong on bond pricing, the others are better at the key characteristics of the bond markets.

Bodie, Z., Kane, A. and Marcus, A. (2012) *Essential of Investments*. McGraw-Hill.

Fabozzi, F., Modigliani, F. and Jones, F. (2010) *Foundations of Financial Markets and Institutions*. Pearson Education.

Pilbeam, K. (2010) *Finance and Financial Markets*. Palgrave Macmillan.

Again, for a more practical guide try:

Chartered Institute for Securities and Investment (2010) *Study Text: Global Operations Management*. BPP Learning.

### Journal article

Perraudin, W. and Taylor, A.P. (2003) Liquidity and bond market spreads. EFA 2003 Annual Conference Paper No. 879.

## Websites

Again, try the websites below. For a thorough understanding of the practical aspects make sure you read the first two references:

The United Kingdom Debt Management Office: *UK Government Securities: A Guide to 'Gilts'*.

The United Kingdom Debt Management Office: *GILTS: An Investor's Guide*.

Ernst & Young: **www.ey.com/UK/en/home**.

FTSE: **www.ftse.com/**.

London Stock Exchange: **www.londonstockexchange.com/home/homepage.htm**.

McKinsey & Company: **www.mckinsey.com/**.

Morgan Stanley: **www.morganstanley.com**.

The Bank of England: **www.bankofengland.co.uk/Pages/home.aspx**.

The European Central Bank: **www.ecb.int/home/html/index.en.html**.

The Federal Reserve: **www.federalreserve.gov/**.

The United Kingdom Debt Management Office: **www.dmo.gov.uk/**.

These sites will have up-to-date data and information on the operation of the capital markets that will enable you to show more understanding and make your answer stand out.

## Companion website

Go to the companion website at **www.pearsoned.co.uk/econexpress** to find more revision support online for this topic area.

**Notes**

# Notes

# 8 Derivatives – forwards, futures and swaps

## Topic map

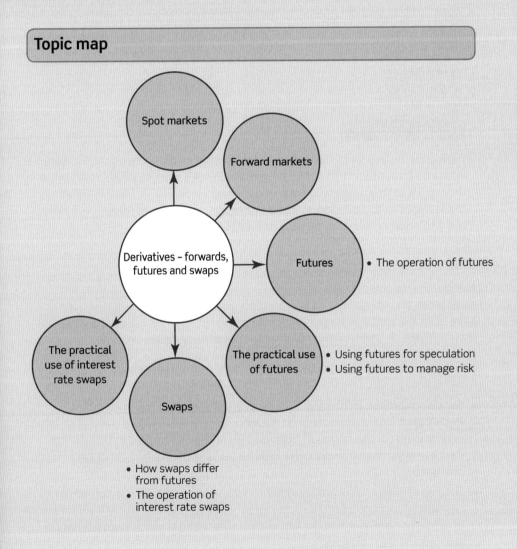

Spot markets

Forward markets

Derivatives – forwards, futures and swaps

Futures
• The operation of futures

The practical use of interest rate swaps

The practical use of futures
• Using futures for speculation
• Using futures to manage risk

Swaps
• How swaps differ from futures
• The operation of interest rate swaps

A printable version of this topic map is available from **www.pearsoned.co.uk/econexpress**

## Introduction

A **derivative** is a financial instrument that 'derives' its value from some other 'underlying' asset. Derivative markets have been around for centuries but their growth has increased spectacularly over the past couple of decades. They originated in Chicago in 1972, and in 1982 London opened the London International Financial Futures Exchange known as LIFFE. Other European derivative markets include those in Paris (MATIF) and Frankfurt (Deutsche Terminborse).

The underlying asset in a derivatives contract could be anything, for example:

- commodities such as grain, tea, metal;
- financial securities such as shares or bonds;
- share indexes;
- currencies;
- or interest rates.

### Recap

Derivative instruments were originated to reduce risk via hedging. Hedging is an investment technique to reduce or eliminate the risk of an asset price moving in such a way as to lose you money. However, derivatives do lend themselves to speculation. In many financial scandals derivatives have been used to speculate rather than to reduce risk.

A derivative contract has a buyer and a seller and gives the right (and also sometimes the obligation) to buy and sell a quantity of the underlying asset at a pre-specified price at a specified date in the future. The value of the derivative contract changes as the value of the underlying asset changes.

The main derivative markets are:

- Forward markets: a forward is an agreement between counterparties to exchange a financial asset of some kind for cash at a future date. They are customised for the needs of both parties and are arranged informally on OTC markets. Traditionally there was no secondary market although this is changing.
- Futures markets: a future is similar to a forward in that it is an agreement between counterparties to exchange a financial asset of some kind for cash at a future date, but futures are standardised and traded on an exchange such as LIFFE in London.

- Swap markets: a swap is an agreement between two parties to exchange two differing forms of payment obligations. This could be to 'swap' the obligation to pay floating rate interest on a bond with that of the obligation to pay fixed rate interest on a bond.
- Option markets: an option is a contract that gives the holder the right but not the obligation either to buy or sell a financial security at a specified price: either at a set point in time or within an agreed time period.

This chapter will look at the dynamics of forwards, futures and swaps. The next chapter will look at options.

 **Revision checklist**

*Make sure that you understand:*
- ❏ use of the term spot price and DvP in derivative markets;
- ❏ the difference between exchange traded and OTC derivative markets;
- ❏ the definition and key features of forwards;
- ❏ the definition of futures and how they differ from forwards;
- ❏ key features associated with the operation of a futures contract;
- ❏ the term 'mark to market' and the different margins that need to be covered by those active in the futures market;
- ❏ the terms tick, open interest and counterparty;
- ❏ practical use of futures for speculation or managing risk;
- ❏ the definition and key features of interest rate swaps;
- ❏ the difference between swaps and futures;
- ❏ practical use of interest rate swaps to restructure debt, hedge risk and reduce the cost of finance.

**✳ Assessment advice**

Derivatives at first glance may seem complicated. Most of the subjects that you are taught during your first finance course will assume the purchase of an asset today in the hope that its price will rise. That is, buying the asset at its spot price to go long on the asset. To understand derivatives ensure that you can explain the basic definitions and the dynamics of each derivative. Forwards, futures, swaps and options all have their own logic – make sure you can explain this logic. The use of fully explained diagrams and examples, which are related to the question being asked, will increase your grade.

**Assessment question**

Derivative markets have witnessed a remarkable growth during the past two decades.

(a) Describe the features of the main derivative instruments. (50 marks)

(b) Examine how futures and swaps can be used to manage risky situations. (50 marks).

Can you answer this question? Guidelines on answering the question are presented at the end of this chapter.

## Spot markets

To understand the operation of derivative markets it is best to introduce what is meant by the **spot market**. In a spot market the underlying asset is traded, paid and delivered immediately. This is known as delivery versus payment (**DvP**) which is a term used widely when analysing the settlement processes of particular financial markets. DvP reduces risk because counterparties do not have to wait for either cash or the asset to be delivered.

A quote for immediate delivery of a share of £6 is known as the spot price. If an investor purchases 1,000 of these shares, they must pay the seller £6,000 (plus any trading costs) immediately and the seller must deliver the shares immediately. Investors use spot markets to **go 'long'** (rather than **go 'short'**) that is, invest now in the hope that the price of the asset will rise.

### Recap

The term 'counterparties' is used to denote the parties in a transaction – the buyer and seller. All transactions in financial markets must have both a buyer and a seller in order to be executed and cleared. In markets today people refer to '**counterparty risk**', which is the risk of either the buyer or seller not being able to honour their financial agreement; that is, not produce payment or not produce the financial assets. In many cases financial markets have a central counterparty which clears trades between buyers and sellers.

### Exchange traded versus OTC derivative markets

Derivative markets can be either:

- over the counter; or
- exchange traded.

## OTC derivative markets

OTC derivative markets trade tailor-made derivatives to the specific requirements of the counterparties and is not tightly regulated. OTC market rules are based on business honesty and courtesy between the derivative buyer and derivative writer. Contracts for the whole range of derivatives are traded including stock, bond, interest rate, **commodity**, and foreign currency derivatives. The market is dominated by large institutional investors, large corporations, financial institutions and government. In most cases the derivative holder is aware of the creditworthiness of the **counterparty**. If the creditworthiness is not known then the credit risk can be mitigated by a collateral guarantee.

## Exchange-traded derivative markets

Exchange-traded derivatives are traded on an exchange which takes the form of a legal corporate entity. The legal entity (for example, LIFFE) provides a physical marketplace for trading with standardised rules and regulations, meaning the exchange specifies the contracts' terms and conditions. For exchange-traded contracts a secondary marketplace is possible where the holder and the writer can sell their obligations to buy or sell the stock before the expiration date.

### Key definitions

**Derivative**

A financial instrument that 'derives' its value from some other 'underlying' asset.

**Commodity**

A physical product, for example grain or metal, which is interchangeable with another if they are of the same type and quality.

**Counterparty**

Refers to the other party in a financial transaction such that every financial transaction to sell must have a counterparty who buys and vice versa.

**Spot market**

This is where a financial security is traded, paid and delivered immediately.

**DvP (Delivery versus Payment)**

Refers to the settlement procedure where financial securities are traded, paid and delivered at the same time.

### Going long

This is where a financial security is bought today in the hope that it goes up in price.

### Going short

This is where you sell a financial security that you do not own, by borrowing it from a counterparty, in the hope that the price will fall. If the security does fall in price you will buy the security at a cheaper price than you borrowed, thus making a profit when you return the security to whom you borrowed it from.

## Forward markets

A **forward** is an agreement between counterparties to exchange a financial asset of some kind for cash at a future date. They are customised (or tailor made) for the needs of both parties and are arranged informally on OTC markets. Originally this made it difficult for the operation of a secondary market. Forward contracts are transacted on a wide range of commodities and are used to lock in a position on the future spot price or interest rate for a commodity or financial security. This reduces the risk of exposure to adverse price movements such that:

- forward contracts take away the risk of an asset appreciating in value that you need to purchase in the future; or
- forward contracts take away the risk of an asset reducing in value that you need to sell sometime in the future.

### Recap

The holder of the forward contract (purchaser) is said to take a long position while the writer (seller) of the forward contract is said to take a short position.

### Test yourself

**Q1.** List the main derivative markets.

**Q2.** What is a counterparty?

**Q3.** What is meant by 'going long' and 'going short'?

For example, for a producer of chocolates the major cost is the raw ingredient, cocoa. The price of cocoa will rise and fall in the markets throughout the year and this may have a significant impact on the cost of chocolate production. In order to eliminate the price uncertainty the chocolatier can enter into a forward contract to buy cocoa at a set price sometime in the future – locking into price certainty. If the actual market price of cocoa is higher than the forward price on the exercise date then the forward contract will be profitable. However, the producer of chocolates bears the risk of prices being lower than the forward contract exercise price – in this case the chocolate producer suffers a loss compared with the then spot price. Note, however, that they have still benefited from price certainty – they knew the price they would pay for cocoa in the future.

Forwards can also be used to lock into an interest rate in the future. These are known as forward rate agreements (**FRAs**) and are based upon some agreed notional amount, for example £100. The seller or writer of the FRA agrees to lend £100 at a stated rate, for example 3%. In this case if the agreement was for delivery in one year's time then the seller of the contract would have to lend £100 at a rate of 3% to the buyer of the FRA in one year's time. The buyer must pay 3% in one year's time to borrow £100. If rates are higher than 3% after one year, then the buyer has benefitted; if not they may lose out, for example if rates were 2% in the spot market. However, note that in both examples forward contracts are liable to the risk of either counterparty defaulting.

Key features of forwards:

- Two parties agree to exchange a real or financial asset on a prearranged date in the future for a specified price.
- They are private agreements, customised to the specific needs of both parties.
- Traditionally there was no secondary market in forwards.
- Traded in the informal OTC market.
- Major players are retail and investment banks.
- The risk of default is higher than for futures.

## Futures

A **future** is an agreement between counterparties to exchange a financial asset of some kind for a pre-specified amount of cash at a future date. A futures contract specifies the amount of the asset to be traded, the delivery date and the process for payment and delivery of assets. **LIFFE** in London was first opened in early 1980s. In 2001 it merged with the Amsterdam, Paris and Belgium exchanges to create Euronext.LIFFE. More recently Euronext also merged with the Lisbon Stock Exchange.

The most popular futures contracts are in commodities like oil, gold, cotton and coffee and financial assets like short-term and long-term interest rates, currency and stock index contracts. Like other derivatives, futures contracts are used both for managing risks and taking speculative positions.

Futures differ from forwards, as follows:

- Forward contracts are traded over the counter. Futures are standardised into a set contract size, a set quality of commodity and a set delivery date, and traded on an exchange such as LIFFE. This reduces search costs associated with forwards as buyers and sellers can enter into a contract immediately using the centralised market.
- Forwards are individual agreements between two parties and so can be high in counterparty default risk. Futures are traded on exchanges that employ a central counterparty and a clearing house and guarantee against default risk.
- Forward contracts are negotiable between two parties and then fixed (in the example above, 3% for £100 in one year's time). Futures contracts are standardised (so the terms of the contract cannot be changed between buyers and sellers) and are then **'marked to market'**. This calls for both the buyer and seller of a futures contract to provide a minimum deposit per contract to the exchange, which then varies as the value of the futures contract changes.
- Futures contracts are more liquid than forwards contracts. This is because futures contracts can be sold in the secondary market before the contract matures. So an investor can sell the futures contract (and their obligation) before maturity. However, traditionally, forwards contracts could not be sold in the secondary market and hence they were less liquid. However, due to a burgeoning secondary market in forwards, the distinction is becoming blurred.

## The operation of futures

The futures contract specifies all necessary details: the commodity to be delivered; the maturity date; and the price. However, in most cases delivery does not actually take place and the buyer and seller of the futures contract close out their positions before the contract matures.

Key features of futures contracts:

- The trader who buys a futures contract, so committing to purchase the commodity on a set date, is taking a long position.
- The trader who sells a futures contract, so committing to delivering the commodity, is taking a short position.

- No money changes hands when the contract is initially agreed and signed.
- The trader going long is fixing a price that they will pay for a set amount of the commodity sometime in the future.
- The seller will lose out when the price rises to exactly the same amount as the purchaser wins. That is, the winner wins what the loser loses; a futures contract is a **zero-sum game**, the loss to one party being exactly equal to the gain of the other party.

## The basic futures contract: an equal-sum game

A trader may buy a futures contract for ethanol delivery in three months' time. Prices will be posted for a three-month ethanol contract on the exchange and this will change daily, up to and including the day when the contract matures. Each ethanol contract requires the delivery of 29,000 gallons of ethanol (standard contract amount) and prices are quoted in dollars per gallon. If the buyer purchases 10 ethanol futures contracts at a price of $2 per gallon then they have gone long; in this case they will benefit if the price rises such that:

profit to those going long = price at maturity − original futures price

profit to those going short = original futures price − price at maturity

If the spot price in three months' time for an ethanol futures contract were $2.05 then the purchaser of the futures contract would win by:

| | | |
|---|---|---|
| the set amount of ethanol to be delivered for each contract | = | 29,000 multiplied by |
| the amount of futures contracts bought | = | 10 multiplied by |
| the price change for the purchaser of the contract | = | +$0.05 |
| **total profit** | = | **$14,500** |

However, the seller of the contract would lose by:

| | | |
|---|---|---|
| the set amount of ethanol to be delivered for each contract | = | 29,000 multiplied by |
| the amount of futures contracts bought | = | 10 multiplied by |
| the price change for the seller of the contract | = | −$0.05 |
| **total profit** | = | **−$14,500** |

## Key definitions

**Forward**

A non-negotiable, customised agreement between counterparties to exchange a financial asset of some kind for cash at a future date.

**FRA**

A forward which is locked into an interest rate in the future.

**Futures**

Standardised negotiable agreements between counterparties to exchange a financial asset of some kind for a pre-specified amount of cash at a future date

**LIFFE**

London International Financial Futures Exchange, where futures are traded, first opened in the early 1980s.

**Initial margin**

The minimum amount of money the investor must deposit with the exchange per derivative contract.

**Marked to market**

The change in the margin required by the exchange as the price moves against those holding a derivative contract.

**Zero-sum game**

Where the loss to one party is exactly equal to the gain to the other party.

- Futures contracts can be traded on the futures exchange at any time up to maturity. In this way investors can realise any profits (or losses), which means they do not have to take delivery of the commodity.

## Realising a profit on a futures contract

Any profit or loss on a futures contract is taken when you sell the contract in the marketplace or at maturity. In this way you can think of futures as any other asset – if the price rises you will make money. This is similar to your buying one company share for £5.00 and then selling it for £5.50 – to realise this gain you must sell the share. This is exactly the same with a futures contract. For example, using the same information as above, if we assume:

- you enter into an agreement for one three-month futures contract to buy ethanol;
- the contract size is for delivery of 29,000 gallons of ethanol (standard contract amount);
- the futures contract was worth a price of $2 per gallon;
- no money changes hands but you are exposed to paying 29,000 × $2 = $58,000 in three months' time to take delivery of 29,000 gallons of ethanol;

Then:

- the price per gallon offered for an ethanol futures contract to be delivered in two months' time (one month after you agreed the contract) rises to $2.10 and then, after two months have elapsed (now one month for the actual delivery of the ethanol), the contract is worth $2.15;
- the contract at this point is worth 29,000 × $2.15 = $62,350;
- you could now 'sell' the futures contract that you own and make a profit of $62,350 − $58,000 = $4,350.

## How do you do this?

To realise this profit the holder of a futures contract must take an offsetting position. So in the above case you had an agreement to *buy* and so you must enter into an agreement to *sell* one ethanol contract. *The contract you sell must be identical to the one you bought (that is, an ethanol futures contract expiring on the same date).* In this way you have agreed to buy 29,000 gallons of ethanol for $58,000 and sell 29,000 gallons of ethanol for $62,350, realising a profit of $4,350.

### Recap

Closing out your position on a futures contract in known as a reversing trade.

- In practice, although you do not have to pay any money to enter into a futures contract, all futures exchanges require buyers and sellers to pay a margin which is then marked to market. This means that the margin that you must maintain changes as the price of the futures contract changes. This limits the exposure of the contract. If the contract is falling in price, which is reducing your original margin payment, then you have to deposit more cash every day. If you fail to do this the exchange has the right to close out your position. There are three margin terms that you must be aware of:

- **Initial margin**: this is the minimum amount of money the investor must deposit with the exchange per contract. If the exchange rules state that you must deposit 10% of the value of one contract using the example above, this would be 29,000 × $2 × 0.10 (or 10%) = $5,800. The initial margin can be paid in cash and/or short-term securities such as Tbills and is referred to as equity.

- **Maintenance margin**: the minimum amount that must be on deposit to cover your position. If you sustain substantial losses in one day then the margin account may fall below this level. For example, if the initial margin is 10% and the maintenance margin is 5% then the initial margin as established is $5,800 and the maintenance margin is 29,000 × 2 × 0.05 (5%) = $2,900. If the price of the contract drops, then you do not have to take any action until it drops below the maintenance margin level of 5%. This would occur if the price of the ethanol future dropped below $1.90 because at this point your contract has dropped in value by $2,900 from its initial value of $58,000 to $55,100 (29,000 × 1.90). You now only have $2,900 in equity left of your initial margin and any further drop will require you to top up to the initial margin level of $5,800.

- **Variation margin**: breaching your maintenance margin triggers a margin call from the exchange and you must then top up your margin account with the amount required to bring your margin back up to the initial margin level. This is known as the variation margin. It must be paid in cash.

## Recap

In the above case the trader who is holding the sell position (to your buy position) will have their margin account credited with positive amounts exactly equal to your losses. This means that they will be covering more than 10% of their initial position – they will be in credit. In this case the seller of the contract can withdraw these excess funds from the margin account.

## Test yourself

**Q1.** How do futures differ from forwards? Is this changing? Why?

**Q2.** What does the term 'negotiable' refer to when discussing derivatives?

**Q3.** What is meant by the term 'reversing trade'?

**Q4.** Define initial margin, maintenance margin and variation margin.

- Central Counterparty Clearing House (CCP). Every futures exchange will have a central counterparty clearing house which sits between those taking a buy position and those taking a sell position. It increases the efficiency and speed of transactions and eliminates counterparty risk. The risks associated with futures contracts are that the buy party will not, or does not, have the capacity to pay or that the sell party does not, or refuses to, deliver the commodity or financial security. This is called default risk. The CCP:

    - Always takes the opposite position taken by a trader. For example, if you buy a contract the clearing house takes the equal and opposite position, in this case a sell position. It will satisfy in full all the terms and conditions of the contract. This eliminates counterparty risk as the trader is no longer exposed to the creditworthiness or integrity of the counterparty.

    - Makes the counterparty in a trade irrelevant. The counterparty is the buyer for every sell contract and the seller for every buy contract. Either party can liquidate their positions immediately with the CCP.

    - Aids reversing trades. Investors looking to unwind their positions in futures can always do so by taking an identical but opposite position to the one they are currently holding.

    - Maintains records of all counterparty transactions and marks their positions – making margin calls when necessary.

    - Closes out positions when traders fail to comply with the rules of the exchange.

- **Open interest**: this is the number of outstanding contracts (long or short) that remain on a particular future, for example ethanol futures to be executed on 1 May. The CCP's position will always net to zero (long positions cancelling out short positions). In the case of the ethanol example, most traders will not want to take delivery of ethanol and so will begin to reverse their trades as the maturity of the contract gets closer. Each reversing trade reduces open interest by 1. Open interest will rise when contracts begin trading, peak and then fall to near zero before the expiry date. Maybe only 1% or 2% of commodity contracts result in actual delivery.

- The futures price at the maturity date should be equal to the spot price. If this is not the case investors will rush to buy the commodity from the cheaper market and sell it in the dearer market. This would allow investors to guarantee an arbitrage profit. However, the price will converge in an efficient, competitive market as trading will take place to eliminate any difference and equate prices. This is known as the **convergence property**.

- Futures exchanges impose **price limits** on a futures contract: this is a maximum and minimum price that the futures contract can be bought or sold for in any single day. This is imposed to provide stability.

- Futures exchanges impose **position limits**: this is the maximum number of contracts that an individual trader may hold.

- **Settlement price**: this is the price used at the end of trading each day to settle trades and call for variation margins if required. It can be the last price at which the contract traded or in some cases an average of the last few trades of the day where contracts see a lot of late activity. The settlement price will be decided by the exchange.

- Cash settlement: suppose an investor invests in the stock index futures. It would be physically impractical to deliver all the stocks in the FTSE 100 index at the required proportions upon expiration of the contract. In this case futures contracts are settled on a cash settlement basis by transferring cash from the losing to the winning party.

---

 **Assessment advice**

### Ticks

When revising futures you may come across calculations which use ticks. A **tick** is the smallest permissible price movement in a futures contract. In the case of ethanol futures the tick size is one-tenth of one cent ($0.001) per gallon, so each cent change in price equals 10 ticks. The tick value is calculated by taking the fixed size of each contract – in the case of ethanol this is 29,000 – and multiplying it by the tick size so that:

tick size (0.001) × fixed contract size (29,000) = $29

Each tick will mean a $29 difference in the cost of buying and selling 29,000 gallons of ethanol. This makes it easier to calculate profits and losses from price movements on futures because it automatically takes into account the size of each contract. Using the example above, when the price for a gallon of ethanol increased by 15 cents from $2 to $2.15 the profit increased by:

ticks × tick value × contracts currently being held = 150 (15 cents × 10 ticks) × 29 × 1 = $4,350

---

## Key definitions

**Counterparty risk**

The same as default risk, that is the risk that the buy party will not, or does not, have the capacity to pay or that the sell party does not, or refuses to, deliver the commodity or financial security.

**Open interest**

The amount of outstanding contracts (long or short) that remain on a particular future.

**Convergence property**

The term for the futures price at the maturity date equalling the spot price.

**Price limits**

The maximum and minimum prices that the futures contract can be bought or sold for in any single day.

**Position limits**

The maximum number of contracts that an individual trader may hold.

**Settlement price**

The price used at the end of trading each day to settle trades and call for variation margins if required.

## The practical use of futures

Derivative instruments such as futures can be utilised effectively to manage risk via **hedging**; however, they also lend themselves ideally to taking on speculative positions which are highly leveraged and can be extremely risky.

### Using futures for speculation

Much of the growth in futures over the past two decades is down to speculators using futures to take highly **leveraged positions** on financial securities, commodities or stock indexes instead of buying (going long) on the actual physical asset and holding it until the price rises. This is because in many cases this is not possible (for example, buying ethanol is not practical as you would need storage space while waiting for the price to rise) but also because:

- investing in the futures market incurs lower **transaction costs** than buying the underlying asset;

- futures allow an investor to leverage their positions above that which is possible when compared with buying the physical asset. This is because futures contracts only require you to provide an initial margin which is much less than the value of the tangible asset in the contract. This can provide investors with higher returns if they 'guess' correctly on the price movement of an asset.

The box below shows how you can leverage your position using futures.

---

## Leveraging your position using futures

### Scenario (a): Purchasing the physical asset

Assume you have £10,000 to invest and after undertaking some research you decide to go long on shares in Bramallco. Each share costs £5.00 and so you purchase 2,000 shares.

### Scenario (b): Entering into a futures contract

However, today you can invest in single stock futures with the contract size being 100. If we assume that a three-month futures contract price can be struck at £5 a share and that each contract is for 100 shares (this means each contract allows you to buy 100 shares at £5 in three months' time), each contract will be worth 100 × £5 = £500. If we assume that the initial margin required by the exchange is 10% then for each contract entered into you will need to give an initial margin of £50. This means that you can purchase 200 contracts with your £10,000, using the £10,000 as the initial margin.

Assume that in two months' time the price, as you had expected, rises to £5.50 and you decide to unwind your position.

Scenario (a): the total profit is the price rise minus the initial spend of £10,000. This is 2,000 × £5.50 = £11,000. Hence, a total profit of **£11,000 – £10,000 = £1,000.**

Scenario (b): you decide to enter a reverse trade and liquidate your position on the exchange. In order to do this you need to agree to sell an equal amount of contracts on exactly the same expiry date. The profit in this case would be as follows.

The initial buy contract was worth 100 × 5 = £500 per contract and you had 200 contracts.

You now enter a sell contract worth 100 × 5.50 = £5.50 per contract and you need to sell 200 contracts

---

You have now agreed to buy 20,000 shares of Bramallco for £5, which equals £100,000, and sell 20,000 shares of Bramallco for £5.50, which equals £110,000. Hence, a total profit of **£10,000**.

## Recap

At maturity the convergence property means that the futures price on the expiry date will equal that day's (spot) price.

## Using futures to manage risk

In contrast to speculators, you can use futures to hedge against market volatility and protect against adverse price movements. This is especially useful if you are a company which is exposed to the market price of an asset or currency. For example, for a gold mining company whose profits rely on the price of gold in the future, a drop in the price of gold would reduce profits. Look at the box below to see how this is achieved.

## Hedging your position using futures

An olive-oil-producing company wants to control against a fall in the price of olive oil reducing its profits. The company knows that in a few months' time it will sell a certain amount of olive oil to the market – it is holding olive oil. As the company is holding a long position in olive oil, it needs to take a short position in olive oil futures in order to hedge against a price drop in the market.

Assume that:

- the company will sell 100,000 litres of olive oil which it has produced on 1 December;
- the company agrees to sell 100 futures contracts of contract size 1,000 litres (equals 100,000);
- the futures contract price is £1.00 per litre for delivery on 1 December so each contract is worth $1000 \times £1 = £1000$;
- there can only be three possible prices of olive oil on 1 December: £0.95, £1.00, or £1.03 per litre;
- on 1 December the company will reverse its position on the futures market.

In the table column (a) shows the effect of the price of olive oil being £0.95 on 1 December.

The company can sell its oil for 100,000 × £0.95 = £95,000. However, it had planned for a price of £1.00 – it can achieve this by reversing (or closing out) its position on the futures market:

- It *sells* its futures contracts for 100 × 1,000 × £1.00 (the agreed price) and receives £100,000;
- it *buys* futures contracts for 100 × 1,000 × 0.95 (the oil price on the expiry date), which cost £95,000;
- In this case it makes **£5,000** on the futures contracts which covers its loss on selling olive oil.

Column (b) shows the effect of the price of olive oil being £1.00 per litre on 1 December:

- The company can sell its oil for 100,000 × £100 = £100,000.
- It *sells* its futures contracts for 100 × 1,000 × £1.00 (the agreed price) and receives £100,000.
- It *buys* futures contracts for 100 × 1,000 × £1.00 (the oil price on the expiry date), which cost £100,000.
- In this case it makes **£0** on the futures contracts but it still receives £100,000 as desired.

Column (c) shows the effect of the price of olive oil being £1.03 per litre on 1 December:

- The company can sell its oil for 100,000 × £103 = £103,000.
- It *sells* its futures contracts for 100 × 1,000 × £1.00 (the agreed price) and receives £100,000.
- It *buys* futures contracts for 100 × 1,000 × £1.03 (the oil price on the expiry date), which cost £103,000.
- In this case it loses **£3,000** on the futures contracts but it still receives £100,000 as desired. What the company wins on selling its oil it loses on the futures contracts.

| | (a) £0.95 | (b) £1.00 | (c) £1.03 |
|---|---|---|---|
| Revenue from sale of oil (£) | 95,000 | 100,000 | 103,000 |
| Profit or loss on the futures contract | 5,000 | 0 | −3,000 |
| **Total revenue** | **100,000** | **100,000** | **100,000** |

## Key definitions

**Hedging**

Taking an offsetting position in a financial security, in which an investment has been made, to reduce or limit risk.

**Speculation**

Purchasing financial securities in an attempt to profit from price changes.

**Leveraged position**

The degree to which an investor is using borrowed money to invest in financial securities. In derivatives this can be achieved by only having to cover the margin requirement of the derivatives exchange.

**Transaction costs**

Costs associated with buying and selling financial securities.

**Ticks**

The smallest permissible price movement in a futures contract

## Swaps

A **swap** is an agreement between two parties (referred to as counterparties) to 'swap' specified cash payments sometime in the future based upon an underlying asset or price. There are many types of swaps including currency swaps, credit risk swaps, commodity swaps and equity swaps. The most common types of swaps are interest rate swaps. All swaps have the same principle: swapping one type of exposure for another, thus allowing (usually) companies to manipulate and manage their exposure to risk. However, the swap market can also help parties raise funds more quickly. The swap market is used by major corporations, international financial institutions and governments and it is an important part of the international bond market.

### Recap

Swaps can be thought of as a series of forward contracts because parties are agreeing swaps over a number of periods; for example, a two-year swap may involve swapping cash payments twice, which is much the same as agreeing two forward rate agreements – in one year and then in two years' time. Remember that a forward is an agreement between counterparties to exchange a financial asset of some kind for cash at a future date.

Swaps differ from futures as follows:

- One of the differences between swaps and forwards is that forwards or futures agreements are usually for less than 24 months, while a swap agreement can be arranged for a period of 10 years or more. Thus firms with longer debt obligations can agree a swap agreement with longer time frames.
- Futures contracts are highly standardised. Swap contracts can be more specific by matching time horizons and payment schedules according to individual requirements.
- Futures contracts are highly regulated. The swap market is free of regulation.
- Futures have an organised secondary market. Swaps, due to their specific nature, are non-standardised and therefore have a less active secondary market.

## The operation of interest rate swaps

Interest rate swaps involve a series of fixed interest cash payments being exchanged (or swapped) for a corresponding series of floating rate cash payments. The aim of the swap is to exploit any comparative advantage in fixed or floating rates in such a way that both parties obtain cheaper financing, manage risk exposure and/or restructure their debt. The interest rate swap market is worth trillions annually.

Key features of interest rate swaps:

- The amount upon which the swap interest is agreed is called the **notional principal amount**.
- The swap buyer (also referred to as the fixed rate payer) agrees to pay a series of fixed rate payments (that were originally agreed by the other party) to the swap seller.

- The swap seller (also referred to as the floating rate payer) agrees to make the floating rate payments (that were originally agreed by the other party) that float or vary on some reference rate to which the original floating rate was agreed. This could be LIBOR or the Tbill rate.
- The counterparties only exchange the net interest payments on set periodic settlement dates.
- Interest rate swaps exchange fixed rate exposure for floating rate exposure and floating rate exposure for fixed rate exposure.
- Basic swaps, like the one explained below, are known as plain vanilla swaps.

## The practical use of interest rate swaps

Interest rate swaps are most commonly used to:

- restructure debt;
- hedge interest rate risk; and
- reduce the cost of finance.

### Restructure debt

As the circumstances of companies change, they may prefer to exchange one type of exposure for another. Rather than retire the form of debt and reissue in the form they require, it may well be cheaper and quicker to swap their current exposure with another firm which has the equal and opposite requirement.

### Hedge interest rate risk

Two companies can swap exposures to fixed and floating rate interest in such a way as to hedge their position and reduce risk.

Assume:

- Two banks: Middleton Bank (A) and Goodwin Bank (B).
- Middleton Bank makes £20 million loans at a fixed rate of 8% for three years.
- Middleton Bank financed these loans by issuing six-month certificates of deposit paying LIBOR plus 100 basis points.
- LIBOR is currently 5%.
- Middleton Bank has a floating rate exposure of LIBOR (currently 5%) + 1% (100 basis points) which equals 6%.

- Middleton Bank on this part of its business is currently earning a spread or profit of 8% minus 6% which equals 2% (or 200 basis points).
- Goodwin Bank has raised £20 million at a fixed rate of 5.2%.
- Goodwin Bank has decided to take the money raised and lend it to customers at a variable rate tracking LIBOR (5%) plus 3%.
- Goodwin Bank on its part of this business is currently earning a spread or profit of 8% minus 5.2% which equals 2.8% (or 280 basis points).

In this scenario both banks are exposed to risk because their liabilities and assets are not matched in terms of their interest rate exposure.

## Recap

Bank liabilities are what a bank owes (a cost to the bank) and assets are what a bank is owed (income for the bank).

## Test yourself

**Q1.** How do swaps differ from futures?

**Q2.** In what three ways are swaps used by companies?

## How banks can hedge using swaps

Both banks are exposed to interest rate movements:

- Middleton Bank: that LIBOR increases from 5% to 7%. This would mean the bank's liabilities are now costing 8% but as Middleton Bank only receives 8% from its fixed loans and now has to pay 8% for its liabilities, the profit on this business has been wiped out.
- Goodwin Bank: that the LIBOR rate will fall from 5% to 2.2%. This would mean the bank's liabilities are still costing fixed 5.2% but the return from loans now equals 3% plus 2.2% or 5.2% which wipes out its profit on this business.

To avoid their exposure the banks decide to enter a swap deal:

- Middleton Bank agrees to pay Goodwin Bank a fixed rate of 7.2%.
- Goodwin Bank agrees to pay Middleton Bank LIBOR + 220 basis points.

The last three columns of the table show the effect of LIBOR on bank profits or spread. Both banks have now locked into certainty regardless of how interest rates move. They have eradicated interest rate risk and maintained their current profit. However, they remain susceptible to the other risks of banking – most notably credit risk.

| Middleton Bank | | | LIBOR 4% | LIBOR 5% | LIBOR 6% |
|---|---|---|---|---|---|
| Income from issuing *fixed rate* loans | + | 8% | 8 | 8 | 8 |
| Expenditure on floating rate debt | − | LIBOR + 100bp | 5 | 6 | 7 |
| Middleton receives from Goodwin floating | + | LIBOR + 220bp | 6.2 | 7.2 | 8.2 |
| Middleton pays Goodwin fixed | − | 7.2% | 7.2 | 7.2 | 7.2 |
| **Spread or profit** | | | **2%** | **2%** | **2%** |

| Goodwin Bank | | | LIBOR 4% | LIBOR 5% | LIBOR 6% |
|---|---|---|---|---|---|
| Income from issuing *floating rate* loans | + | LIBOR + 300bp | 7 | 8 | 9 |
| Expenditure on fixed rate debt | − | 5.2% | 5.2 | 5.2 | 5.2 |
| Goodwin receives from Middleton fixed | + | 7.2% | 7.2 | 7.2 | 7.2 |
| Goodwin pays Middleton floating | − | LIBOR + 220bp | 6.2 | 7.2 | 8.2 |
| **Spread or profit** | | | **2.8%** | **2.8%** | **2.8%** |

## Reduce the cost of finance

If companies are exposed to different interest rates in different markets, there may well be a potential to swap for mutual benefit. This may be the case for domestic companies raising finance in their own market. For example, a new issue of bonds issued by a British company in London may well obtain cheaper finance than an Australian company as investors may well have more information and confidence in the British company. Likewise the Australian company may well be able to obtain finance cheaper in Australia. If a British company requires Australian dollars and the Australian company requires British pounds, there is an opportunity for both to raise finance in their own markets and swap exposures.

Assume:

- Bramallco can borrow at a floating rate of LIBOR plus 1.2%.
- Bramallco can borrow at fixed rate of 5%.
- Shoreham Plc can borrow at a floating rate of LIBOR plus 0.7%.
- Shoreham Plc can borrow at a floating rate of 5.6%.
- Bramallco wants to borrow £10 million for five years at a floating interest rate.
- Shoreham Plc wants to borrow £10 million for five years at a fixed interest rate.

### Using swaps to reduce the cost of finance

|  | Fixed rate | Floating rate |
|---|---|---|
| Bramallco | 5.0% | LIBOR + 1.2% |
| Shoreham Plc | 5.6% | LIBOR + 0.7% |

Note that:

- Bramallco can borrow at a fixed rate of interest which is 0.6% or 60 basis points cheaper than Shoreham Plc.
- Shoreham Plc can borrow at a floating rate of interest which is 0.5% or 50 basis points cheaper than Bramallco.
- Bramallco has an absolute advantage over Shoreham Plc in the fixed rate market.
- Shoreham Plc has an absolute advantage over Bramallco in the floating rate market.

If Bramallco borrows the £10 million at a fixed interest rate of 5% and Shoreham Plc borrows the £10 million at the floating rate of LIBOR + 0.7% then a mutually beneficial swap deal can be agreed. The companies do not exchange the principal since they have both borrowed £10 million:

- Bramallco pays LIBOR + 0.7% to Shoreham Plc; and
- Shoreham Plc pays Tbill + 5% to Bramallco.

If LIBOR is currently known to be 4.5% then Bramallco will have to pay Shoreham Plc 5.2% (4.5% + 0.7%). These payments can be paid net, with Bramallco paying Shoreham Plc 20 basis points on the £10 million.

The result:

- Bramallco receives floating rate finance which is 50 basis points cheaper than if it had raised floating rate financing without the swap; and
- Shoreham Plc receives fixed rate finance which is 60 basis points cheaper than if it had raised fixed rate finance without the swap.

## Key definitions

**Swap**

An agreement between two parties (referred to as counterparties) to 'swap' specified cash payments sometime in the future based upon an underlying asset or price

**Notional principal amount**

The amount upon which the swap interest is agreed.

## Examples & evidence

The decade from 1999 to 2009 has been the most remarkable in the derivatives market's history, with exceptionally fast growth in many markets and product lines. That was brought to a sharp halt in 2008 by the financial slump. But when the crisis eases, can the derivatives market go back to the steep upwards path of the past 10 years? Colin Packham investigates.

The exchange-traded derivatives market has enjoyed a decade of unprecedented growth, until the past 12 months – a time disfigured by the worst financial crisis since the Great Depression. As the graphs on these pages show, the acceleration in European and US futures and options trading has been so fast that common sense suggests it cannot continue at the same rate forever. Was the financial crisis of 2008 an inflexion point, after which the market will grow more slowly?

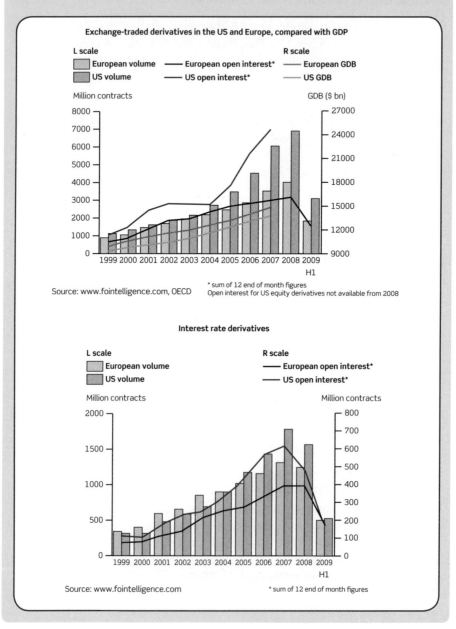

**Exchange-traded derivatives in the US and Europe, compared with GDP**

L scale
■ European volume —— European open interest* ----- European GDB
■ US volume —— US open interest* —— US GDB

R scale

Million contracts

GDB ($ bn)

Source: www.fointelligence.com, OECD

* sum of 12 end of month figures
Open interest for US equity derivatives not available from 2008

**Interest rate derivatives**

L scale
■ European volume
■ US volume

R scale
—— European open interest*
—— US open interest*

Million contracts

Million contracts

Source: www.fointelligence.com

* sum of 12 end of month figures

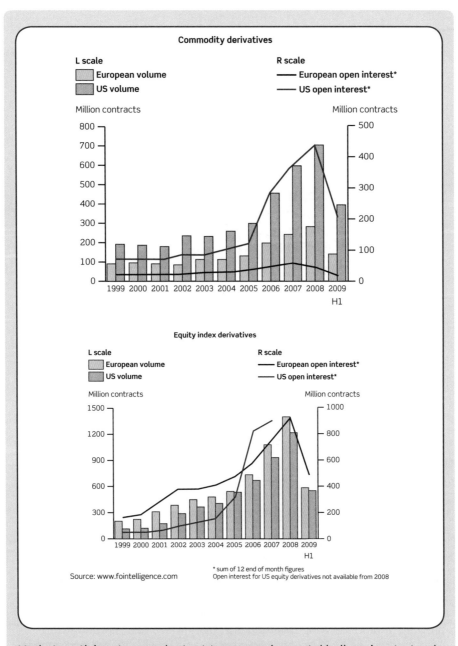

**Commodity derivatives**

L scale
- European volume
- US volume

R scale
- — European open interest*
- — US open interest*

Million contracts (L scale): 800, 700, 600, 500, 400, 300, 200, 100, 0
Million contracts (R scale): 500, 400, 300, 200, 100, 0

1999 2000 2001 2002 2003 2004 2005 2006 2007 2008 2009 H1

**Equity index derivatives**

L scale
- European volume
- US volume

R scale
- — European open interest*
- — US open interest*

Million contracts (L scale): 1500, 1200, 900, 600, 300, 0
Million contracts (R scale): 1000, 800, 600, 400, 200, 0

1999 2000 2001 2002 2003 2004 2005 2006 2007 2008 2009 H1

Source: www.fointelligence.com

\* sum of 12 end of month figures
Open interest for US equity derivatives not available from 2008

Market participants are reluctant to engage in crystal ball-gazing. Instead, they point out that the growth in derivative markets in the past decade can be accounted for by specific factors. And they highlight several concrete reasons why, far from slowing down, exchange-traded derivative markets, even in developed countries, could be on the threshold of another period of fast growth.

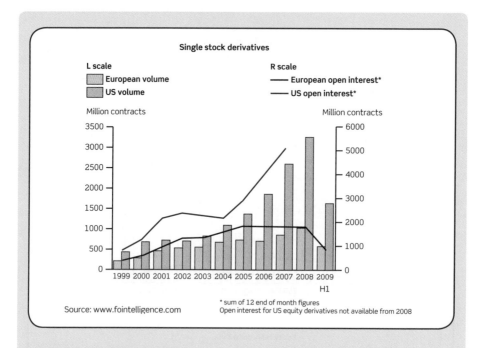

**Single stock derivatives**

L scale
▨ European volume
▨ US volume

R scale
—— European open interest*
—— US open interest*

Million contracts (L scale): 3500, 3000, 2500, 2000, 1500, 1000, 500, 0

Million contracts (R scale): 6000, 5000, 4000, 3000, 2000, 1000, 0

1999 2000 2001 2002 2003 2004 2005 2006 2007 2008 2009 H1

Source: www.fointelligence.com

\* sum of 12 end of month figures
Open interest for US equity derivatives not available from 2008

## A golden decade

In 1999, the economies of Europe and the US were both strong, but the growth of the listed futures and options markets was still more impressive. The annual percentage growth of trading on the US exchanges hovered in the high teens between 1999 and 2003, before accelerating to around 25% in 2004–5 and over 30% in 2006–7. In Europe volume growth was usually more moderate, staying between 10% and 20% every year except 2001, when a big jump in fixed income pushed the whole market up by 43%, and 2007, when it almost reached 25%. Even in 2008, volume grew by 14% on both continents.

## Euro sparks rates explosion

The explosion of derivatives in Europe came at the turn of 2000, which coincided with a period of vigorous economic growth. Exchange trading swelled by 17.39%, as economic output rose 3.86%. The good times continued for Europe in 2001 as 1.44bn contracts were traded, 43% up on the previous year. Underlying this furious activity was a fast maturing European market, led by Eurex and the creation of a newly merged exchange in London. Euronext was formed in September 2000 with the merger of the Amsterdam, Brussels and Paris stock exchanges, to take advantage of the harmonisation of European Union financial markets. In December 2001

Euronext acquired the London International Financial Futures and Options Exchange, renaming it Euronext Liffe – now NYSE Liffe.

However, Brendan Bradley, global head of product strategy at Eurex, says the real catalyst for the take-off at Eurex and Liffe was the introduction of the euro at the beginning of 1999, which united the government bond markets of 11 countries under a single currency, greatly increasing liquidity. "In fixed income, there was a de facto benchmark for the whole of the euro zone which became the German yield curve – and by virtue of the fact that Eurex had the Bund, Bobl and the Schatz products available, trading tended to concentrate on the most liquid market," says Bradley.

The short term interest rate derivatives market, led by Liffe, also profited from the consolidation brought by the euro. Bradley also highlights the capital efficiencies brought by exchange-traded derivatives, particularly encouraged by the Basle Accord. "The exchange-traded derivatives market offered participants the opportunity to use margined products within a centrally cleared environment – which was particularly beneficial to them," Bradley says.

## New sophistication in equities

The new millennium brought with it strong equity markets in the financial capitals of the US and Europe. With that came a rapidly expanding equity derivatives market. As the graphs show, US trading in single stock derivatives outnumbered trades in equity index derivatives by four to one in 1999. In Europe, the two markets were level. Over the next 10 years, the US stock index market grew more than tenfold, the European market sevenfold, to a point where the US had nearly caught up with Europe by number of contracts.

On the single stock side, European growth over the decade was a shade under five times, but the US market ballooned from 445m contracts in 1999 to 3.27bn in 2008 – growth of more than seven times. European single stock trading is now just a third of that in the US. The substantial increase in equity index derivatives owes much to the success of CME Group's E-Mini S&P 500 contract – which started the decade with just over 10m trades and reached 309m in 2008.

The contract, which is particularly popular with retail investors, offers traders leveraged exposure to the most widely traded equity index in the US. Other successful contracts such as the Chicago Board of Trade's Volatility Index and CME's Russell 2000 contract, which moved to the Intercontinental Exchange last year, all enjoyed sustained growth. In

Europe, the individual equity derivatives market in the early 2000s was dominated by what is now NYSE Liffe Paris, with its suite of equity options.

However, Eurex was chasing, and by 2003, the German exchange's equity products outperformed those of Euronext Liffe. That success hit its peak in 2008, when 480m single stock contracts were traded at Eurex – of which 349m were options. Bradley highlights what he calls the "growing sophistication" of market participants who embraced the use of equity options with a new willingness, and also showed a preference for exchange-traded over OTC products.

## Processor power

From another perspective, the soaring volumes on derivatives exchanges can be explained almost entirely by technological innovation. The adoption of new trading gateways and platforms, and the implementation of algorithmic trading made it far easier for traders to access exchanges, and to trade in greater volumes.

Giles Nelson, director of technology and co-founder of Progress Apama, a software company that specialises in services for algorithmic trading, says the high-frequency style of trading has been a "significant factor in the growth of exchange-traded derivatives". "Being able to get a machine to do the trading in place of a human means you can do more of it. Inevitably trading volumes have tended to go up," Nelson says.

Bradley agrees, but also notes that with the rise of algorithmic trading and the tendency to trade in and out of the market quickly, traditional proprietary traders have lost ground in comparison.

*Source:* Futures market set for another glorious decade? *Futures & Options World*, 20 July 2009.

## Question

This is an excerpt from an article printed in 2009 in *Futures and Options World*. What led to the explosion in derivatives? What was the role of technology? How would you interpret the graphs and the effect of the financial crisis of 2008? Undertake some research on the growth of derivative markets since 2009.

# Chapter summary – pulling it all together

By the end of this chapter you should be able to:

| | Confident ✓ | Not confident? |
|---|---|---|
| Define a spot price and explain what is meant by going long | | Revise page 212 |
| Explain the difference between exchange traded and OTC derivative markets | | Revise page 213 |
| Define a forward and its key features | | Revise pages 214–215 |
| Describe the difference between futures and forwards | | Revise page 216 |
| Provide an example of how a futures contract works in practice showing that it is an equal-sum game between the buyer and seller of a future | | Revise pages 216–217 |
| Define marked to market/initial, maintenance and variation margin | | Revise pages 217–220 |
| Explain the role of a central counterparty and define open interest and tick | | Revise pages 221–222 |
| Provide examples of how futures can be used for speculation and risk management | | Revise pages 223–227 |
| Define a swap and its key features | | Revise pages 227–229 |
| Describe how swaps differ from futures | | Revise page 228 |
| Give examples of how interest rate swaps can be used to restructure debt; hedge risk and reduce the cost of finance | | Revise pages 229–233 |

Now try the sample question at the start of this chapter, using the answer guidelines below.

## Answer guidelines

### ✳ Assessment question

Derivative markets have witnessed a remarkable growth during the past two decades.

(a) Describe the features of the main derivative instruments. (50 marks)

(b) Examine how futures and swaps can be used to manage risky situations. (50 marks)

### Approaching the question

Begin this question by showing that you understand what is meant by a derivative. Explain the spot market and what going long and going short mean. You should then introduce the main derivative instruments: forwards, futures, swaps and options. Provide an explanation of each before going into a more detailed description of them – provide full explanations of their key features. Avoid using bullet points as this looks like a list and fails to give you the opportunity to analyse or describe in detail. Explain the key differences between each derivative instrument. Part (b) requires you to examine the use of futures and swaps. Begin this part by linking the main features discussed in part (a) with the oncoming discussion: you should relate futures and swaps to risk management. Provide a definition of risk. The rest of this section should concentrate on examples of how futures and swaps can help manage risk. These should be fully explained.

### Important points to include:

- Key definitions.
- An explanation of each type of derivative instrument – avoid bullet points and take time to describe in full.
- A definition of risk and how this can be managed using derivatives.
- As many numerical examples of how futures and swaps can help manage risk.

### Make your answer stand out

Ensure that you have fully explained each derivative instrument and contrasted the differences clearly – to make an answer stand out in this type of question you must get the basics right. You will see your grade increasing with the use of more examples to show how futures and swaps can be utilised to manage risk. Use examples that your lecturer did not use in their lecture slides – the best way of doing this is to use a wide selection of books. Derivatives will be discussed in finance, corporate finance, financial management and banking books. Spread your search wide for good examples to use in your examination.

## Read to impress

### Books

Here is a selection of books that introduce the above concepts in an understandable way – each offering a slightly different perspective. It is recommended to start with Bodie *et al.*:

Bodie, Z., Kane, A. and Marcus, A.J. (2010) *Essentials of Investments*. McGraw-Hill.

Fabozzi, F., Modigliani, F. and Jones, F. (2010) *Foundations of Financial Markets and Institutions*. Pearson Education.

Madura, J. (2012) *Financial Markets and Institutions*. South-Western.

Pilbeam, K. (2010) *Finance and Financial Markets*. Palgrave Macmillan.

Saunders, A. and Cornett, M.M. (2012) *Financial Markets and Institutions*. McGraw-Hill.

### Journal articles

Jong, F.D. and Driessen, J. (2001) LIBOR market models versus swap market models for pricing interest rate derivatives: an empirical analysis. *European Finance Review*, Vol. 5 (3), pp. 201–37.

Longstaff, F.A., Mithal, S. and Neis, E. (2005) Corporate yield spreads: default risk or liquidity? New evidence from the credit default swap market. *Journal of Finance*, Vol. 60 (5), pp. 2213–53.

### Websites

Chicago Mercantile Exchange (CME) Education: **www.cmegroup.com/ education/**.

Ernst & Young: **www.ey.com/UK/en/home**.

FTSE: **www.ftse.com/**.

LIFFE Investor Learning Center: **www.liffeinvestor.com/learning-centre**.

London Stock Exchange: **www.londonstockexchange.com/home/ homepage.htm**.

McKinsey & Company: **www.mckinsey.com/**.

Morgan Stanley: **www.morganstanley.com**.

NYSE Euronext Global Derivatives: **https://globalderivatives.nyx.com/**.

The Bank of England: **www.bankofengland.co.uk/Pages/home.aspx**.

The European Central Bank: **www.ecb.int/home/html/index.en.html**.

The Federal Reserve: **www.federalreserve.gov/**.

## Companion website

Go to the companion website at **www.pearsoned.co.uk/econexpress** to find more revision support online for this topic area.

## Notes

# 9

# Derivatives – options

## Topic map

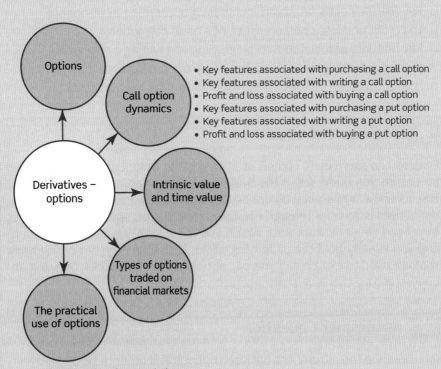

Options

Call option dynamics
- Key features associated with purchasing a call option
- Key features associated with writing a call option
- Profit and loss associated with buying a call option
- Key features associated with purchasing a put option
- Key features associated with writing a put option
- Profit and loss associated with buying a put option

Derivatives – options

Intrinsic value and time value

Types of options traded on financial markets

The practical use of options

- Using options for speculation
- Using options for risk management

A printable version of this topic map is available from **www.pearsoned.co.uk/econexpress**

## Introduction

This chapter continues to analyse derivatives, focusing upon options. An option is a contract that gives the holder the right but not the obligation either to buy or sell a financial security at a specified price – either at a set point in time or within an agreed time period. Options can be quite confusing – ensure that you take time to consider the logic behind them including the role of the buyer of an option and the writer (or seller) of an option. Once you understand this you will begin to realise the logic of options.

###  Revision checklist

*Make sure that you understand:*

- ❏ the difference between an American option and European option;
- ❏ how options differ from futures;
- ❏ common terminology used in options;
- ❏ key features associated with purchasing and writing a call option;
- ❏ the profit and loss characteristics of a basic call option;
- ❏ key features associated with purchasing and writing a put option;
- ❏ the profit and loss characteristics of a basic put option;
- ❏ how options can be used for speculation and for managing risk.

### ✳ Assessment advice

Options can seem more complicated than other basic types of derivatives so ensure you understand the basic operation of an option including all the common terms used by option traders. Key to understanding option derivatives is to work through examples from the perspective of both the buyer and seller (writer). Note that if you are a seller (writer) of an option and you already hold the underlying asset, it changes the basic diagrams that are used to explain **call and put options** in the textbooks. Showing an understanding of this will help increase your grade.

### ✳ Assessment question

(a) Describe the differences between options and other basic derivatives. (30 marks)

(b) Fully explain the dynamics of a call option and consider the advantages and disadvantages of writing a call option. (70 marks)

Can you answer this question? Guidelines on answering the question are presented at the end of this chapter.

# Options

An **option** is a contract that gives the holder the right but not the obligation to buy or sell an underlying asset at a fixed price on or before a specified date. For example, an option on a house may give the owner the right (but not the obligation) to buy the house for £200,000 on or at anytime before a given date. Options enable investors to take positions on assets without being fully exposed to the full risk of prices moving against them.

For example, if you believe shares in Bramallco are going to rise in price over the next three months from £1 to £1.30 you could go long and buy some shares in Bramallco. If they increase in price like you expected you will realise the full benefit of 30p per share. However, if you miscalculated and the share price dropped to 90p then you would lose 10p per share. If you had taken out an option to buy Bramallco shares at £1.05 in two months' time and the shares were trading for £1.30 in two months' time, by exercising your right to buy the shares at £1.05 you would again be in profit. If the price dropped to 90p you would leave the option unexercised. So, options are only exercised if it is advantageous for the holder to do so, otherwise the options remain unexercised.

Options also require two parties: the person buying the option and the person selling the option, the person selling the option being referred to as the **writer.** Options protect **holders** from **downside risk**, which is not the case for writers of options who are exposed to risk in some scenarios.

Options come in two types:

1 **American option:** this gives the option holder the right to buy or sell the underlying asset anytime during the time period until the option expires. An option that expires in three months can be acted upon anytime within this three-month period.
2 **European option:** this gives the option holder the right to buy or sell the underlying asset on a particular date known as the expiry date.

As with other derivatives, options can be purchased on an exchange (exchange-traded options) or direct from an institution over the counter (OTC). Exchange-traded options are standardised in terms of expiration date and contract size while OTCs are tailor made to suit the individual.

Options differ from futures in the following ways:

- Futures commit both parties to transacting at a later date. Options allow one party the 'option' to transact while the other party, the writer, is committed to transacting if the option is exercised.

- Futures do not involve a fee. However, with an option the buyer pays the writer (seller of the option) an **option fee or premium.**

- Futures contracts provide a sliding scale of profit or loss for the buyers and sellers as the price moves in their favour or against them – the buyer 'wins' what the seller 'loses'. Options allow the buyer to restrict their loss to the option fee. The writer's maximum profit is the fee but they are exposed to large losses.

## Common terminology

When discussing options (and other derivative instruments) there is a common terminology used in books, with which you must become familiar. These are given in the following Key definitions box:

### Key definitions

**Option**

A contract that gives the holder the right but not the obligation to buy or sell an underlying asset at a fixed price on or before a specified date.

**Call option**

Gives the holder the right but not the obligation to buy an underlying asset at a given price on or before a pre-specified date.

**Put option**

Gives the holder of the option the right but not the obligation to sell an underlying asset at a given price on or before a pre-specified date.

**Downside risk**

Risk that an investment will move in such a way that the investor will lose money.

**Holder**

The person who buys an option.

**Writer**

The person who sells a call or put option.

**Option premium, price or fee**

The fee that is paid by the purchaser of the option to the writer of the option.

**Exercising the option**

The act of buying or selling the option at the specific price.

**Strike or exercise price**

The price that has been agreed in the option contract to buy or sell the underlying asset.

**Expiration date**

The maturity date of the option – the option does not exist past this date.

**'In the money' option**

An option is 'in the money' when it is profitable to exercise the option at the given strike price.

**'Out of the money' option**

An option is 'out of the money' when it is not profitable to exercise the option at the given strike price.

**Going long on an option**

Buying an option is called taking a long position.

**Going short on an option**

Selling an option is called taking a short position.

## Test yourself

**Q1.** How do options differ from futures?

**Q2.** What does 'call' and 'put' refer to in option markets?

**Q3.** What is an options' exercise price?

## Call option dynamics

All options have a purchaser and a writer and the benefits accrue/dissipate to each symmetrically.

Key features associated with *purchasing* a *call* option:

- A call option gives the purchaser the right to buy the underlying asset at a specified price known as the **strike price**.

- Buying a call option is called a **long call**.
- The purchaser of the option must pay the writer immediately when they agree to enter into a deal; you may not wait to pay at the expiry date or until you **exercise the option**.
- The amount that the purchaser pays for each option is subtracted from any **'in the money'** profit.
- The amount of money that the purchaser can make on a call option is potentially limitless.
- If the option is 'in the money' such that the strike price (including the option fee) is lower than the current market price for the asset then the holder can exercise the option, purchase the asset and sell it immediately in the marketplace to realise a profit.

### Recap

A profit is made only when the strike price plus the fee for each option is above the current market price. For example, the strike price on a share is £2.00, the fee is 10p and the price of the share on the day of expiration is £2.20; then you are 'in the money' by 10p.

- If the option is **'out of the money'** such that the strike price is higher than the current market price, the holder would not exercise the option but would still incur the option premium or fee.
- If the option is 'at the money', which means the strike price equals the current market price, there is little point in exercising the option. For example, the strike price is £2.00, the fee is 20p and the price of the share on the day of expiration is £2.00, so whether you exercise the option or not you lose 20p.
- The purchaser will exercise the option if the strike price is above the current market price but not at a price to cover the entire option fee. In this case the holder will lose money but not as much as they would if they left the option unexercised. For example, the strike price is £2.00, the fee is 10p and the price of the share on the day of expiration is £2.05. In this case you can buy at £2.00, incur a fee of 10p, so it will cost you £2.10, and sell immediately at £2.05. You lose 5p as compared with not exercising the option, which would incur a cost of 10p.

Key features associated with *writing* a *call* option:

- The writer will be 'in the money' as long as the price of the underlying asset is equal to or less than the market price when the option is exercised. In this case the option will not be exercised and the writer will benefit to the amount of the fee.

- If the strike price equals the current market price then any further movement upwards of the market price will begin to erode the writer's profit. For example, if the strike price and the market price are equal at £2, and the option fee was 10p, the holder will not exercise the option. If the market price increases to £2.01 the holder will buy at £2.10 (strike price plus fee) and sell at £2.01, losing 9p instead of 10p when the prices were equal. In this case the writer loses 1p, making only 9p instead of 10p.

- The writer is exposed to limitless losses as the underlying stock rises in price. If the underlying asset is higher on expiration than the strike price plus option fee, the holder will exercise the option and force the writer to buy the underlying asset at the current market price and sell at the lower strike price. Each movement of the market price upwards, which is potentially unlimited, means that the writer could suffer heavy losses.

## An example of profit and loss associated with buying a call option

Assume:

- You have bought a call option which gives you the right to buy one share of Bramallco for £8 in three months' time.
- The option fee was £1.
- Total price of exercising the option = £9.

Possible outcomes at the expiry date:

- If the price of a Bramallco share is less than £8 exercising the option would be futile – you would be buying the share for £8 when it is cheaper just to buy it at the current market price. Not exercising the option will cost you £1. In this case, the maximum loss to you as the option holder is £1; even if the price of Bramallco is £4 on expiry, you do not exercise the option and incur the £1 fee.

- If the share price on the expiry date is exactly £8 (point A in Figure 9.1) you would not exercise the option as this would also be futile. You would be buying the Bramallco share at exactly £8, incur the fee of £1 and so the total price would be £9, but you could only sell at £8. This is the same as not exercising the option; you would still incur a loss of £1.

- Once the share price of Bramallco rises above £8 then it is economically rational to exercise the option. If the price is more than £8 but less than £9 (the points in the figure between A and B) you would exercise the option but still lose money. For example, if Bramallco is trading at £8.50, you could buy at £9 and sell at £8.50 incurring a loss of 50p rather than £1.

- If Bramallco is trading at £9 you would exercise the option and break even exactly as the cost of purchase equals the current selling price.

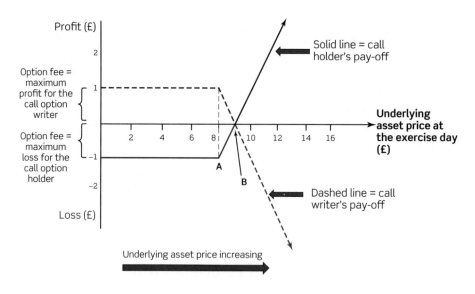

**Figure 9.1** Buyer's and writer's profit and loss on call options.

- Any price above £9 for Bramallco sees you in profit, so if on the day of expiry the price of one Bramallco share is £15, you receive a profit of £6 (£15 – £9).
- The writer is in an equal and opposite position to the holder. At any current market price under £8 they will realise their maximum profit of £1. Any price between £8 and £9 (between A and B in the figure) will see them begin to lose some of their profit. At a market price of £8.70, the writer would have to buy at £8.70 and sell at £8.00 to the holder of the option. This would incur a loss of 70p, but the writer would have received the fee of £1 so they would realise a profit of 30p.
- At a market price of £9 the writer breaks even, mimicking the holder of the option.
- At any market price over £9 the writer begins to lose money – since prices can rise to any level – so the writer's exposure is limitless and risky.

### Test yourself

**Q1.** When purchasing a call option when will you be 'in the money'?

**Q2.** The purchaser of a call option will exercise the option if the strike price is _____ the current market price. Fill in the gap.

**Q3.** Explain why the writer of a call option is exposed to limitless losses.

**Recap**

Due to the limitless risk exposure of the writer, most exchanges would require the *writer* to deposit the fee received for the option as a margin. As the price moves against the writer they would have to add a variation margin – the position would be being marked to market.

Key features associated with *purchasing* a *put* option:

- A put option gives the purchaser the right to sell the underlying asset at a specified price known as the strike price.
- Buying a put option is called a long put.
- The purchaser of the option must pay the writer immediately when they agree to enter into a deal; you may not wait to pay at the expiry date or until you exercise the option.
- The amount that the purchaser pays for each option is subtracted from any 'in the money' profit.
- The amount of money that the purchaser can make on a put option is limited as the underlying asset cannot trade below a price of zero.
- The option is 'in the money' when the strike price (taking into account the option fee) is higher than the current market price for the asset. In this case the holder of the option will buy the underlying asset in the marketplace and sell it to the option writer at the agreed lower strike price.

**Recap**

A profit is made only when the strike price plus the fee for each option is lower than the current market price. For example, the strike price on a share is £2.00, the fee is 10p and the price of the share on the day of expiration is £1.80; then you are 'in the money' by 10p. You buy the share from the market on the day for £1.80, you then sell it to the writer of the option for £2.00, but you have paid 10p for the option to sell it to them, thus realising a profit of 10p.

- If the option is 'out of the money' such that the strike price is lower than the current market price, the holder would not exercise the option but still incur the option premium or fee.
- If the option is 'at the money', which means the strike price equals the current market price, there is little point in exercising the option. For

example, the strike price is £2.00, the fee is 20p and the price of the share on the day of expiration is £2.00; whether you exercise the option or not, you lose 20p.

- The purchaser will exercise the option if the strike price is below the current market price but not at a price to cover the entire option fee. In this case the holder will lose money but not as much as they would if they left the option unexercised. For example, the strike price is £2.00, the fee is 10p and the price of the share on the day of expiration is £1.95. In this case you can buy the share for £1.95 from the market and sell it the writer for £2.00 less costs of 10p, which equals £1.90. You lose 5p on the deal compared with 10p.

Key features associated with *writing* a *put* option:

- The writer will be 'in the money' as long as the price of the underlying asset is equal to or more than the market price when the option is exercised. In this case the option will not be exercised and the writer will benefit to the amount of the fee.
- If the strike price equals the current market price then any further movement downwards of the market price will begin to erode the writer's profit. For example, if the strike price and the market price are equal at £2, and the option fee was 10p, the holder will not exercise the option. If the market price decreases to £1.99 the holder will buy from the market at £1.99 and sell at £1.90 (strike price minus fee), losing 9p instead of the 10p when prices were equal. In this case the writer loses 1p, making only 9p instead of 10p.
- The writer is exposed to limited losses as the underlying stock price cannot fall below zero. If the underlying asset is lower on expiration than the strike price minus the option fee, the holder will exercise the option. This will force the writer to buy the underlying asset at the higher strike price than they can resell in the marketplace. So if the price in the market is £1.50 and the writer is exposed to a strike price of £2.00, they will be committed to buying at £2.00; when they try to resell the share they will only receive £1.50. The writer loses 50p minus the option premium.

## An example of profit and loss associated with buying a put option

Assume:

- You have bought a put option which gives you the right to sell one share of Bramallco for £8 in 3 months' time;
- The option fee was £1;
- Effective selling price of the option including option premium = £7.

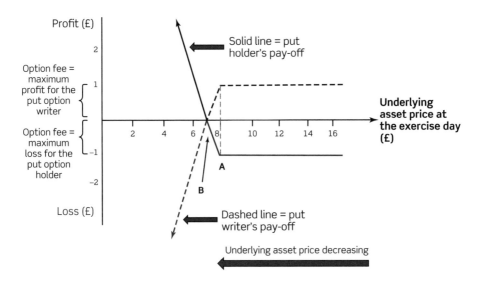

**Figure 9.2** Buyer's and writer's profit and loss on put options.

Possible outcomes at the expiry date:

- If the price of a Bramallco share is more than £8 exercising the option would be futile – you would be selling the share for £8 when it would be more beneficial just to sell it at the current market price. Not exercising the option will cost you £1.

> ### Recap
> The maximum loss to you as the option holder is £1 even if the price of Bramallco is £15 on expiry. You do not exercise the option and incur the £1 fee.

- If the share price on the expiry date is exactly £8 (point A in Figure 9.2) you would not exercise the option as this would also be futile. You would be buying the Bramallco share on the market for £8, selling the share at exactly £8 to the writer, incurring the fee of £1 and so the effective net share price you receive would be £7. This is the same as not exercising the option; you would still incur a loss of £1.
- Once the share price of Bramallco drops below £8 then it is economically rational to exercise the option. If the price is less than £8 but more than £7 (the points in the figure between B and A) you would exercise the option but still lose money. For example, if Bramallco is trading on the market for £7.50, you could buy at £7.50 and sell the share to the writer for £8.00, incurring a

loss of 50p rather than £1 (buying at £7.50, selling at £8.00, but incurring the £1 option premium, an effective selling price of £7).

- If Bramallco is trading at £7 you would exercise the option and break even (point B in the figure) buying on the market at £7 with an effective selling price to the writer of £7, the current market price being equal to your agreed effective selling price.
- Any market price below £7 for Bramallco sees you in profit, so if on the day of expiry the price of one Bramallco share is £4, you buy on the market at £4 and sell at £7 (including the cost of the option premium), realising a profit of £3.
- The writer is in an equal and opposite position to the holder. At any current market price above £8 they will realise their maximum profit of £1. Any price between £8 and £7 (between B and A in the figure) will see them begin to lose some of their profit.
- At a market price of £7 the writer breaks even, mimicking the holder of the option.
- At any market price under £7 the writer begins to lose money; since prices are constrained to zero the writer's exposure is limited.

## Recap

Once again, due to the risk exposure taken by the writer, most exchanges would require them to deposit the fee received for the option as a margin. As the price moves against the writer they would have to add a variation margin – the position would be being marked to market.

## Test yourself

**Q1.** When purchasing a put option when will you be 'in the money'?

**Q2.** The purchaser will exercise the option if the strike price is _____ the current market price but not at a price to cover the entire option fee. Fill in the gap.

**Q3.** Explain why the writer of a put option is exposed to limited losses.

## Intrinsic value and time value

The examples given above are based upon the price when the option matures or expires. Any profit or loss is provided by the difference between the strike price agreed with the option writer and the price of the underlying asset on the date you choose, if you do choose to exercise the option. This difference is the **intrinsic value** of the share such that:

call option intrinsic value = underlying asset price − exercise price

and:

put option intrinsic value = exercise price − underlying asset price

However, before the expiry date there is an inbuilt **time value** associated with the option, which usually means that the option premium (referred to by some textbooks as the 'value' of the option in this instance) is always greater than the intrinsic value before the expiration date:

time value = the option price, fee or premium − the intrinsic value of the option

For example, take a call option for one share of Bramallco with a strike price of £10 and a current market price of £12. This makes its intrinsic value £12 − £10 = £2. However, if the option is currently being offered by an option writer for £3, then the time value is £3 − £2 = £1. Essentially, the time value takes into account that the intrinsic value could increase in the future; it covers the writer of the call option for volatility or risk that the value will rise in the future and leave them exposed to losses. The option writer will increase the option price to cover themselves for the price moving against them. Remember, they have limitless downside risk when writing a call option. In the example above, an investor will buy the option at £3 if they believe the intrinsic value will increase to allow for a profit; taking into account the option premium, the buyer believes the writer has underestimated the time value of the option.

Option premiums or fees will be determined by:

- The market price of the underlying asset: the greater the market price of the underlying asset relative to the strike price, the higher the call option premium but the lower the put option premium.
- The underlying asset's volatility: the greater the volatility, the greater the premium. This is because the option writer cannot clearly assess the next movement in the underlying asset with any confidence. The larger option premium allows the option writer a wider margin of error.
- Time to maturity: the longer the time to maturity, the higher the option premium. As with all financial instruments, this reflects the greater risk of adverse price movements.

## Types of options traded on financial markets

There are many different types of options traded on the markets throughout the world. See the following Key definitions box for some examples:

## Key definitions

**Stock index option**

An option that gives the holder the right but not the obligation to buy or sell a stated stock index at a particular price at some time in the future.

**Interest rate option**

An option that gives the holder the right but not the obligation to lend or borrow a given amount at a pre-specified interest rate for a given period of time.

**Currency option**

An option that gives the holder the right but not the obligation to buy or sell a particular amount of currency at a pre-specified given exchange rate.

**Executive stock option**

A long-term call option that is given to executives as part of their compensation package. It gives the executives the right, but not the obligation, to buy or sell shares at an agreed-upon price within a certain period or on a specific date.

**Warrants**

An option to buy shares from a company at a stipulated price before a set date.

**Convertible bond**

These are bonds that the holder may exchange for a specific number of shares.

**Callable bond**

These are bonds that may be repurchased by the issuer before maturity at a specified call price.

## The practical use of options

As with all derivatives, a variety of techniques have emerged to utilise options for either speculation or risk management purposes. Below we run through an example of each.

## Using options for speculation

Speculating with options allows you, much like futures, to take a position without the initial cash outlay. So a call option allows you to leverage your position and benefit from a price rise while limiting your risk exposure.

### Using a call option to speculate

Assume you:

- expect the share price of Bramallco to increase from its current price of £2;
- do not want to 'go long' and purchase the share (because you do not have the money);
- purchase a call option (option to buy) with a strike price of £2.10;
- are charged an option fee of £0.02 or 2p;
- learn before the option expires that Bramallco's share price has increased to £2.20.

At this point you decide to exercise your option so you:

- purchase a share in Bramallco at the strike price of £2.10 as per your option;
- sell the share at the current market price of £2.20.

In this case you make the following profit:

| | |
|---|---|
| Revenue from selling the share | £2.20 |
| Outlay for the share | −£2.10 |
| Option premium or fee | −£0.02 |
| **Profit** | **£0.08** |

### Recap

The advantage of buying the option is that if the share had not increased in price then the total loss would have been limited to 2p. Compare this with going long, where you would have had to lay out £2.00. Also notice as with all financial transaction that if you had bought the share and borne the risk you would have made a profit of £2.20 minus £2.00 minus the cost of trading. This is higher than the return that you realised with the option. However, you can greatly increase your leverage by purchasing multiple options and also greatly reduce downside risk.

# Using options for risk management

Two techniques used to reduce risk exposure are:

- **covered call;** and
- **protective put.**

## Covered call

This is where an option is used to protect against a decline in price on tangible asset holdings over a period of time, for example a block of £100,000 Bramallco shares. In order to achieve this, shareholders can *sell* or *write* a call option to hedge against the potential decline in price (remember, by writing a call option it gives the option to buy the underlying stock to the purchaser of the option). This is called a covered call because the writer is covered by the shares they already own.

> ### ✳ Assessment advice
>
> You may have questioned why anybody would sell or write a call option which exposes them to limitless risk in exchange for a maximum return of the option premium. Writing such a call option without already holding the underlying asset is known as naked option writing. However, if you already hold the asset that you have written a call option on, this is called a covered call and helps manage risk. Be aware of this in case you are tested on this logic in your assessments.

In this scenario:

- If the price of Bramallco shares rises above the strike price agreed with the option buyer then the option will be exercised and the writer (who already holds the shares) will deliver the shares at the agreed price; the writer/owner has locked themselves into the near certainty regarding the price they will receive for the shares in the future (near certainty because, even if the option is 'in the money', it may still not be exercised).
- If the market price of Bramallco shares declines below the strike price then the option will not be exercised, the Bramallco shares will not be sold and the option premium will partially offset the fall in share price.

A covered call (nearly) guarantees a price for the writer in the future while partially offsetting downside risk.

Assume that you:

- purchased Bramallco shares for £2 some time ago;
- write (sell) a call option with an exercise price of £2;
- charge an option premium of £0.04 or 4 pence (Figure 9.3).

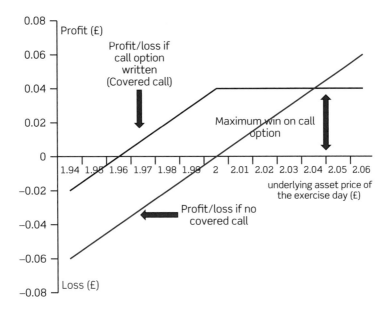

**Figure 9.3** Profit/loss of a covered call versus not writing a covered call.

This shows that:

- The covered call writing is beneficial when the stock performs poorly, for example you break even with a covered call in the above example at £1.96. Without the covered call you break even at £2.00 (which is the purchase price you paid for Bramallco).
- If the share performs well then the covered call will reduce your profits. In the above example, your profit is constrained to £0.04 or 4p (see table 9.1 on p. 260).

**Recap**

The black line in Figure 9.3 shows the call option writer – this does not look the same as the line for the call option writer in Figure 9.1. This is because in the example above the call writer already owns the share (they are not exposed to buying the underlying asset at the market price on the expiry date).

### Protective put

An alternative to a covered call is a protective put (remember, a put option is an option to sell). A protective put can be used to protect downside risk: just as the covered call limits the potential profits, a protective put limits the

**Table 9.1** Possible outcomes from the covered call.

| Market price of Bramallco at expiration date | Price at which you sell Bramallco stock | Add the premium received from writing the call option | Subtract the price paid for Bramallco stock | Profit/ loss | Profit/ loss if no covered call |
|---|---|---|---|---|---|
| 1.94 | 1.94 | +0.04 | −2.00 | −0.02 | −0.06 |
| 1.95 | 1.95 | +0.04 | −2.00 | −0.01 | −0.05 |
| 1.96 | 1.96 | +0.04 | −2.00 | 0.00 | −0.04 |
| 1.97 | 1.97 | +0.04 | −2.00 | 0.01 | −0.03 |
| 1.98 | 1.98 | +0.04 | −2.00 | 0.02 | −0.02 |
| 1.99 | 1.99 | +0.04 | −2.00 | 0.03 | −0.01 |
| 2.00 | 2.00 | +0.04 | −2.00 | 0.04 | 0.00 |
| 2.01 | 2.00 | +0.04 | −2.00 | 0.04 | 0.01 |
| 2.02 | 2.00 | +0.04 | −2.00 | 0.04 | 0.02 |
| 2.03 | 2.00 | +0.04 | −2.00 | 0.04 | 0.03 |
| 2.04 | 2.00 | +0.04 | −2.00 | 0.04 | 0.04 |
| 2.05 | 2.00 | +0.04 | −2.00 | 0.04 | 0.05 |
| 2.06 | 2.00 | +0.04 | −2.00 | 0.04 | 0.06 |

potential loss. Risk is eliminated by buying (or already holding) the underlying asset and also buying a put option.

Assume:

- You already hold one share of Bramallco which cost you £2.00.
- You buy one put option with an exercise price of £1.95.
- The option premium is £0.05.
- The expiration date is in one year.

Your expense is the £2.00 price of the share plus the option premium of £0.05. If the share price at expiration is below £1.95, say £1.90, then you will exercise your put option and sell the share at £1.95. The maximum loss that you have to bear in this case is £2.00 + £0.05 − £1.95 = −£0.10.

This strategy of buying a share and buying a put on the share is also called a protective put strategy, because it protects against losses beyond a particular limit. If you were to work through a table such as the one completed for the covered call (Table 9.1) then the diagram would look like that in Figure 9.4.

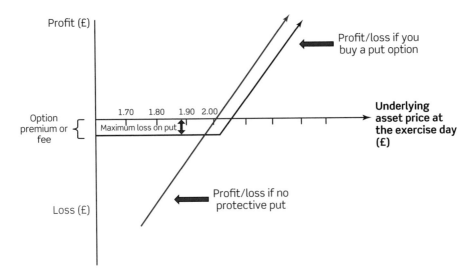

**Figure 9.4** Profit/loss of a protective put versus not holding a protective put.

## Recap

- When the price rises above £2.00 you do not exercise the put option but you still suffer the £0.05 fee – this is the difference between holding the share without a put option and holding the option if the share performs well.
- If your share performs badly you are protected by the put option – maximum loss is the option fee.

**You have reduced your risk but also your potential profit**

## Test yourself

**Q1.** What is meant by the intrinsic value of an option?

**Q2.** What can determine option premiums?

**Q3.** What is meant by naked option writing?

**Q4.** How does already holding the underlying share change the curve for a call option writer?

## Key definitions

**Intrinsic value**

The underlying asset price minus the exercise price.

**Time value**

The option price minus the underlying asset price.

**Covered call**

Where an option is used to protect against a decline in price on tangible asset holdings over a period of time.

**Protective put**

Buying (or already holding) an underlying asset and also buying a put option.

## Examples & evidence

HOW did bankers so misunderstand their own creations? The Frankensteins of Wall Street thought they had protected themselves from harm by holding only the safest slices of collateralised-debt obligations (CDOs), enticingly known as "super senior" tranches, while selling the riskier bits to other investors. A report issued this week by JPMorgan, an investment bank, estimated that banks alone held around $216 billion worth of super senior tranches of CDOs backed by assets such as mortgages and issued over the past two years. It now expects losses on these tranches to be "immense".

The super senior tranches did have some attractions for banks. They protected investors from initial losses on the mortgages backing the CDOs, while offering better returns than bonds with a similar rating.

But as Erik Sirri, a senior official at the Securities and Exchange Commission, pointed out in a speech on November 28th, other forces were at work too. Many banks got rid of the riskier and more junior CDO tranches, because their own risk-management systems designated them as too dangerous. By offering better returns on these riskier slices in order to attract investors, they had to lower the yields on the super senior tranches (since the overall cash flows from the assets backing a CDO are fixed). That made it harder to find buyers for the super senior tranches and forced many banks to keep them on their own books instead.

As the banks offloaded the junior CDO tranches and kept the safer ones, the risks they were exposed to became less obvious. But that does not mean they should have been missed. As Mr Sirri points out, the dangers inherent in super senior tranches of CDOs were similar to those in put options, instruments that have been around in financial markets for decades and entail risks that are well understood. Put options are a form of insurance that allow investors to sell an asset to the "insurer" at a set price (the "strike" price) at an agreed time in the future. A put option is to a CDO what a horse-drawn carriage is to a Ferrari. There are big differences between put options and super senior CDO tranches: most obviously, options are widely traded on exchanges whereas CDOs are notoriously illiquid. Even so, there are some striking parallels.

When markets are booming, or even just stable, selling "out-of-the-money" put options, with a strike price far below the current market price of the asset, is a route to easy money. Since such options expire without being exercised (because the investor can sell the asset in the market for a better return), the money goes straight to the bottom line.

The problem comes when the market crashes and prices drop below the strike price of the option. When that happens, the insurer can suddenly find itself facing huge losses that can not only wipe out the premiums earned in good times, but also cut into its capital as well. Put options are so dangerous because when markets are volatile, their riskiness does not rise steadily, but spikes very sharply within a very short space of time. An insurer that had thought itself well protected can suddenly find the vultures circling. During the sterling crisis of 1992, when the pound dropped out of the exchange-rate mechanism, one expert estimated that option sellers would have made losses even if they had hedged themselves every hour. To make matters worse, liquidity tends to disappear during times of turmoil, making it hard, if not impossible, to shed risk.

Aware of these flaws, most banks and fund managers avoid selling more than a small number of such instruments. But as Mr Sirri points out, "the risk profile of an out-of-the-money put can be manufactured in many different ways through a wide and ever-growing variety of instruments". A whole range of products, from bonds to super senior tranches of CDOs, exhibit this same property of yielding steady (if unspectacular) returns in good times, and then going quite horribly wrong in bad ones. That is dangerous—like picking up coins in front of a steamroller. The risks are especially great given that extreme events seem to occur more often than standard statistical theory suggests they should.

The bewitching thing about financial innovation is its novelty and its complexity. But when the next crisis comes, its roots will almost certainly lie in some vulnerability that is as old as finance itself.

*Source:* Put out: the risks posed by CDOs should have been familiar to Wall Street's finest. *The Economist,* December 6, 2007.

## Question

This article from *The Economist* shows the dynamics of options and how dangerous they can be if misunderstood. Ensure you understand who is writing the options in the above scenario and who is buying.

## Chapter summary – pulling it all together

By the end of this chapter you should be able to:

| | Confident ✓ | Not confident? |
|---|---|---|
| Define the difference between an American option and a European option | | Revise page 245 |
| State how options differ from futures (and how futures differ from forwards) | | Revise pages 245–246 |
| Define the common terminologies used when discussing options | | Revise pages 246–247 |
| Discuss the key features associated with buying and writing a call option | | Revise pages 247–249 |
| State the profit and loss situation of a call option to both buyers and writers | | Revise pages 249–250 |
| Draw the profit and loss on a call option in diagrammatic form | | Revise page 250 |
| Discuss the key features associated with buying and writing a put option | | Revise pages 251–252 |

| | Confident ✓ | Not confident? |
|---|---|---|
| State the profit and loss situation of a put option to both buyers and writers | | Revise pages 252–254 |
| Draw the profit and loss on a put option in diagrammatic form | | Revise page 253 |
| Discuss and draw the appropriate diagrams to show how call and put options can be used to manage risk and for speculation | | Revise pages 257–262 |

Now try the sample question at the start of this chapter, using the answer guidelines below.

## Answer guidelines

### ✳ Assessment question

(a) Describe the differences between options and other basic derivatives. (30 marks)

(b) Fully explain the dynamics of a call option and consider the advantages and disadvantages of writing a call option. (70 marks)

### Approaching the question

For part (a) begin with the basics and clearly define options. This should include an explanation of a call and put option and the different positions taken by the buyer of an option and the seller (or writer) of a call and put option. Ensure you show that you understand the difference. Contrast your definition of options with that of the other basic derivative instruments: forwards, futures and swaps. Part (b) takes most of the marks and so you should concentrate your efforts here – start with linking part (a) with (b) concentrating on call options. This should be followed by a diagram showing the profit and loss associated with both the buyer and writer (seller) of a call option. Finish part (b) with a discussion of the advantages/disadvantages of writing a call option – at first this may not be apparent – and spend time explaining how the writer can make a profit.

## Important points to include

- Key definitions such as put option and call option.

- Detailed discussion of the differences with other basic derivatives.

- Distinguish between the writer of an option and the buyer.

- Explain the pay-off structure of a call option and illustrate it graphically.

- Graphically illustrate a covered call, showing how the writer of a call option can benefit if they already own the underlying asset.

## Make your answer stand out

Get the basics right and ensure your explanations are clear. Key to making your answer stand out is drawing the diagrams clearly and linking them to the practical operations of a call option. To obtain higher marks illustrate a covered call and show the differences between the basic call option pay-off and the covered call option pay-off structure.

## Read to impress

Here is a selection of books that introduce the above concepts in an understandable way, each offering a slightly different perspective. It is recommended to start with Bodie *et al.*:

### Books

Bodie, Z., Kane, A. and Marcus, A.J. (2010) *Essentials of Investments*. McGraw-Hill.

Fabozzi, F., Modigliani, F. and Jones, F. (2010) *Foundations of Financial Markets and Institutions*. Pearson Education.

Madura, J. (2012) *Financial Markets and Institutions*. South-Western.

Pilbeam, K. (2010) *Finance and Financial Markets*. Palgrave Macmillan.

Saunders, A. and Cornett, M.M. (2012) *Financial Markets and Institutions*. McGraw-Hill.

## Journal articles

Jong, F.D. and Driessen, J. (2001) LIBOR market models versus swap market models for pricing interest rate derivatives: an empirical analysis. *European Finance Review,* Vol. 5 (3), pp. 201–37.

Longstaff, F.A., Mithal, S. and Neis, E. (2005) Corporate yield spreads: default risk or liquidity? New evidence from the credit default swap market. *Journal of Finance,* Vol. 60 (5), pp. 2213–53.

## Websites

Chicago Board Option Exchange Education: **www.cboe.com/LearnCenter/Default.aspx**.

Chicago Mercantile Exchange (CME) Education: **www.cmegroup.com/education/**.

Ernst & Young: **www.ey.com/UK/en/home**.

FTSE: **www.ftse.com/**.

LIFFE Investor Learning Center: **www.liffeinvestor.com/learning-center**.

London Metal Exchange: **www.lme.com/education/home.asp**

London Stock Exchange: **www.londonstockexchange.com/home/homepage.htm**.

McKinsey & Company: **www.mckinsey.com/**.

Morgan Stanley: **www.morganstanley.com.**

NYSE Euronext Global Derivatives: **https://globalderivatives.nyx.com/**.

The Bank of England: **www.bankofengland.co.uk/Pages/home.aspx**.

The European Central Bank: **www.ecb.int/home/html/index.en.html**.

The Federal Reserve: **www.federalreserve.gov/**.

## Companion website

Go to the companion website at **www.pearsoned.co.uk/econexpress** to find more revision support online for this topic area.

**Notes**

# 10 The central bank, money and the money supply

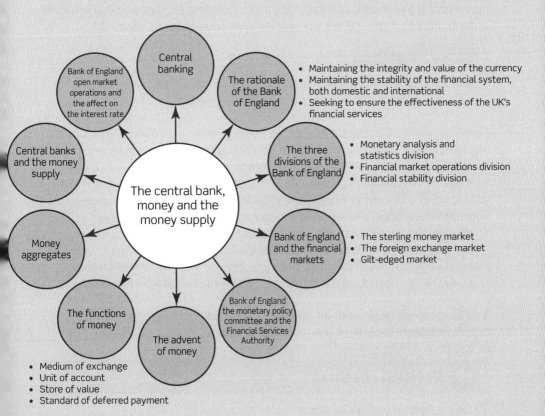

**Central banking**

**The rationale of the Bank of England**
- Maintaining the integrity and value of the currency
- Maintaining the stability of the financial system, both domestic and international
- Seeking to ensure the effectiveness of the UK's financial services

**The three divisions of the Bank of England**
- Monetary analysis and statistics division
- Financial market operations division
- Financial stability division

**Bank of England and the financial markets**
- The sterling money market
- The foreign exchange market
- Gilt-edged market

**Bank of England the monetary policy committee and the Financial Services Authority**

**The advent of money**

**The functions of money**
- Medium of exchange
- Unit of account
- Store of value
- Standard of deferred payment

**Money aggregates**

**Central banks and the money supply**

**Bank of England open market operations and the affect on the interest rate**

*The central bank, money and the money supply*

A printable version of this topic map is available from **www.pearsoned.co.uk/econexpress**

## Introduction

The central bank sits at the top of the financial system and is the 'banker's bank' – watching over a nation's financial institutions and overall financial system, ensuring that the system operates at its most efficient. Many of the functions of a central bank require an understanding of the possible manipulation of money and the supply of money, usually referred to as monetary policy. The term 'money' will usually conjure up interest as most individuals will desire more money all of the time, but what is money and how do you control its supply? If individuals are suffering poverty, why don't governments and central banks just print more money and give it to the poor? The answer to this question lies with inflation. It is paramount to a well-functioning economy that rises in prices (inflation) are kept at a reasonable and stable level because, as inflation increases, people become uncertain of the future value of goods and services. This uncertainty in turn will affect the functioning of the financial markets and the overall economy as people demand a higher nominal return in order to maintain the real return on their investments (see Chapter 2).

### Recap

Inflation is where the general level of prices for goods and services is rising and the purchasing power per pound or dollar is falling.

Some economists in the past, such as Milton Friedman, believed that controlling the money supply would help control inflation (a rise in prices and the devaluation of money). However, controlling the money supply is not easy as it will be determined by complex interactions within the economy which will include banks, other financial institutions and the financial markets. One way of manipulating the demand for money, as we saw earlier (Chapter 3), is to change the price of money – the interest rate. Think what this entails: in many cases the central bank is responsible for the setting of an economy's interest rate, but in a freely functioning economy with billions of transactions every day how does a central bank manipulate the interest rate?

This chapter will begin with an overview of the Bank of England, a leading central bank, before looking at the functions of money, open market operations by the Bank of England and monetary policy.

###  Revision checklist

*Make sure that you understand:*

- ❑ The various roles that a central bank may undertake within an economy.
- ❑ The ownership structures that central banks may take.
- ❑ The rational of the Bank of England and its three core purposes.

- ❏ The three divisions within the Bank of England.
- ❏ The financial markets in which the Bank of England is active.
- ❏ The role played by the Monetary Policy Committee (MPC) and the Financial Services Authority (FSA).
- ❏ The rise of money as a medium of exchange and the benefits this brings to an economy.
- ❏ The definitions of money M0, M1, M2, M3 and M4.
- ❏ The role of the central bank in manipulating the money supply.
- ❏ The Bank of England's open market operations to set the interest rate at the level desired by the MPC.

## ✳ Assessment advice

This topic will test your knowledge as well as your understanding of how the financial system works on a day-to-day basis. Make sure you understand the basics of why an economy needs a central bank and the role it plays. Provide examples of a central bank – in this chapter we have used the Bank of England but the US central bank, the Federal Reserve, works in a similar way. Obtaining information regarding different banks will show greater knowledge and help increase your grade. One key tip is to go to the central bank websites around the globe as they have some excellent articles on how they operate – start with the Bank of England (**www.bankofengland.co.uk**). Also visit the DMO (Debt Management Office: **www.dmo.gov.uk**) which has some excellent articles on the money markets which may help your understanding. In addition, work through as many examples as you can regarding the relationship between money supply manipulation/the central bank and the banking sector.

## ✳ Assessment question

(a) Explain, using a central bank of your choice, the guiding principles that a central bank should follow within a developed economy. (40 marks)

(b) Describe, using T-accounts, how a central bank can affect the interest rate. (60 marks)

Can you answer this question? Guidelines on answering the question are presented at the end of this chapter.

## Central banking

In general, a **central bank** in any economy will have the following roles:

- ensuring the integrity of the financial system via supervision and regulation;
- serving as the commercial banker's bank and government's bank;
- helping to control the **monetary policy** of the economy;
- managing the national debt;
- maintaining the stability of the currency;
- managing the foreign exchange reserves;
- issuing national currency;
- providing liquidity when a systemic financial crisis occurs.

They may differ somewhat in their ownership structure such that the central bank may be:

- a government agency – wholly owned by the country' government;
- a privately owned bank – independent of the government in undertaking its roles; or
- a combination of the above two ownership structures.

To look at the operations of a central bank we will look at the Bank of England, the central bank of the United Kingdom.

## The rationale of the Bank of England

The Bank of England is at the head of the UK financial system, is owned by the government (having been nationalised in 1946) and has a monopoly on the note issue in England and Wales. As the central bank of the UK, the Bank is committed to maintaining a stable and efficient monetary and financial framework. The Bank was granted independence in setting interest rates in 1997 and this is undertaken by the **Monetary Policy Committee** as part of the Bank of England. This type of independence is known as **instrumental (not full) independence** as the Bank does not have policy goal independence.

In pursuing its goal, it has three core purposes:

- maintaining the integrity and value of the currency;
- maintaining the stability of the financial system, both domestic and international;
- seeking to ensure the effectiveness of the UK's financial services.

## Maintaining the integrity and value of the currency

This involves maintaining price stability (defined by the inflation target set by the government) while achieving the wider economic goals of sustainable growth and high employment. The Bank pursues this core purpose through its decisions on:

- interest rates taken at the monthly meetings of the Monetary Policy Committee (MPC);
- by participating in international discussions to promote the health of the world economy;
- by implementing monetary policy through its open market operations and its dealings with the financial system; and
- by maintaining confidence in the note issue.

## Maintaining the stability of the financial system, both domestic and international

The Bank seeks to achieve this through monitoring developments in the financial system both at home and abroad by:

- analysing the links between individual institutions and the various financial markets;
- analysing the health of the domestic and international economy;
- closely co-operating with financial supervisors, both domestically and internationally; and
- developing a sound financial infrastructure including efficient payment and settlement arrangements.

### Recap

In exceptional circumstances (in consultation with the Financial Services Authority and HM Treasury as appropriate) the Bank may also provide, or assist in arranging, last-resort financial support where this is needed to avoid systemic damage. That is, crisis management.

## Seeking to ensure the effectiveness of the UK's financial services

The financial system should offer opportunities for firms of all sizes to have access to capital on terms that give adequate protection to investors and which enhances the international competitive position of the City of London and other UK financial centres. It aims to achieve these goals by:

- utilising its expertise in the marketplace;
- bringing financial institutions together to act in the best interests of the economy when the market alone is deficient or has failed;

- supporting the development of a financial infrastructure that furthers these goals;
- advising government; and
- encouraging British interests through its contacts with financial authorities overseas.

(see Bank of England Annual Report, 2000, p. 14)

## Key definitions

**Central bank**

A bank that sits at the top of the financial system and is the 'banker's bank', watching over a nation's financial institutions and overall financial system.

**Monetary policy**

Using techniques, including varying interest rates, to manipulate money and the supply of money.

**Instrumental independence**

Refers to a type of independence that gives freedom to a central bank to use 'instruments' to manipulate the economy, most commonly the setting of interest rates.

**MPC (Monetary Policy Committee)**

A committee within the Bank of England that is charged with setting the base interest rate for the UK economy.

## The three divisions of the Bank of England

In order for it to achieve its core purposes, the Bank is split into three main divisions, each of which has its own responsibilities to the UK financial system. These are the:

- **Monetary Analysis and Statistics Division**
- **Financial Market Operations Division**
- **Financial Stability Division**.

## Monetary Analysis and Statistics Division

This division is responsible for providing the Bank with economic analysis that helps the MPC (see below) formulate its monetary policy to aid economic growth and control inflation. Within this division, economists at the Bank conduct research and analyse developments in the international and UK economies and publish reports which are then made publicly available.

## Financial Market Operations Division

This division has three main areas of responsibility:

- Operations in the financial markets. It is responsible for planning and conducting the Bank's operations in the core financial markets, especially the sterling wholesale money markets. It aims to establish short-term interest rates at the level required by government in order to meet its monetary policy objectives (see below). This division also manages the UK's foreign exchange and gold reserves and contributes market analysis to aid the MPC and the Financial Stability Committee in their operations.
- Banking and market services. The Bank undertakes the traditional role of providing banking services to the government, banks and other central banks and managing the note issue. In addition, this division plays an important role in providing (and monitoring) a safe and efficient payment and settlement system for the UK financial markets and the wider economy.
- Risk analysis and monitoring. The Bank is responsible for analysing any risks that may arise in the financial markets and assess the effects that these may have on the Bank and the UK economy.

## Financial Stability Division

The Bank of England has no direct regulatory power over the UK financial system but this division attempts to maintain the stability of the financial system as a whole. Its main areas of responsibility are domestic finance, financial intermediaries, international finance, financial market infrastructure and regulatory policy.

The division works closely with the Financial Stability Committee, which is chaired by the Governor of the Bank of England. In general, the work of this division covers the functioning of the international financial system as well as that of the UK and it carries out research into developments in the structure of financial markets and institutions, making proposals to increase safety. The division is responsible for publishing the **Financial Stability Review**.

### Test yourself

**Q1.** List five roles that a central bank may undertake.

**Q2.** What are the three core purposes of the Bank of England?

**Q3.** Explain the operations of the three divisions of the Bank of England.

## The Bank of England and the financial markets

In operational day-to-day terms the Bank has an important influence on three major markets. These are:

- the sterling money market;
- the foreign exchange market, and
- the gilt-edged market.

## The sterling money market

The Bank is a major player in the sterling money market (see Chapter 5), buying and selling Treasury Bills on a daily basis. The object is twofold:

- The Bank buys or sells Tbills in order to ease cash shortages or to withdraw cash surpluses which arise as a result of daily transactions between the government and the public. Such transactions by the Bank affect commercial bank clearing balances, alter the liquidity of these banks and hence their willingness to lend (see Chapter 11).
- The Financial Market Operations Division of the Bank trades in Tbills to achieve the government's desired interest rate. The buying and selling of Tbills by the Bank affects yields and therefore influences interest rates throughout the market.

## The foreign exchange market

The Bank has a major role in the foreign exchange market as it is responsible for carrying out government policy with regard to the exchange rate. A strong pound has been seen by successive governments as essential if inflation is to be kept low. The Bank also uses the **Exchange Equalisation Account** to intervene in the foreign exchange market by buying up surplus sterling should it need to support the external value of the pound.

## The gilt-edged market

The Bank is influential in the gilt-edged market as it administers the issue of new bonds when the government wishes to borrow money. Various methods are used, depending on market circumstances. The 'tap' method is where bonds (gilts) are issued gradually in order not to flood the market and depress the price; the 'tender' method is where institutions are invited to tender for a given issue; and the 'auction' method is where bonds are sold to the highest bidders among the 20 or so gilt-edged market-makers (GEMMs – see Chapter 7).

The Bank also manages the redemption of existing bonds in such a way as to smooth the demands on the government's financial resources. For example, it buys up bonds which are nearing their redemption date so as not to have to make large repayments over a short period of time.

## Key definitions

**Monetary Analysis and Statistics Division**

The division responsible for providing the Bank with economic analysis that helps the MPC formulate its monetary policy.

**Financial Market Operations Division**

The division responsible for planning and conducting the Bank's operations in the core financial markets and banking markets, and for risk analysis and monitoring of the financial system.

**Financial Stability Division**

The division that attempts to maintain the stability of the financial system as a whole.

**Financial Stability Review**

Published twice a year and covering an assessment of the outlook for the stability and resilience of the financial sector.

**Exchange Equalisation Account**

The account that holds the UK's reserves of gold, foreign currencies and International Monetary Fund (IMF) Special Drawing Rights (SDRs). It was established in 1932 to provide a fund which could be used for 'checking undue fluctuations in the exchange value of sterling'.

## Recap

**Issues with the central bank operating in the financial markets**

The Bank faces a continual problem in that its actions in each of these markets have repercussions for the functioning of other markets. For example:

Intervention to purchase sterling in the foreign exchange market in order to support the sterling exchange rate is often ineffective because of the size of speculative outflows of short-term capital from the sterling money and gilt-edged markets.

As a result interest rates may need to be raised in order to deter these short-term capital outflows. This often proves difficult, however, because of the way in which daily transactions between the government and the public affect the balances of the clearing banks with the Bank.

For example, if the banks are short of liquidity the Bank may purchase bills from the banks in order to help replenish their cash balances. However, purchasing existing bills by the Bank will raise their market price and lower their yield – that is, lower interest rates. This may then conflict with the need to keep interest rates high to prevent short-term capital outflows from depressing the sterling exchange rate.

## Bank of England, the MPC and the Financial Services Authority

The three main purposes of the Bank were defined in May 1997, when the Chancellor of the Exchequer, Gordon Brown, proposed a number of institutional and operational changes:

- The Bank was given operational independence in setting interest rates which would now be the responsibility of a newly created Monetary Policy Committee (MPC) working within the Bank.
- The regulation of the banking sector was taken away from the Bank and given to a newly established 'super' regulator called the **Financial Services Authority (FSA)**.
- The government retained responsibility for determining the exchange rate regime; the Bank could now intervene at its discretion in support of the objectives of the MPC.
- The management of the national debt was transferred from the Bank to the **Treasury**. These changes were set out in The Bank of England Act which came into force on 1 June 1998. The most important of these changes involved the creation of the MPC and the FSA.

### The Monetary Policy Committee (MPC)

The MPC consists of the Governor of the Bank, two deputy governors, two members appointed by the Bank in consultation with the Chancellor, and four 'experts' appointed by the Chancellor. The MPC meets monthly, publishes its decisions within days of concluding any meeting and publishes minutes of the meeting within six weeks.

Key features:

- The Bank of England Act established that the responsibility for monetary policy and therefore for setting short-term interest rates was to reside with the MPC.
- The MPC would be free from government intervention in all but extreme economic circumstances.

- The aim of short-term interest rate setting would be to restrict the growth of inflation to within a target range set by the government and announced in the annual Budget Statement.
- The target was set at 2.5% for annual retail price inflation, excluding mortgage interest payments (RPIX). If inflation is more than 1% either side of this figure then the MPC is required to write an open letter of explanation to the Chancellor.

## The Financial Services Authority (FSA)

In May 1997 the Chancellor reformed the regulatory structure of the financial system. As noted, regulation and supervision of the banking sector was traditionally the responsibility of the Bank, covering mainly risks associated with the banking sector such as capital adequacy, liquidity, and foreign currency exposure.

In contrast, the regulation and supervision of the non-bank sector was historically the responsibility of numerous different bodies, such as the Building Societies Commission and the Securities and Investment Board which itself headed three other self-regulating bodies. The Bank of England Act of 1998 transferred the regulatory functions of the Bank to a new regulatory authority called the Financial Services Authority (FSA), which was now to be responsible for regulating all financial institutions, whether bank or non-bank.

The Bank retained responsibility for monitoring the financial system, with the government establishing a structure whereby the Treasury, the Bank of England and the FSA work together to achieve stability. In a Memorandum of Understanding (known as the '**tripartite agreement**') published in October 1997 the Chancellor set out the various roles of the Treasury, the Bank and the FSA, making it clear that these organisations should exchange information and consult regularly. A standing committee was established to provide the means for the three bodies to discuss any foreseeable problems.

In 2009, this regulatory structure was complemented by the establishment of a Financial Stability Committee (FSC) whose functions were to oversee the stability of the system and detect any risk of system-wide failure – reflecting the new statutory duty then given to the Bank to enhance financial stability in the UK financial system. This committee has the responsibility of liaising with the Standing Committee created by the Memorandum of Understanding. Figure 10.1 provides an overview of the new regulatory structure.

As a result of a review of the role of the FSA and the Bank in dealing with the financial crisis in 2007–8, and particularly the lack of effectiveness of the tripartite agreement, the government decided to alter the structure of financial regulation in the UK. In 2010 it announced plans to create a '**twin peaks' approach** to regulation.

In 2013, the FSA will be replaced by two separate bodies, the Prudential Regulation Authority (**PRA**) and the Financial Conduct Authority (**FCA**). The PRA, a subsidiary company of the Bank, will be responsible for the prudential regulation of deposit-taking banks, insurance companies and systemically significant investment firms (micro-prudential regulation). The FCA (effectively the FSA renamed) will be a company separate from the Bank and responsible for regulating the conduct of business of all financial services firms in the UK, as well as the prudential regulation of those financial services firms not regulated by the PRA.

---

## Test yourself

**Q1.** In which financial markets is the Bank of England active?

**Q2.** List the key features of the Monetary Policy Committee.

**Q3.** Which new body is replacing the Financial Services Authority?

---

In addition, in 2011 the Bank created an interim Financial Policy Committee (FPC). This is a committee of the Court of Directors of the Bank of England, and is responsible for identifying, monitoring and taking action to reduce or remove systemic risk in order to enhance the resilience of the UK financial system (macro-prudential regulation). As well as making recommendations to the Bank and the Treasury, this committee will be able to make recommendations and give directions to both the PRA and FPC concerning the furtherance of financial stability and macro-prudential regulatory policy. When the new regulatory system comes into effect, the FPC will take the place of the FSC. Figure 10.1 shows the new structure.

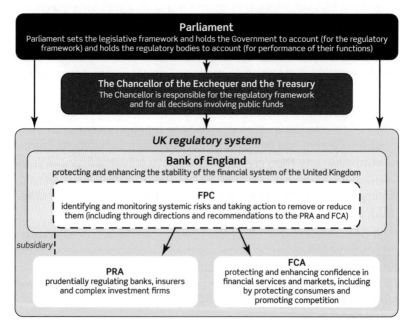

**Figure 10.1** Roles and accountabilities in the new system
HM Treasury (2011) *A New Approach to Financial Regulation: The Blueprint for Reform.* London: TSO, p. 8.

Key definitions

## Key definitions

**FSA (Financial Services Authority)**

An independent body that regulates the financial services industry in the UK.

**UK Treasury**

The UK government department responsible for developing and executing the government's public finance policy and economic policy.

**Tripartite agreement**

An agreement between the Treasury, the Bank of England and the FSA on working together to provide and maintain financial stability.

**'Twin peaks' approach**

Refers to the new financial stability structure involving the FCA and PRA.

**FCA**

The Financial Conduct Authority.

**PRA**

The Prudential Regulation Authority.

## The advent of money

Much of what central banks are trying to achieve is the stabilisation of prices and retention of the value of money. Money affects all individuals' lives in an active economy, but remember that the £10 in your pocket has very little actual tangible worth – essentially it is a piece of paper. It gains its worth from its acceptability in the economy. You know how much you can purchase with £10; you know in essence what it is worth.

Before the existence of money, in primitive economies, people lived by combining various attributes, including personal abilities, land and labour, to produce goods which they themselves consumed. In such economies, people are self-sufficient and trade is limited. However, producers of goods soon realised that they could obtain increasing utility by swapping, or bartering, some of their production with that of somebody else's and trading begins. At first people have to take the time to find others who are willing to barter their production and trade only occurs where there is a 'double coincidence of wants'.

## Recap

Barter is where goods are exchanged for other goods without using a medium of exchange.

The major problem with this primitive system is that it requires a vast amount of valuable time to search for other people who are willing to trade. The time it takes for individuals to find each other and transact means that few trades are undertaken and this results in inefficiency and low growth within the economy. Therefore, gradually, two processes evolve:

- marketplaces develop as people begin to meet at a certain time and place in order to trade their goods with other producers;
- indirect exchange is initiated and people begin to accept goods which they have no use for in order that they can exchange them for commodities that they do require.

These help reduce transaction and search costs and allow for more economic activity, eventually leading to growth in the economy and a rise in the standard of living. This is achieved by:

- reducing the time spent looking for a trading partner;
- allowing individuals to specialise in a trade in which they excel and exchange their labour for money to spend elsewhere.

As more intermediate trade takes place there is a narrowing of goods which are acceptable for the process and one good tends to become dominant. In most cases, a precious metal, usually gold, becomes the dominant good (but other goods have been used, for example cigarettes in prison communities) and the price of other goods are referred to in the amount of gold for which they can be exchanged.

Eventually, producers will begin to sell their produce for more gold than they can spend in a single time period and they will begin to increase their stock of gold. The use of gold, even in coinage form, is costly to the producers because it is difficult to store, protect and move. These additional expenses led to the evolution of people who are willing to absorb these costs of transacting in gold. **Goldsmiths** were in the ideal position to offer to store gold due to their secure and large storage facilities. Therefore, traders began to deposit gold with the goldsmiths in return for receipts or claims on the amount of gold deposited. In time these receipts began to be accepted for exchange purposes on the good name of the goldsmith and evolved into the medium of exchange and goldsmiths became banking institutions. The operations of banks will be analysed later (see Chapter 11).

## The functions of money

A general definition of money is anything that is readily accepted for goods and services or in repayment of a debt. Today, this will most commonly be coins, banknotes, or bank deposits, usually transacted using your debit card. Money has four main functions, as follows.

## Medium of exchange

Money must be readily acceptable by all in the economy. For this to occur, it requires the medium of exchange to have certain characteristics which enhance its ability to trade for goods. The characteristics which a medium of exchange should have include something which:

- is frequently traded and therefore marketable;
- has a certain exchange value;
- is easily portable;
- is non-perishable.

## Unit of account

Money must be able to be used to measure the value of disparate items within an economy, enabling all prices to be quoted in terms of the money amount. This again reduces transaction costs as there is one unit of account (compared with barter where it is necessary to have an individually agreed exchange for every transaction).

## Store of value

Money must be able to be stored and maintain its value over time. This allows purchasing power to be 'saved' until later. This can be referred to as allowing inter-temporal transactions, which are transactions between times. Money can be an efficient store of value as it is liquid – it can be spent immediately. However, when the price level is increasing and the inflation rate is high, the value of money in the future will be uncertain and may provide a poor store of value.

## Standard of deferred payment

Money must be able to be used to agree a price for goods and services to be delivered sometime in the future. It must act as a standard benchmark for future payments for current purchases.

## Money aggregates

Given that money plays the key role in transactions throughout the economy, it is important that the authorities are able to measure the amount of money in the economy, but first they must know what they are measuring, which is commonly referred to as the money aggregate and the amount of money in the economy as the money supply. **Money aggregates** are definitions of money used by a country (or economic area in the case of the European Union) and are based upon what is acceptable as a medium of exchange. Money aggregates are defined as being 'narrow', which usually includes just 'notes and coins in circulation' and commercial banks' reserves with the central bank (referred to as the monetary base or M0), or 'broad', which includes financial claims that are easily convertible into cash and so can be thought of as money.

## Definitions of euro area monetary aggregates (as defined by the European Central Bank)

| Liabilities[1] | M1 | M2 | M3 |
|---|:---:|:---:|:---:|
| Currency in circulation | × | × | × |
| Overnight deposits | × | × | × |
| Deposits with an agreed maturity up to two years | | × | × |
| Deposits redeemable at a period of notice up to three months | | × | × |
| Repurchase agreements | | | × |
| Money market fund (MMF) shares/units | | | × |
| Debt securities up to two years | | | × |

[1]Liabilities of the money-issuing sector and central government liabilities with a monetary character held by the money-holding sector.

**M1** = narrow money and includes currency (banknotes and coins) as well as balances which can immediately be converted into currency or used for cashless payments (overnight deposits).

**M2** = 'Intermediate' money and comprises narrow money M1 and, in addition, deposits with a maturity of up to two years and deposits redeemable at a period of notice of up to three months. Depending on their degree of moneyness, such deposits can be converted into components of narrow money, but in some cases there may be restrictions involved, such as the need for advance notification, delays, penalties or fees. The definition of M2 reflects the particular interest in analysing and monitoring a monetary aggregate that, in addition to currency, consists of deposits which are liquid.

**M3** = Broad money comprising M2 and marketable instruments issued by the monetary financial institutions sector. Certain money market instruments, in particular money market fund (MMF) shares/units and repurchase agreements, are included in this aggregate. A high degree of liquidity and price certainty make these instruments close substitutes for deposits. As a result of their inclusion, M3 is less affected by substitution between various liquid asset categories than narrower definitions of money, and is therefore more stable.

**MMF** = A mutual fund portfolio which consists of short-term (less than one year) financial securities of high-quality, liquid debt and monetary instruments.

The Bank follows these definitions with exceptions:

- The Bank publishes a figure referred to as 'Notes and Coins in circulation', which is the narrowest measure of money published. This comprises sterling notes and coins in circulation outside the Bank (including those held in banks' and building societies' tills). It also includes all holdings of notes and coins in banks, non-banks and the non-building society private sector.
- The Bank also publishes figures for a monetary aggregate M4 and retail M4 which also substitutes as M2.
- M4 = the private sector's (which is the UK private sector other than monetary financial institutions (MFIs)) holdings of:
  - sterling notes and coin;
  - sterling deposits, including certificates of deposit;
  - commercial paper, bonds, floating rate notes (FRNs) and other instruments of up to and including five years' original maturity issued by UK MFIs;
  - claims on UK MFIs arising from repos (from December 1995);
  - sterling bank bills (estimated).
- Retail M4 (or M2) comprises:
  - M4 private sector's holdings of sterling notes and coin; and
  - sterling-denominated 'retail' deposits with UK MFIs.

## Recap

Monetary Financial Institutions (MFIs) are generally all deposit-taking institutions within the UK which have legal permission to accept deposits (but does not include credit unions or friendly societies).

## Test yourself

**Q1.** What benefits do marketplaces bring to a primitive economy?

**Q2.** List the functions of money.

**Q3.** What constitutes M1, M2 and M3 as defined by the European Central Bank?

## Central banks and the money supply

Bringing this together and remembering what we discussed previously regarding interest rate determination, it is widely believed that by influencing the money supply the central bank can either stimulate the economy or repress it. If the central bank expands the supply of money, *ceteris paribus*, then there will be more money in the economy and increased demand for products, leading eventually to expansion or growth to absorb this demand. However, this depends on many inter-related factors and increasing the money supply can lead to price rises and inflation as more money chases fewer products. In addition, the new money pushed into the economy may not be spent but held in the balance sheet of banks or companies – thus not leading to any stimulation.

### Recap

It is often asked why in economies that are suffering from a recession (a decline in economic activity in an economy leading to contraction) the authorities do not print more money and give it to society to spend. The quick answer to this is to do with the economic problem of scarcity, that is resources are not limitless. Think of three men suffering dehydration in the desert, each of whom is carrying £5. A woman passes by with just one flask of water; the value of the water in the city where there is plenty of water is £1, but here the woman demands £5 for the flask. We can see already that due to scarcity the price has increased by £4 (compared with the price in the city). Scarcity has led to a price rise or inflation. Just then a money lender passes by and agrees to lend another £5 to each man. Essentially this has increased the money supply by £15. Armed with more money they bid more: the first man bids £6, the second £8 and the third £9; they then all shout out £10 at the same time. The flask has not changed in any way (there has been no increase in production – the quality has not changed) *but* there has been a price rise of £5 – that is, the amount of money and the scarcity of water in the desert have led to inflation. Without an increase in the money supply the price could not have increased above £5 cash.

So you can see that the money supply can affect the price of goods and services (if they are finite) within the economy. Given this importance you should begin to understand how the money supply is determined within an economy. Essentially this will be influenced by the interaction between:

- the central bank;
- banks;
- depositors.

The major or largest banks in an economy are important in this process (as you will see later in Chapter 11) as they provide loans and take in deposits (that are spendable and included in the monetary aggregates). Their position in the financial system allows them to create credit, which increases the money supply. However, the central bank is the biggest player as it can manipulate the money supply via its dealings in the financial markets.

## The use of the T-account to analyse the banking sector and open market operations

Many textbooks utilise the T-account to picture what is happening within a bank. It can be used here to show how the Bank can manipulate the money supply. The narrowest definition of money is referred to as the monetary base or M0, which equals notes and coins in circulation plus reserves held at the central bank. This can be shown as being directly affected by the purchase of securities by the central bank.

### Key definitions

**Money**

Something tangible that is accepted and can be exchanged for goods and services. Also used as a measure of value.

**Goldsmith**

An entity or person who, in the past, would store gold, issue a receipt and charge a fee for this service.

**Money aggregates**

Definitions of money used by a country (or economic area in the case of the European Union) based upon what is acceptable as a medium of exchange. Money aggregates are defined as being 'narrow' or 'broad'.

**Bank liabilities**

What a bank owes to its customers.

**Bank assets**

Generally what a bank is owed sometime in the future (excepting cash money), the same as its financial investments.

## The central bank's balance sheet

All banks have:

- **liabilities** – which is what they owe;
- **assets** – which is what they are owed.

It is slightly different for a central bank because its liabilities are currency in circulation, as this is the medium of exchange and in the past could be exchanged for gold. This is no longer the case but if you look on any note issued in the UK it will state 'I promise to pay the bearer on demand the sum of ... ' say, £10 (this would have been 10 pounds of gold). It is now the Bank's solid reputation that underpins the acceptance of pound notes. On the asset side of the balance sheet, what the Bank is owed is made up of securities issued by the government. The Bank has invested in government bonds.

| Liabilities (£) (owe) | | Assets (£) (owed) | |
|---|---|---|---|
| Currency in circulation | 1,000 | Government securities held | 2,000 |
| Reserves | 1,000 | (for example, Tbills) | |
| **Total** | **2,000** | **Total** | **2,000** |

In the above T-account the Bank has £2,000 in liabilities and £2,000 in assets but wishes to purchase securities from four of the leading retail banks in the UK.

---

✱ **Assessment advice**

Note that when analysing T-accounts, *assets* always equal *liabilities*. Also, if the Bank wants to buy government-issued securities such as Tbills then a number of **primary participants** stand ready to purchase the securities (see the Debt Management Office for a list of these participants: **www.dmo.gov.uk**).

---

**Open market operations by the Bank of England**

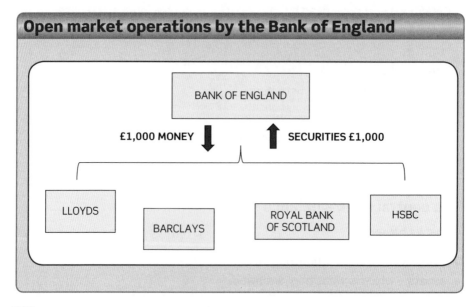

The Bank at the top of the financial system is buying £1,000 worth of securities from four of the main high street banks. As a result of this:

- Security holdings at the Bank will increase.
- Money held on the balance sheets of the four main high street banks will increase or reserves held at the Bank will increase.

This is because securities will flow from the high street banks to the Bank and in return they receive money for the securities. *There has been an increase in the money supply.*

This can be shown on the T-accounts of the Bank and the banking sector.

## Purchasing Tbills by the Bank of England

The Bank's balance sheet:

| Liabilities (£) (owe) | | Assets (£) (owed) | |
|---|---|---|---|
| Currency in circulation | 1,000 | Tbills | 3,000 |
| (increase by £1,000) Reserves | 2,000 | (increase by £1,000) | |
| **Total** | **3,000** | **Total** | **3,000** |

When the Bank purchases Tbills, the primary participants (in the example this is represented by the four large retail banks) sell them, so they sell £250 each (£250 × 4 = £1,000). If we initially assume that the Bank places the money they pay for the Tbills in the each of the bank's reserve account held at the Bank, the effect on their balance would be the same for each bank.

## A bank's balance sheet

A retail bank's balance sheet before the purchase of Tbills:

| Liabilities (£) (owe) | | Assets (£) (owed) | |
|---|---|---|---|
| Deposits | 1,000 | Cash | 350 |
| | | Reserves held at the Bank of England | 250 |
| | | Tbills | 400 |
| **Total** | **1,000** | **Total** | **1,000** |

The effect of the purchase of Tbills by the Bank (£250 each from four banks = £1,000):[1]

---

[1]This will be replicated across all four retail banks for this example.

| Liabilities (£) (owe) | | Assets (£) (owed) | |
|---|---|---|---|
| Deposits | 1,000 | Cash | 350 |
| | | Reserves held at the Bank of England | 500 |
| | | Tbills | 150 |
| **Total** | **1,000** | **Total** | **1,000** |

The effect:

- Holdings of Tbills at the four retail banks will fall by £250 each to £150 (£400 − £250 = £150).
- Reserves held at the Bank by the retail banks initially increases by £250 each.
- Monetary base M0, which equals notes and coins in circulation plus *reserves held at the central bank*, increases by £250 × 4 banks = £1,000. *There has been an increase in the money supply.*
- Finally, if the banks decide to reduce their reserve holdings at the Bank and hold the reserves as cash then the balance sheet will look like this:

| Liabilities (£) (owe) | | Assets (£) (owed) | |
|---|---|---|---|
| Deposits | 1,000 | Cash | 600 |
| | | Reserves held at the Bank of England | 250 |
| | | Tbills | 150 |
| **Total** | **1,000** | **Total** | **1,000** |

This can be done in reverse: that is, the Bank can *sell* Tbills to the banking sector via the primary participants.

### Recap

The buying of Tbills is equivalent to printing new money and lowering the supply of Tbills. Work through how this will affect the balance sheet at the Bank.

## Selling Tbills by the Bank of England

The Bank of England's balance sheet:

| Liabilities (£) (owe) | | Assets (£) (owed) | |
|---|---|---|---|
| Currency in circulation | 1,000 | Tbills | 1,000 |
| (decrease by £1,000) Reserves | 0 | (decrease by £1,000) | |
| **Total** | **1,000** | **Total** | **1,000** |

The retail bank's balance sheet: the effect of selling Tbills by the Bank (if we start from the initial balance sheet and assume again that £250 are sold to each of the four banks = £1,000):[1]

| Liabilities (£) (owe) | | Assets (£) (owed) | |
|---|---|---|---|
| Deposits | 1,000 | Cash | 350 |
| | | Reserves held at the Bank of England | 0 |
| | | Tbills | 650 |
| **Total** | **1,000** | **Total** | **1,000** |

The effect:

- Holdings of Tbills at the four retail banks will increase by £250 each to £650 (£400 + £250 = £650).
- Reserves held at the Bank by the retail banks will initially decrease by £250 each.
- Monetary base M0, which equals notes and coins in circulation plus **reserves held at the central bank**, decreases by £250 × 4 banks = £1,000. *There has been a decrease in the money supply.*
- Finally, if the banks decide to decrease their cash holdings and hold more reserves at the Bank, in this case the balance sheet may look like this:

| Liabilities (£) (owe) | | Assets (£) (owed) | |
|---|---|---|---|
| Deposits | 1,000 | Cash | 150 |
| | | Reserves held at the Bank of England | 200 |
| | | Tbills | 650 |
| **Total** | **1,000** | **Total** | **1,000** |

### Recap

The selling of Tbills has led to a contraction of the monetary base and in this example a lower cash ratio (cash to total assets) at the banks. *There has been a reduction in the money supply.*

### Test yourself

**Q1.** Define what is meant by a 'primary participant'.

**Q2.** What is the effect of the Bank purchasing Tbills from the primary participants?

**Q3.** What is the effect of the Bank selling Tbills to the primary participants?

[1]This will be replicated across all four retail banks for this example.

## Bank of England's open market operations and the effect on the interest rate

It can be seen from the above simple analysis that a central bank, in this case the Bank of England, can manipulate the money supply within an economy by undertaking what are known as **open market operations**, that is operations to buy and sell securities to influence money aggregates. The Bank undertakes this on behalf of the MPC in order to guide the interest rate to the one set by the MPC. The following extract is from the Bank's website:

> The MPC meets every month to set the interest rate. Throughout the month, the MPC receives extensive briefing on the economy from Bank of England staff. This includes a half-day meeting – known as the pre-MPC meeting – which usually takes place on the Friday before the MPC's interest rate setting meeting. The nine members of the Committee are made aware of all the latest data on the economy and hear explanations of recent trends and analysis of relevant issues. The Committee is also told about business conditions around the UK from the Bank's Agents. The Agents' role is to talk directly to business to gain intelligence and insight into current and future economic developments and prospects.

(See **www.bankofengland.co.uk**)

The aim of a central bank's operations in the money markets is to guide short-term interest rates to the level set by the government or the independent body responsible for setting interest rates. In the UK this is the MPC. The Bank accomplishes this aim by providing liquidity or cash to the banking system when the system is short of liquidity (or is starved of liquidity). Importantly, the price of money or the marginal liquidity or the price (interest rate) at which the Bank will provide liquidity in the markets is set at the rate imposed by the independent body or MPC.

Key features:

- Major retail banks who bank with the Bank (referred to as **settlement banks**) are obliged to maintain a minimum balance of zero on their Bank settlement accounts at the end of each day; they cannot go into debt.
- Settlement of **sterling obligations** (which are just the transactions in the economy that require money to be transferred out of one settlement bank into another settlement bank). For example, if you purchase a pair of shoes and pay with your debit card then the money will be transferred from your account to the account of the shoe seller which may be at a different bank.
- Settlement occurs over the accounts which the banks hold at the Bank.
- During or after the settlement process it may become apparent that a bank may require liquidity in order to ensure that its account at the Bank is positive.

- In addition, the Bank's lending operations in the money markets ensures that the banks regularly need to go to the Bank to refinance their lending.
- Commercial banks need to seek refinancing from the Bank when the demand for banknotes rises or if the level of sterling-denominated deposits (reserves) held at the Bank by banks increases.
- The financing requirements of the banks can be filled either by a reduction in the size of the banks' operational deposits at the Bank (their reserves in the above example) or by an increase in the stock of refinancing (which would be achieved through the Bank's open market operations – in the example above, buying Tbills) or a combination of the two.
- The Bank therefore provides the liquidity needed by the banks in order for them to achieve positive end-of-day balances on their accounts.
- It acts as the marginal supplier of money to the banking system, enabling effective system-wide liquidity management in normal market conditions.

Importantly, the price of the **marginal liquidity** or the price at which the Bank will purchase money market instruments and provide the required money is set at the rate imposed by the MPC.

- By acting in this way it exerts pressure on the short-term money market rate of interest to move to the 'official' rate set by the MPC.
- The Bank maintains demand for liquidity in a variety of ways:
  - Through taxation and government borrowing in the market. When people pay their taxes they do so from their bank accounts; the flow of these payments drains the banking sector of liquidity. Likewise, the selling of government instruments has the same effect.
  - Through acquiring via its money market operations short-term claims on banks. A number of these claims mature throughout the day and must be redeemed by the financial institutions, draining them of liquidity.
  - By ensuring that the clearing banks have to maintain positive end-of-day balances with the Bank.
  - By draining liquidity from the money markets each week by issuing Tbills (or gilt repos) which are bought by the banking sector or their customers. Either way there is a flow of liquidity from the banks to the Bank.
  - By ensuring it works because banks want equilibrium in their balance sheets, that is a pre-determined **liquidity ratio** (this is the ratio of cash to total assets).

## Test yourself

**Q1.** Explain the process whereby the Bank can set the price of marginal liquidity.

**Q2.** How does the Bank maintain the demand for liquidity?

Therefore, the Bank manipulates interest rates by first starving the banking sector of money and then via open market operations manipulates the money supply at the lending or borrowing rates required to get the interest rate to that officially set by the MPC.

## Key definitions

**Primary participants**

Those financial institutions standing by to purchase government-issued securities such as Tbills when issued.

**Open market operations**

The buying or selling of government securities such as Tbills to primary participants in order to manipulate the money supply and/or the interest rate.

**Settlement bank**

Major retail banks which bank with the Bank and which must maintain a positive balance on their Bank settlement accounts at the end of each day.

**Sterling obligations**

Transactions in the economy which require money to be transferred out of one settlement bank into another settlement bank.

**Marginal liquidity rate**

The price at which the central bank will purchase the next 'lot' of money market instruments and provide money.

**Liquidity ratio**

The ratio of cash to total or average assets at a bank.

## Examples & evidence

Read the paper 'The Bank of England's operations in the sterling money markets' which can be accessed at: **www.bankofengland.co.uk/markets/money/stermm3.pdf**. Below is a brief extract:

> The fulcrum of the system is the underlying demand for Bank of England money as the final settlement asset for sterling payments, principally in the form of Bank of England bank notes and banks' settlement accounts held with the Bank of England. Settlement banks are obliged to maintain a minimum balance of zero on their Bank of England settlement accounts at the end of each day (i.e.

there is, in effect, a one-day maintenance requirement in the United Kingdom, and, unlike some other countries' systems, no positive reserve requirements and no reserve averaging over a maintenance period). Although the Bank of England holds accounts for some other commercial banks, the vast majority of banks in the United Kingdom hold accounts with the settlement banks. Settlement of sterling obligations between settlement banks occurs in the United Kingdom's Real Time Gross Settlement (RTGS) system, operated by the Bank of England. Whether payments are between customers of different banks, between settlement and/or non-settlement banks, through whichever payment system (CHAPS Sterling, CREST, BACS, Cheque or Credit clearings), or whether between the Bank of England and the rest of the system, settlement ultimately occurs over the accounts which settlement banks hold at the Bank of England. In its money market operations, the Bank of England, by providing the liquidity needed by the banking system, for same-day settlement, enables the settlement banks to achieve positive end-of-day balances on these accounts. In this, way it acts as the marginal supplier of money to the banking system, enabling effective system-wide liquidity management in normal market conditions.

## Question

Consider how the Bank of England's operations rely on the interaction of the whole financial system.

## Chapter summary – pulling it all together

By the end of this chapter you should be able to:

| | Confident ✓ | Not confident? |
| --- | --- | --- |
| Define the roles that a central bank may have in an economy | | Revise page 272 |
| Describe the three core purposes of the UK's central bank, the Bank of England | | Revise pages 272–274 |
| Explain the three divisions of the Bank of England and their roles | | Revise pages 274–276 |

| | Confident ✓ | Not confident? |
|---|---|---|
| Describe the markets in which the Bank of England is active | | Revise pages 276–278 |
| Explain the functioning of the MPC and the FSA | | Revise pages 278–280 |
| Elucidate the rise of money as a medium of exchange; the functions of money; and how money reduces transaction costs | | Revise pages 281–283 |
| Describe the difference between M0, M1, M2, M3 and M4 | | Revise pages 284–285 |
| Fully explain how the Bank of England can manipulate the money supply and how this can lead to interest rates converging on the rate set by the MPC | | Revise pages 286–294 |

Now try the sample question at the start of this chapter, using the answer guidelines below.

## Answer guidelines

### ✻ Assessment question

(a) Explain, using a central bank of your choice, the guiding principles that a central bank should follow within a developed economy. (40 marks)

(b) Describe, using T-accounts, how a central bank can affect the interest rate. (60 marks)

### Approaching the question

Begin this question by explaining the basics. This should include the roles that central banks can take on within a developed economy, such as ensuring the integrity of the financial system or managing the national debt. After showing that you understand the basic need for a central bank, you should introduce the central bank of your choice and weave into your analysis the guiding principles that you believe to be important, with an analysis of the central bank's actual operations and how it undertakes these. Guiding this analysis should be information from the central bank's website and any research articles you have read. The second part of this question is testing your basic knowledge of a central bank's position within an economy and how it manipulates the money supply to keep the major banks always demanding some liquidity in the form of cash. It is this daily demand for liquidity that forms the basis of the central bank's ability to move interest rates to the level set by the government or – in the case of the UK – the MPC.

## Important points to include

- Provide an explanation of the possible roles that a central bank may undertake.

- Fully elucidate the possible guiding principles and link these to a central bank in practice.

- Contrast the principles you have outlined with any evidence emanating from the central bank you have chosen.

- Explain how central banks manipulate the money supply.

- Show how this manipulation can lead to interest rate changes.

- Use T-accounts to show how this happens in practice.

## Make your answer stand out

Key to a high mark will be using the research literature and the publications from the central bank so ensure that you understand these:

- Read the articles by Mishkin and by Goodhart recommended below and refer to them in your answer. Correctly referring to and interpreting leading economists in your exam answers is impressive.

- Take time to understand fully the T-accounts and remember not only to draw them but also to explain your diagrams (many students can draw the diagrams but fail to explain or interpret them correctly).

- Show the T-accounts from the perspective of the central bank and a large retail bank.

## Read to impress

### Books

The most easily understandable book in this area is by Frederic Mishkin, who is a leading expert on central banking:

Mishkin, F.S. (2012) *The Economics of Money, Banking and Financial Markets*, 10th edition. Pearson Education.

Mishkin, F.S. and Eakins, S. (2011) *Financial Markets and Institutions*, 7th edition. Pearson Education.

Also try:

Goodhart, C.A.E. (1989) *Money Information & Uncertainty*. MIT Press.

### Journal articles

Goodhart, C.A.E. (1994) What should central banks do? What should be their macroeconomic objectives and operations? *Economic Journal*, Vol. 104 (427), pp. 1424–36.

Goodhart, C.A.E. (2010) The changing role of central banks. Special Paper 197, LSE Financial Markets Group Paper Series, December.

Mishkin, F.S. (2000) What should central banks do? *Review, Federal Reserve Bank of St. Louis*, Vol. 82 (5), pp. 1–13.

O'Driscoll, G.P. Jr (2012) Central banks: reform or abolish? Working Paper no. 11, The Cato Institute.

### Websites

Bank of England (2002) The Bank of England's operations in the sterling money markets. Available at: **www.bankofengland.co.uk/markets/money/stermm3.pdf**.

*The Economist* (2012) Don't give up: central banks cannot substitute for incompetent politicians. But they can do more to support weak economies. June 30.

Again, try the websites below. For a thorough understanding of the practical aspects make sure you read the first two references:

The Federal Reserve: **http://www.federalreserve.gov/**.

The European Central Bank: **http://www.ecb.int/home/html/index.en.html**.

FTSE: **http://www.ftse.com/**.

The Bank of England: **http://www.bankofengland.co.uk/Pages/home. aspx**.

The Cato Institute: **http://www.cato.org**.

The United Kingdom Debt Management Office: **http://www.dmo.gov.uk/ index.aspx?page=publications/money_markets**.

## Companion website

Go to the companion website at **www.pearsoned.co.uk/econexpress** to find more revision support online for this topic area.

## Notes

**Notes**

# 11 Banking

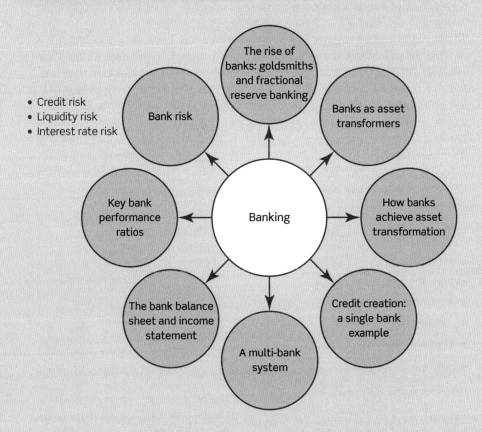

- Credit risk
- Liquidity risk
- Interest rate risk

Bank risk

The rise of banks: goldsmiths and fractional reserve banking

Banks as asset transformers

Banking

How banks achieve asset transformation

Key bank performance ratios

Credit creation: a single bank example

The bank balance sheet and income statement

A multi-bank system

A printable version of this topic map is available from **www.pearsoned.co.uk/econexpress**

## Introduction

Large retail banks in developed economies dominate the high street and are instrumental in the financial system. They perform unique functions that place them at the heart of the financial system and, after the recent financial crisis, at the centre of controversy. Many textbooks that you will read will have chapters titled 'What makes banks special?' and to a large extent the large banking groups are special. They have the ability to create credit, and as we discussed earlier (see Chapter 10) their deposits are included in the money aggregates M1 to M4 because bank deposits are spendable immediately via your debit card. Traditionally, the core function of the large retail banking groups was taking in deposits from individuals and bundling these deposits into loans to be used by retail customers (you and me) and business, both small and large. For example, in the past UK retail bank liabilities have been dominated by deposits making up 60–70% of total liabilities. In contrast, loans dominated assets, making up around 60–65%.

Taking in deposits and providing loans is inherently risky. Deposits and loans have strikingly different characteristics and most of us will deposit our money in banks thinking that it is 100% safe. Loans, however, are risky as they are linked to the ability of the borrower to pay back the money over time and this will be difficult to assess at the time of providing the loan. This is just one example of how banks are exposed to risk. Theoretically, academics analyse banks as asset transformers – transforming the characteristics of their deposits into different forms as they become assets. Banks transform their assets in four ways: maturity, liquidity, risk and size. More practically, this transformation exposes banks to risk, which requires managing to ensure the survival of the bank.

The main risks that banks are exposed to are:

- credit risk;
- liquidity risk;
- interest rate risk;
- market risk; and
- operational risk.

These will all have their own specialist department within a bank to manage them on a day-to-day basis.

Over the past two decades banking has evolved and retail banks have diversified and become involved in a wider range of products and services. So, along with their deposit and loans business they now offer insurance, mortgages and investment banking services. They have also altered their funding model, becoming more reliant on the financial markets. It has been argued it is the move into investment banking and more reliance on the financial markets that led to the 2008 financial crisis. This chapter will look at the rationale for banks, their operations, risk exposure and management.

---

### → Revision checklist

*Make sure that you both understand and can explain:*

- ❏ the rise of the goldsmith and fractional reserve banking;
- ❏ the characteristics of bank liabilities and assets;
- ❏ bank asset transformation: maturity, risk, liquidity and size;
- ❏ how banks achieve asset transformation;
- ❏ how banks can create credit in a single and multi-bank system;
- ❏ how reserve ratios and capital adequacy ratios affect credit-creating capabilities at a bank;
- ❏ the balance sheet and income statement of banks;
- ❏ key bank performance ratios;
- ❏ credit risk, liquidity and interest rate risk.

---

### ✳ Assessment advice

It is important that you understand the basics of banking from the rise of the goldsmith onwards. Ensure that you fully understand fractional reserve banking and what the goldsmith is doing. Take this knowledge and apply to the banking firm. Remember, in any question regarding banking your lecturer will usually ask something on asset transformation – make sure you can define it and explain the different types. Practising the T-accounts and using them in your answer will increase your grade. On this foundation, if you can relate the theory of asset transformation to the balance sheet and income statement, key ratios, and define and analyse the key risks facing banks, then all these will garner marks.

---

### ✳ Assessment question

(a) Examine the theoretical benefits that banks may bring to those undertaking financial transactions. (40 marks)

(b) Explain the risks that banks expose themselves to in their day-to-day operations and any techniques used to manage these risks. (60 marks)

Can you answer this question? Guidelines on answering the question are presented at the end of this chapter.

## The rise of banks: goldsmiths and fractional reserve banking

To understand what banks do you need to go back to where it all began – the creation of money as a medium of exchange as explained earlier (see Chapter 10). In very primitive markets, households and businesses transact using barter, which is trading one tangible good for another, for example a pig for a sheep. However, it is time consuming to find people willing to trade and it requires a 'double coincidence of wants'.

The major problem with this primitive system is that it requires a vast amount of valuable time to search for other people who are willing to trade. It was stated previously that a precious metal such as gold becomes acceptable as a medium of exchange and that goldsmiths began to store gold in their secure storage facilities. Traders begin to deposit gold with the goldsmiths, who charged a fee for this storage service. In return for the gold, the goldsmith would issue a receipt or claim on the amount of gold deposited. Initially every transaction would require the purchaser of a good to return to the goldsmith to obtain gold, pay for the good and then require the seller of the good to return the gold they received back to the goldsmith. This process remains high in transaction costs.

Eventually, to circumvent the need to make several trips to the goldsmith to exchange receipts for gold, the receipts begin to be accepted as a medium of exchange. The receipts are accepted as long as the goldsmith's reputation remains strong and there is a belief that the receipts can, at any time, be exchanged for gold. If everybody is using receipts for transactions then:

- the inflow and outflow of gold through the goldsmith reduces and becomes more predictable as there are no longer people withdrawing and depositing gold after every transaction;
- the stock of gold held by the goldsmith attains a certain level but then stabilises – not increasing or decreasing (as receipts replace the need to keep depositing gold stock).

Initially, goldsmiths took in gold and offered receipts to the same amount; however, they soon realised that receipts were not being redeemed for gold and there was little need to have equal amounts of gold to receipts in issue. If nobody withdraws gold and you hold enough to cover any small withdrawals then why not begin to issue more receipts than you have gold? As long as the additionally printed receipts look identical to the ones issued (which were backed by gold) they can be loaned, at a rate of interest, to borrowers who require more 'medium of exchange'. We now have a fractional reserve banking system which looks like this:

| RECEIPTS | |
|---|---|
| GOLD | SHORTFALL OF GOLD = LOANS = RISK |

This can be shown using a T-account as introduced earlier (see Chapter 10). Here is the position when receipts = gold deposited. The goldsmith is not undertaking **fractional reserve banking**:

| Liabilities (ounces of gold) | | Assets (ounces of gold) | |
|---|---|---|---|
| Receipts | 1,000 | Gold | 1,000 |
| **Total** | **1,000** | **Total** | **1,000** |

Here is the position when the goldsmith undertakes fractional reserve banking – they have issued more receipts than gold reserves:

| Liabilities (ounces of gold) | | Assets (ounces of gold) | |
|---|---|---|---|
| Receipts | 1,100 | Gold | 1,000 |
|  |  | Loans | 100 |
| **Total** | **1,100** | **Total** | **1,100** |

Key features:

- When analysing bank balance sheets, **liabilities** always equal **assets** – what you owe in liabilities equals what you have in assets (gold in the above example plus what you are owed, which is loans).
- Remember that the borrower in the above example borrows the receipts and will begin to use them as a medium of exchange to purchase goods; the receipts will disperse in the economy.
- As the loan is repaid with receipts, the receipts in issue fall and this reduction is shown on both sides of the balance sheet.
- The liability of paying back the receipts (loans) rests with the borrower.
- Once the loan has been agreed and the receipts issued, remember that the borrower can exchange the receipts for gold at any time by presenting them to the goldsmith – the goldsmith is exposed to the risk of not having enough gold.

- Issuing more receipts than gold exposes the goldsmith to risk in initially two forms: liquidity risk, which is the risk that they will not have enough gold in storage to satisfy receipts issued; and credit risk, which is the risk that the additionally issued receipts in the form of loans will default (not be repaid).
- Issuing more receipts increases profit from the interest charged but increases liquidity and credit risk.

The goldsmith is the basis of today's bank operations. While there are no longer any real claim on gold in most economies, the claim we have on banks is on liquidity or obtaining your deposited cash money. Banks must hold enough cash to satisfy the daily demand of people cashing in their deposits; that is, withdrawing cash from their bank branches.

Today, banks have exactly the same problem as the early goldsmiths: they can keep issuing loans for which they receive a healthy rate of interest but each loan becomes a deposit and increases their requirement for cash liquidity as people exchange their deposits for money. Liquidity risk increases and the bank will need to hold more cash to cover potential demand. Like the goldsmiths, the banks are aware that not all claims on deposits will come in at the same time and they can calculate the amount of new cash that will be incoming to the bank every day. For example, in 2010 the UK bank Barclays held just over 6.5% of its total assets as cash. An equivalent T-account to that used to analyse goldsmiths may look like this for a bank:

| Liabilities (£m) | | Assets (£m) | |
|---|---|---|---|
| Deposits | 500 | Cash | 50 |
| | | Loans | 450 |
| **Total** | **500** | **Total** | **500** |

## Banks as asset transformers

As gold is replaced in society by receipts and the receipts become accepted in their own right, we move to using '**fiat money**', which is money backed by the government but which has no intrinsic value – goldsmiths develop into banks and begin to develop their operations, based on fractional reserve banking. They become asset transformers. We introduced the use of the T-account to analyse central bank and bank balance sheets in the previous chapter, which helps to explain bank operations.

## Recap

Remember the key features concerning banking and the use of T-accounts:

- Assets always equal liabilities.
- Liabilities are what the bank owes.
- Assets are what the bank is owed (except cash).
- Cash is held on the balance sheet as an asset to service deposits when individuals want to convert their deposits into cash.
- Cash is held at a minimum as it yields no return.

## Test yourself

**Q1.** How do goldsmiths expose themselves to risk?

**Q2.** Are loans assets or liabilities for a bank?

**Q3.** Cash is held on the balance sheet as an _____ to service deposits when individuals want to convert their deposits into cash. Fill in the gap.

**Asset transformation** can be observed in the balance sheet by looking at the different characteristics of bank liabilities: mainly deposits and their assets, mainly loans. If we use the goldsmith example again, the goldsmith was issuing receipts that could be exchanged for gold at any time; however, when the goldsmith began to issue loans, the loans would be issued and repayable over time, perhaps up to 20 years. In this way the goldsmith is undertaking asset transformation:

- Their liabilities can be withdrawn immediately but some of their assets, the loans, will take much longer to pay back (or mature) – perhaps up to 20 years or more. The goldsmith is undertaking maturity transformation.
- The receipts are perceived to be low risk but the loans carry credit risk – the risk they may not be paid back. The goldsmith is undertaking risk transformation.
- In a major retail bank deposits tend to be short term and have the characteristics outlined in the left hand column of Figure 11.1. Loans tend to be long term and have the characteristics shown in the right hand column of the figure.

## Key definitions

**Bank liabilities**

What a bank owes to its customers.

### Bank assets

Generally what a bank is owed sometime in the future (excepting cash money), the same as its financial investments.

### Fractional reserve banking

Originally referred to as the system where goldsmiths would keep only a 'fraction' of gold to underpin their issued receipts. In today's banking system, a term used to denote a type of banking whereby institutions only hold a 'fraction' of their liabilities (mainly deposits) as actual ready cash.

### Fiat money

Money that is backed by the government but has no actual value.

### Asset transformation

A process that involves banks 'transforming' the characteristics of their liabilities as they become assets. They do this in four ways: risk, size, liquidity and maturity.

Banks transform assets in four ways:

● Maturity
● Risk
● Liquidity
● Size.

| Liabilities – What banks owe | Assets – What banks are owed |
|---|---|
| Deposits (Approximately 60–70% of total liabilities) | Loans (Approximately 60–65% of total liabilities) |
| Characteristics (generally): | Characteristics (generally): |
| • Perceived to be risk free<br>• Liquid<br>• Certain<br>• Secure | • Risky<br>• Illiquid<br>• Uncertain<br>• Long term (5–25 years) |

Changing the characteristics of liabilities as they become assets increases risk

**Figure 11.1** Basic asset transformation on a retail bank's balance sheet.

## Maturity transformation

Banks bridge the gap between the desire of lenders to be able to get their money back quickly if needed and the desire of borrowers to borrow for a long period. In fulfilling this function the bank holds liabilities (mainly deposits) that have a shorter term to maturity than their assets (mainly loans). They borrow short and lend long.

## Liquidity transformation

Liquidity is the ability of the deposit holder in a bank to redeem their deposit quickly and without cost in the event that they desire or need cash. Banks issue claims in the form of deposits which do not require their holders to give the bank any notice or pay any penalties for premature withdrawal. In contrast, banks hold assets that are largely illiquid and costly to convert back into cash.

## Risk transformation

This involves the bank shifting the burden of risk from the depositors (who lend to the bank) to themselves. Deposits are safe. Loans are risky.

## Size transformation

Banks transform the nature of their assets through the collection of a large number of small amounts of funds from depositors and parcelling them into larger amounts required by borrowers. Often the banks have relied on obtaining many small deposits from conveniently located branches. This benefits borrowers because they obtain one large loan from one source, thus reducing transaction costs.

## How banks achieve asset transformation

Banks are able to perform asset transformation in part because:

- they know that not all deposit holders will want to redeem their deposits for cash at the same time;
- individuals and businesses will be depositing more cash with them every day;
- a portion of each loan will gradually be repaid, usually monthly, swelling their cash reserves; and
- they hold a privileged position within the financial system.

Banks can undertake asset transformation with more certainty if they are larger and have more branches. More branches equals more customers depositing and withdrawing cash from around the country. As the number of customers that a bank has increases, the ability to measure the amount of daily cash required by the bank becomes more predictable.

A larger bank will be able to calculate, with some certainty, the value of cash that will be needed on any one day and hold enough cash reserves to meet this demand. In addition, having more branches allows banks to pool small deposits into larger loans for consumer and business use. This is referred to as the '**law of large numbers**', which is a general theorem that asserts that as sample size increases, the average of these samples moves towards the mean of the whole population.

Transforming risk depends on economies of scale in risk management. The large amounts of deposits that banks collect allow them to diversify their assets across a wide variety of types and sectors. 'Pooling' risk in this way means that no individual is exposed to a situation where the default of one or more borrowers is likely to have a significant effect.

Large banks can also predict their asset and liability levels with more certainty because their position in the economy is hierarchical. At the top is the central bank where large banks do their banking, and then come the large retail banks, then the non-bank financial intermediaries. The large retail banks benefit from being just below the central bank in terms of hierarchy. Think what happens when you spend cash in a shop. Your money is transferred from your bank account to the bank account of the shop, if you both bank at the same bank, then the liquidity at the bank is unaffected, just transferred from your account to the shop's account.

The large banks dominate the deposit business; in the UK the largest four banks have approximately 80% of all retail deposits and so they can be pretty sure that, as cash is spent, that cash will be retained among themselves – allowing them to reduce the amount of cash they need to hold on a day-to-day basis. Of course there will be some withdrawals from the retail sector, for example cash going abroad to a non-domestically owned bank. In addition, the bank can also calculate how much cash will be coming in from asset investments (what a bank is owed). For example, its loans will be being paid off and it will receive cash (most likely) on a monthly basis which it can retain as cash. Banks can therefore asset transform and 'create credit' for the economy, but must be aware of the risks to which they are exposed. Let's look at how this works.

## Test yourself

**Q1.** List the general characteristics of deposits in a retail bank.

**Q2.** List the general characteristics of loans in a retail bank.

**Q3.** Define asset transformation.

**Q4.** In what ways do banks transform their assets?

# Credit creation: a single bank example

Large retail banks can create credit, which boosts the money supply and becomes the concern of the government, central bank and regulators. In a single bank model **credit creation** can be demonstrated by looking at three T-accounts: the initial position; the issuing of a new loan; and then the depositing of new money. You will notice that the T-accounts now have capital in the liabilities column. **Bank capital** has become a key concern of bankers, governments and regulators. It is the difference between the value of a bank's assets and its liabilities. In the T-accounts below it is £20 million, which is the £520 million of assets minus £500 million of liabilities (in this case deposits). It is the amount that the assets can drop in value before deposit holders can no longer be provided with money:

CAPITAL = ASSETS − LIABILITIES

You can also observe below each T-account's two ratios:

- **Reserve ratio:** this is the percentage amount of total deposits a bank must hold as cash money, enabling banks to return cash immediately to deposit holders. Deposit holders demanding cash once a bank's holdings of cash have been expended must wait for their bank to sell other short-term securities' holding such as Tbills. The reserve ratio will affect the credit-creating abilities of banks and the money supply in a country and for this reason some countries set a minimum reserve requirement.

- **Capital to assets ratio (CAR):** this is the percentage of a bank's assets covered by capital. You can think of this as a cushion before the bank becomes insolvent. For example, if everything else remains the same but assets revalue, in the T-account below think of loans now having a market value of £460 million; then capital has dropped to £10 million (that is, nothing else has changed – deposits are at the same level and so is cash). In reality the authorities impose a CAR that only includes assets that carry risk; cash is therefore excluded. It is excluded in the CAR estimates below.

**The initial position:**

| Liabilities (£m) | | Assets (£m) | |
|---|---|---|---|
| Deposits | 500 | Cash | 50 |
| Capital | 20 | Loans | 470 |
| **Total** | **520** | **Total** | **520** |

Reserve ratio = cash/deposits = 50/500 = 10%
CAR = capital/total assets (not cash) = 20/470 = 4.26%

### (a) Issuing a new loan of £100 million:

| Liabilities (£m) | | | Assets (£m) | | |
|---|---|---|---|---|---|
| | Deposits | 600 | | Cash | 50 |
| | Capital | 20 | | Loans | 570 |
| | **Total** | **620** | | **Total** | **620** |

Reserve ratio = cash/deposits = 50/600 = 8.34%
Capital assets ratio = capital/total assets (not cash) = 20/570 = 3.50%

### (b) Issuing another new loan of £200 million:

| Liabilities (£m) | | | Assets (£m) | | |
|---|---|---|---|---|---|
| | Deposits | 800 | | Cash | 50 |
| | Capital | 20 | | Loans | 770 |
| | **Total** | **820** | | **Total** | **820** |

Reserve ratio = cash/deposits = 50/800 = 6.25%
CAR = capital/total assets (not cash) = 20/770 = 2.60%

### (c) New deposits received of £50 million:

| Liabilities (£m) | | | Assets (£m) | | |
|---|---|---|---|---|---|
| | Deposits | 850 | | Cash | 100 |
| | Capital | 20 | | Loans | 770 |
| | **Total** | **870** | | **Total** | **870** |

Reserve ratio = cash/deposits = 100/850 = 11.76%
CAR = capital/total assets (not cash) = 20/770 = 2.60%

Take time to consider what has happened in the above T-accounts:

- No new deposits have entered the system until T-account (c); however, the money aggregate has increased – the banks created credit.
- Loans have increased in (a) by £100 million and this has resulted in a £100 million increase in deposits. This occurs because the bank credits your deposit account with an amount equal to your loan and because there is only one bank in the system. When the person that borrowed the money undertakes expenditure, those receiving the expenditure deposit the money back with the bank and deposits increase by the amount of the loan.
- THE MONEY SUPPLY HAS INCREASED – THE BANK HAS CREATED CREDIT.

The reserve ratio has declined from 10% to 8.34%. This is an indication that risk has increased within the bank. Prior to the loan being issued the bank could provide cash immediately for 10% of its deposits; it can now provide only 8.34% cash. Liquidity risk has escalated. Risk is increased further on the issue of the £200 million loan, now the bank can cover only 6.25% of its deposits.

- You can also observe that the capital ratio has decreased from 4.26% to 2.60%. This also indicates that risk has increased because in the new scenario if only 2.6% of loans revalue (or default) then the bank has no capital underpinning its operations.
- In T-account (c) we observe a new deposit in the bank; this is retained as cash and boosts the reserve requirement. It has no effect on the capital ratio, thus liquidity risk is reduced but the bank remains susceptible to credit risk.
- If the bank uses the new deposit to issue new loans then both liquidity and credit risk will increase. The banks will create or multiply the credit available in the economy. However, if they want to maintain their capital ratio new capital will be required.

## Key definitions

**Law of large numbers**

A general theorem that asserts that, as sample size increases, the average of these samples moves towards the mean of the whole population. This means that as deposit inflows and outflows increase as a result of a bank holding more deposit accounts (usually via a large bank branch network), then the bank can calculate with more certainty the net cash position.

**Credit creation**

The term used to denote how large retail banks can 'create' money by issuing loans based upon deposited money. Note that issuing loans also creates deposits. In banking, liabilities always equal assets.

**Bank capital**

What is left if a bank sells all its assets and repays all its liabilities.

**Reserve ratio**

The percentage amount of total deposits a bank holds as cash money.

**Capital to assets ratio**

The percentage of bank assets covered by capital.

## The bank money multiplier

You must be aware of the **bank money multiplier**: if the bank has a set reserve requirement of 10% (as in the T-account on page 311) then this will constrain the bank's credit creation abilities to:

$$D = \frac{1}{r} \times C$$

where:

$D$ = amount of deposits
$r$ = reserve requirement
$C$ = cash held within the bank
So if a bank initially had a deposit of £5,000 and held this as cash:

| Liabilities (£) | | Assets (£) | |
|---|---|---|---|
| Deposits | 5,000 | Cash | 5,000 |

it could create deposits equal to:

$D = (1/0.1) \times 5,000$

$D = 50,000$

and retain a reserve ratio of 10% cash to assets 5,000/50,000 = 10%. The new balance sheet would look like this:

| Liabilities (£) | | Assets (£) | |
|---|---|---|---|
| Deposits | 50,000 | Cash | 5,000 |
| | | Loans | 45,000 |
| **Total** | **50,000** | **Total** | **50,000** |

Or, viewed another way, the bank could create loans equal to:

$$L = \left(\frac{1}{r} \times C\right) - C$$

where:

$L$ = amount of loans

Using the example as proof:

$$L = \left(\frac{1}{0.1} \times 5,000\right) - C$$
$L = 50,000 - 5,000$
$L = 45,000$

You can also calculate the effect of an additional deposit of cash on total deposits by using the formula:

$$\Delta D = \frac{1}{r} \times \Delta C$$

where:

$\Delta D$ = the change in total deposits held at the bank (to be added to the original amount)

$\Delta C$ = the change in cash deposits

For example, in T-account (c) the fresh injection of cash deposited equals £50 million. If the bank wanted to keep the reserve ratio at the level before it received the cash, which was 6.25% as shown in T-account (b), then it could expand deposits by:

$\Delta D = (1/0.0625) \times 50$

$\Delta D = £800$

The level of deposits would increase to £1,600 million, cash to £100 million and loans issued would increase to £1,520 million. The reserve ratio remains unchanged at 100/1,600 = 6.25%.

| Liabilities (£m) | | Assets (£m) | |
|---|---|---|---|
| Deposits | 1,600 | Cash | 100 |
| Capital | 20 | Loans | 1,520 |
| **Total** | **1,620** | **Total** | **1,620** |

Reserve ratio = cash/deposits = 100/1,600 = 6.25%

CAR = capital/total assets (not cash) = 20/1520 = 1.32%

However, credit creation will also be constrained by the banks chosen, or the authorities impose a capital requirement so that capital will only support a certain amount of loans such that:

maximum amount of loans = S/CAR

where:

$S$ = capital in the bank

CAR = capital to assets ratio set by the authorities (or self-imposed)

So if the bank had capital of £20 million and an imposed CAR of 8% then the maximum amount of loans this capital would support would be:

maximum amount of loans = 20/0.08 = £250m

## Recap

Putting all this together, you can observe that banks can create credit but that their ability to do so will be constrained by:

- the reserve requirement; and
- the capital to assets ratio that banks choose or is set by the authorities.

The bank money multiplier is constrained by cash; the capital adequacy ratio is constrained by levels of capital. If we assume the bank has a set amount of capital in the medium term, then an increase in new cash will be constrained by the capital adequacy ratio such that:

$$\frac{S}{CAR} \geq \left( \frac{1}{r} \times \Delta C \right) - \Delta C$$

This imposes a constraint on the bank's credit creation linked to its levels of capital. That is, given their chosen (or imposed) reserve requirement, banks cannot keep creating credit – given levels of cash – over and above the imposed (self or otherwise) capital requirement. If this relationship does not hold then the bank will be contravening set capital requirements. Of course, it can increase capital, which will allow more loans to be issued (as long as the set reserve ratio is not contravened).

Also note that credit creation will also be constrained by the demand for loans – if there is no demand then the bank cannot issue loans.

## A multi-bank system

The above example shows a single bank's system but this can be extended to a multi-bank system that more clearly represents the real world. This will show the effect of credit creation on the money supply and how the position of the large retail banks within the economy enables large banks to undertake asset transformation.

| GOODWIN BANK (£m) | | MIDDLETON BANK (£m) | | BANK OF HESTOR (£m) | |
|---|---|---|---|---|---|
| Liabilities | Assets | Liabilities | Assets | Liabilities | Assets |
| Deposits 360 | Cash 15 | Deposits 615 | Cash 40 | Deposits 855 | Cash 50 |
| | Loans 375 | | Loans 625 | | Loans 875 |
| Capital 30 | | Capital 50 | | Capital 70 | |
| **Total 390** | **390** | **Total 665** | **665** | **Total 925** | **925** |

Assume:

- there are only three banks in the economy;
- all banks initially have a CAR of 8% (capital/risky assets, in this case loans).

Consider what happens when Goodwin Bank increases loans by £4 million to its own customers and this is immediately spent on goods and services with companies that have accounts with Middleton Bank and Bank of Hestor. Assume £1 million transfers to Middleton Bank and £3 million to Bank of Hestor.

Initially Goodwin Bank's balance sheet expands by the size of the loans granted:

| GOODWIN BANK (£m) | | | |
|---|---|---|---|
| **Liabilities** | | **Assets** | |
| Deposits | 360 **(+ 4)** | Cash | 15 |
| | | Loans | 375 **(+ 4)** |
| Capital | 30 | | |
| **Total** | **394** | | **394** |

But as the money loaned is spent with companies that hold accounts with the other banks, money is transferred to their balance sheets, increasing deposits and cash holdings:

| MIDDLETON BANK (£m) | | | | BANK OF HESTOR (£m) | | | |
|---|---|---|---|---|---|---|---|
| **Liabilities** | | **Assets** | | **Liabilities** | | **Assets** | |
| Deposits | 616 | Cash | 41 | Deposits | 858 | Cash | 53 |
| | | Loans | 625 | | | Loans | 875 |
| Capital | 50 | | | Capital | 70 | | |
| **Total** | **666** | | **666** | **Total** | **928** | | **928** |

Once the money has been transferred Goodwin Bank's balance sheet will look like this:

| GOODWIN BANK (£m) | | | |
|---|---|---|---|
| **Liabilities** | | **Assets** | |
| Deposits | 364(− 4) | Cash | 15(− 4) |
| | | Loans | 379 |
| Capital | 30 | | |
| **Total** | **390** | | **390** |

## Recap

**Note that in the above example:**

- On granting the loans Goodwin Bank's balance sheet size increases.
- When the borrowers of the loans begin to spend, the money is transferred from Goodwin Bank to the bank accounts held by those receiving the money. In this case £1 million to Middleton Bank and £3 million to Bank of Hestor.
- Middleton Bank sees deposits increase by £1 million and cash reserves increase by £1 million. Its reserve ratio increases slightly.
- Bank of Hestor sees deposits increase by £3 million and cash reserves increase by £3 million. Its reserve ratio also increases slightly.
- After the money has been transferred Goodwin Bank once again has liabilities and assets of £390 million but it has a lower reserve ratio – it has moved out of cash into loans. Deposit levels remain the same.

## Recap

Banks can asset transform due to the law of large numbers but also by their place within the financial system. From the above example you can see that if all these banks are providing loans every day and these are being spent, a large proportion of the money will remain held within these three banks. They can determine that they only need to hold cash reserves to cover the net daily change in cash. That is because, as people are spending money from their deposits, the money is being received by one of the other two banks. Cash levels will remain stable and predictable. As with the one-bank system, credit creation will be constrained by the reserve ratio, the capital to assets ratio and demand.

In addition individuals can withdraw money from the banking system by:

- spending money outside the economic area/nation, for example going on holiday abroad;
- holding cash and notes outside the banking system, for example at home.

## Test yourself

**Q1.** Provide a definition of bank capital.

**Q2.** Define reserve ratio.

**Q3.** What is meant by the bank money multiplier?

**Q4.** What factors may constrain the growth of loans in a retail bank?

## The bank balance sheet and income statement

The analysis of banking so far has been theoretical and it is important that you understand the rationale for banks before looking at the more practical elements, not least because it is their asset transformation functions that underpin their daily operations. So far we have looked at the T-account and placed deposits in liabilities and cash and loans in assets. An actual **bank balance sheet** will have a variety of different liabilities and deposits. At least once a year, a large retail bank will publish its annual report; this will include a wealth of information on the operations of the bank, allowing us to analyse the bank's performance. The annual report will include the balance sheet and the income statement:

- The balance sheet is the stock of what the bank has when the auditors look at the bank's operations. It is the items it is holding in cash terms at that point in time.

- The income statement in contrast is the inflow and outflow of income from the holdings of assets and the costs of liabilities including operating costs.

## Recap

All large retail banks report slightly differently and can have different terminology/classifications for their assets or liabilities. If analysing, ensure you are comparing like with like. The best way of doing this is to check the 'notes' section in the accounts. Below we run through the most commonly found liabilities and assets.

## Key definitions

**Bank money multiplier**

Signifies how many deposits can be created given a level of cash and a set cash ratio, remembering that bank deposits are counted as money.

**Bank balance sheet**

A table showing the stock of assets and liabilities in pounds sterling (in the UK) that are held within a bank at a point in time.

**Bank income statement**

A table showing the flow of income from held financial assets and expenditure on financial liabilities plus any other income and expenditure.

## What is on a bank's balance sheet?

| Major liabilities | Explanation |
|---|---|
| Deposits:<br>• deposits from banks<br>• demand deposits<br>• time deposits<br>(49% of total liabilities[1] at Lloyds Banking Group 2011) | Money received from other banks – about half of these could be securities sold under repurchase agreements<br>Demand deposits – deposits that can be withdrawn immediately and pay a small amount of interest<br>Time deposits – pay higher rates of interest and are usually held for a specified amount of time; if withdrawn early usually suffer an interest fine |

| Major liabilities | Explanation |
|---|---|
| Debt securities issued (20% of total liabilities[1] at Lloyds Banking Group 2011) | This will include medium-term notes, covered bonds, certificates of deposit, securitised notes and commercial paper. A covered bond is issued and backed by a pool of loans. Securitised notes are loans securitised under a bank's securitisation programme. Banks will issue all these to boost funding into the bank in addition to deposits |
| Derivative financial instruments (6.3% of total liabilities[1] at Lloyds Banking Group 2011) | These are held by banks and now reported fully as both a liability and asset. Usually held to help manage risk Derivatives used: interest rate swaps, forward rate agreements and options. Exchange rate related forward foreign exchange contracts, currency swaps and options. Credit derivatives |
| Subordinated debt (3.8% of total liabilities[1] at Lloyds Banking Group 2011) | These are notes and bonds with maturities in excess of one year. They are subordinated to the claims of depositors and all other creditors of the bank |
| Capital (Tier 1 capital levels were 10.8% of risk-weighted assets[2] at Lloyds Banking Group 2011) | The difference between a bank's liabilities and assets such that assets − liabilities = capital; held on the balance sheet to reduce bank risk; to provide leeway to absorb losses and remain solvent (reduce obligated outflows); to provide access to financial markets allowing access to liquidity; and to constrain growth. Tier 1 capital mainly consists of shareholders' equity and retained earnings |
| **Major assets** | **Explanation** |
| Cash and balances at the central bank (6.3% of total assets at Lloyds Banking Group 2011) | Notes and coins held in bank's vault to meet any daily outflows of money Deposits with central bank – used to meet any legal reserve requirements, clearance requirement and Tbill transactions |
| Short-term securities (14.4% of total assets at Lloyds Banking Group 2011) | This will include: certificates of deposit (CDs) purchased, repurchase agreements (repos), Tbills and other government securities. They are held on balance sheet to earn interest; to meet liquidity needs; and to speculate on interest movements. They are low in transaction costs and low in risk – a way of employing attracted funds but due to their high liquidity they earn less interest |

| Major assets | Explanation |
|---|---|
| Loans (63% of total assets at Lloyds Banking Group 2011) | Primary earning asset of banks and the largest item on the asset side of the balance sheet. Three major categories:<br>● commercial loans<br>● consumer loans<br>● real estate loans or mortgages |

1 Excludes equity.
2 Assets that carry risk have a risk weighting depending on the level of risk. Consumer loans carry a weight of 100%. This means that if a bank wanted to have 8% capital for every consumer loan, it would need to have £8 of capital for every £100 consumer loan.

## The income statement

- The **bank income statement** starts with the interest income then subtracts interest expense to produce net interest income (NII).
- The other source of bank income is non-interest income – this is mainly fee income.
- From this the bank subtracts non-interest expense.
- Then the bank subtracts provisions for loan losses.
- Then it adds realised gains or losses from the sale of securities minus tax to get net income.

| Income from: | Costs from: |
|---|---|
| **Interest income:** short-term instruments, securities, retail loans, commercial loans and real estate loans | **Interest expense:** all interest-bearing liabilities, all deposit accounts, savings accounts, CDs, short-term borrowing, any other liabilities |
| **Non-interest income:** fees and deposit service charges, commissions on insurance premiums and mutual fund sales, safety deposit rental fees, underwriting and accepting | **Non-interest expense:** on salaries, fringe benefits to employees, premises (occupancy) and technology |

| Income from: | Costs from: |
|---|---|
| **Realised securities gains:** gains occur when bank sells securities from its portfolio at prices above the initial cost to the bank (this could also be a loss) | **Loan losses (known as provision for loan losses):** it is the amount charged against earnings to establish a reserve sufficient to absorb expected loan losses. It is subtracted from net interest income because some of the reported interest income overstates what will be received after loan defaults |

So that to find the net income (or profit) at a bank you would take the negatives from the positives:

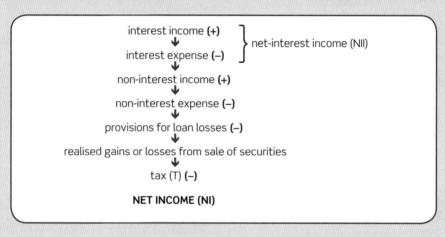

# Key bank performance ratios

When publishing its annual report a bank will state the results using key ratios from the data in the balance sheet and income statement. You will also see these ratios reported in the media. Important ratios include:

**Return on asset (ROA):**

$$\frac{\text{Net income}}{\text{Total assets}}$$

This is the rate of return on total assets or net income per pound or dollar of assets owned.

**Return on equity (ROE):**

$$\frac{\text{Net income}}{\text{Total equity}}$$

This is the rate of return to shareholders or the percentage return on each pound or dollar of equity.

**Net interest income (NII)** is not a ratio but is:

Interest income − interest expense

This is the returns from a bank's interest-bearing assets minus what it costs a bank for its interest-bearing liabilities (the bank's funding sources).

**Net interest margin:**

$$\frac{\text{Net interest income}}{\text{Earning assets}}$$

This is the net interest return on income-producing assets or net interest yield on intermediation.

**Efficiency ratio or cost/income ratio:**

$$\frac{\text{Non-interest expense (total costs)}}{\text{Net interest income + non-interest income (total income)}}$$

This is a quick test of efficiency and currently much used; it reflects how well a bank is maximising income while reducing costs.

## Bank risk

Retail banking is a trade-off between pushing for high returns and risk. As we saw with the goldsmith and in our banking examples, many of the risks in banking arise from the fact that banks mismatch their assets and liabilities. Banks absorb risk and price it at a level which is attractive to businesses requiring credit for investment today. However, banks must be aware of the dangers of pushing too much credit into the marketplace and bearing too much risk, but also of being too conservative and not maximising returns to shareholders. Banks can 'match' their assets and liabilities more closely and reduce risk levels, for example matching maturities or liquidity. This is known as having a tight matching structure, but it would also reduce profitability. Generally, the more risky assets the bank holds, the more profit the bank expects to make. In order to manage risk the bank needs to set clear priorities and must decide upon its risk appetite. This must emanate from the very top of the bank, from the chief executive officer and the executive board.

Here is an example adapted from Santomero and Babbel (2001) showing just how quickly a bank can find itself in trouble if it miscalculates risk:

| GOODWIN BANK (£) | | | |
|---|---|---|---|
| **Liabilities** | | **Assets** | |
| Deposits | 95 | Cash | 5 |
| | | Loans | 95 |
| Capital (or equity) | 5 | | |
| **Total** | **100** | | **100** |

Goodwin Bank:

- earns 11% on loans     $(0.11 \times 95) = £10.45$
- pays 8% for its deposits $(0.08 \times 95) = £7.60$
- if we define capital narrowly as shareholders' equity then Goodwin Bank earns £2.85 on the equity of £5 = 57% ROE (Return on Equity)

However, the bank has operating expenditures (for example staff costs) = £2.25

Shareholders left with 65p (£2.85 − £2.25) in return = 13% ROE (65p/£5.00)

Due to Goodwin Bank's levels of capital underpinning its balance sheet, see what happens if loans decline in value and begin defaulting. That is, if a misjudgement of risk means that loans fall in value by 5.27%, to £90, deposits remain unchanged and the entire £5 (100%) of capital is wiped out. *The capital is wiped out quickly and Goodwin Bank becomes insolvent.* It is no longer viable and will have to recapitalise or close.

| GOODWIN BANK (£) | | | |
|---|---|---|---|
| **Liabilities** | | **Assets** | |
| Deposits | 95 | Cash | 5 |
| | | Loans | 90 |
| Capital (or equity) | 0 | | |
| **Total** | **95** | | **95** |

## Recap

- The more cash the bank holds, the fewer loans will be in issue, reducing the exposure to risk, *but, ceteris paribus*, the bank will make less profit (as cash receives no return).
- The more capital the bank holds, the lower the risk, but capital has no return and so, *ceteris paribus*, profit will be reduced.

Therefore, it should be apparent that banks accept risk onto their balance sheets and mismatch assets and liabilities because it increases expected profitability. Banks must price loans expecting losses, price deposits to attract savers, but try not to lower the net interest income. The net interest income must cover losses to risk and operating costs. Generally a bank must:

- identify areas where risk can arise;
- measure the degree of risk – for example, when deciding on a loan, evaluate the customer, analyse the industry, the purpose of the loan and the nature of project to be undertaken;
- balance risk and return trade-offs and determine prudent levels of total risk exposure for individual or firm, setting the line of business activity management to agreed levels of risk;
- set up monitoring procedures.

## Key definitions

You should be aware of the main risks to which banks are exposed:

**Credit risk**
The risk that the borrower will not be able or willing to pay off the loan and therefore default.

**Liquidity risk**
The risk of the bank being unable to meet its money commitments on time as a result of deposit holders demanding their money, or commitments falling due to the financial markets.

**Bank interest rate risk**
The risk of loss due to changes in market interest rates affecting either the bank's net interest income or the capital levels of the bank.

**Market risk**

The risk that changes in interest rates will affect traded assets or liabilities.

**Foreign exchange risk**

The risk that exchange rate changes will adversely affect bank assets and liabilities.

**Off-balance-sheet risk**

Risks associated with contingent liabilities such as guarantees, letters of credit or underwriting business.

**Operational risk**

The risk that support systems, people or technology fail to operate as expected.

We shall look at the first three in more detail.

# Credit risk

The Global Association of Risk Professionals (GARP) defines **credit risk** as the 'potential for loss due to failure of a borrower to meet its contractual obligation to repay a debt in accordance with the agreed terms'. This could be when a business stops making payments on its loan. Much of a bank's credit risk arises in its banking book, which includes all its loans and bonds held to maturity. However, credit risk can arise in the trading book as counterparty credit risk. Credit risk is also commonly referred to as default risk.

Banks generally manage credit risk by setting up a loan division and collecting information regarding the borrower. They will assess what are known as the **5Cs**:

1 Character: refers to the willingness of the borrower to repay.
2 Capacity: refers to cash flow and the ability of that cash flow to service the debt.
3 Capital: refers to the strength of the borrower's balance sheet.
4 Collateral: refers to the security backing up the loan.
5 Conditions: refers to the borrower's sensitivity to external forces such as interest rate and business cycles and competitive pressures.

Credit risk management concerns building up information on the individual or business and then making a decision. Banks can make decisions by analysing information and interviewing the borrowers in order to reduce 'asymmetric' information flows. These are flows of information that may not be the whole truth; the borrower has an incentive to be over-optimistic about the future; they have more information than the bank about future performance. Many banks around the world still prefer to meet individuals face to face and make a loan decision. Other banks collect information and place it into models. Commonly used models include:

- Qualitative risk models, ratios and financial data: qualitative risk models are reliant on the collection of information from private sources and/or the purchase of information which will give the bank a clearer indication of the reliability and credit quality of the borrower. The bank will continue collecting information as long as it deems it necessary to make an informed decision. However, this will be a function of the size of the borrower, the amount of the loan, the economics of the sector. To enable the decision the bank will run key financial ratios such as return on assets and will also run credit scoring models.
- Quantitative models: these are more complex models which look for trends in the data to guide loan decisions; they include econometrics-based models such as the linear probability model, logit and probit models and the linear discriminant model.

Overall, once a bank has assessed risk it can decide to manage risk via a combination of:

- Limiting: limiting risk by investing in high-grade instruments.
- Diversifying: selecting loans from a broad range of different geographic and business areas.
- Reserving: holding strong reserves of capital to offset any losses.

## Liquidity risk

**Liquidity risk** is the risk to the bank that it will not have enough money to pay back depositors if they are suddenly called upon. Banks must have enough liquid funds to meet contractual or relationship obligations at reasonable prices at all times. As we have seen throughout this chapter, banks need to keep money and near liquid instruments such as Tbills in order to service any net outflows of money during, and at close of business, each day. Banks generally have access to two forms of liquidity:

- **Stored liquidity**: this is 'stored' in the balance sheet and emanates from the bank's traditional operations of deposit taking and lending. Banks will receive and return money to their customers each day and the overall cash position can be measured, managed and stored. Remember, the bank will receive cash payments each month from its borrowers paying back the principal of and interest on their loans. In addition, the bank can sell its short-term securities such as Tbills to absorb any net outflow of money.

- **Purchased liquidity** from the wholesale markets: more recently banks have utilised the financial markets to manage their liquidity. This can be attractive because stored liquidity can be expensive as near liquid instruments produce low returns and cash (no return). The bank can manage its liquidity by holding less cash and short-term instruments and buying the liquidity from the markets when required. In addition, on the liability side of the balance sheet, it allows banks to move away from awaiting new deposit inflows from customers and towards boosting funding by selling financial instruments to the financial markets to raise money. This has allowed banks to become less reliant on deposits and cash. The amount that the bank becomes reliant upon the financial markets for additional finance is known as the **funding gap**:

$$\text{FUNDING GAP} = \text{AVERAGE LOANS} - \text{AVERAGE DEPOSITS}$$

## Recap

The 2008 financial collapse exposed the banks for being over-reliant on the risky financial markets (which collapsed) leaving the banks short of liquid funds. There has therefore been a retrenchment towards more stable stored funding. To this end, the authorities are imposing stricter regulations on funding and liquidity. A ratio that is commonly used is the loan to deposit ratio, which is a percentage indication of the funding gap. For example, if the bank has £120 million of loans and £100 million in deposits, the loan to deposit ratio would be 120%, indicating that 20% of loans are being funded by the financial markets. Banks in the UK and Europe are trying to reduce their financial market exposure and lower their loan to deposit ratio to 100%. The Royal Bank of Scotland stated in its 2012 Annual Report: "we want to put our balance sheet on a more secure footing by lending only as much as we have in deposits". This saw its loan to deposit ratio fall to 108% in 2011, down from 118% in 2010, reflected in short-term funding from the markets being down from £130 to £102 billion.

## Interest rate risk

**Interest rate risk** is the risk that unanticipated changes in interest rates affect the price and value of a bank's liabilities and assets.

### *Price effect risk of interest rate changes*

Banks are at risk to a price effect when interest rate changes leave them with a negative spread across their liabilities and assets; that is, the interest rates they are receiving on their assets fall while the interest payments for their liabilities remain stable or increase. In this case they will suffer a reduction in their net interest income.

### *Value effect risk of interest rate changes*

In addition to a price effect, there will be a value effect because, as interest rates change, the value of a bank's assets and liabilities will change. More specifically, the value effect of interest rate changes will be most acute:

- when the value of a bank's liabilities begins rising more rapidly when interest rates decline than does the market value of its assets; or
- when the value of its liabilities falls more slowly when interest rates increase than does the market value of its assets.

In the case of a value effect the bank will suffer a reduction in its capital levels.

The price effect is best explained by Saunders and Cornett (2011):

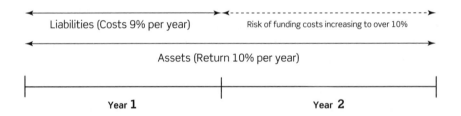

In this case the bank issues a liability of one year maturity which finances the issue of assets, in this case a loan with two years to maturity. This is known as short funding, which means that the maturity of liabilities is less than the maturity of assets.

- Assume that the cost of funds = 9%
- Return on assets = 10%

In this case the bank can benefit from a spread of 1% in the first year by bor-rowing short term and lending long term – over two years. It can also make money in the second year if the cost of refinancing stays the same. However, there is a risk that interest rates may change between years 1 and 2, which exposes the bank to losses. For example, if the cost of funds during the sec-ond year increases to 11% this would equate to a negative spread or net interest income of 1% (return on assets of 10% minus the cost of liabilities of 11% $= -1$). So, the 1% earned in the first year is wiped out. In this scenario the bank exposes itself to the following risks.:

**Refinancing risk** is the risk that the cost of rolling over or reborrowing funds could be more than the return earned on asset investments.

Alternatively the bank could borrow long so that it holds longer-term liabilities than assets:

This exposes the bank to shifts in interest rates again but this time to the fol-lowing risk.

**Reinvestment risk** is the risk that the returns on funds to be reinvested will fall below the cost of funds. This can be witnessed in the real world where banks have borrowed fixed rate deposits while investing in floating rate loans.

The value or market value effect occurs because, as we showed earlier, when interest rates increase, the value of financial securities falls – there is an inverse relationship. This is because rising interest rates increase the discount rate on future cash flows, reducing its current market value. In addition, the reverse is true: falling interest rates increase the present value of cash flows from financial securities, increasing the security's current market value. Banks as maturity transformers hold longer-term assets than liabilities so that when interest rates rise, the value of a bank's assets fall by a greater amount. This was shown earlier: the more cash flows a security has, which implies that the security has a longer term to maturity, the greater is the effect of discounting. Thus, in the example below, a rise in interest rates reduces capital from 20 to 15 – the market value of the bank has decreased.

| GOODWIN BANK (£) | | | | |
|---|---|---|---|---|
| Liabilities | Rise in interest rates | Assets | | Rise in interest rates |
| Certificate of deposit    100 | 95 | Cash    5 | | 5 |
| | | Bond    115 | | 105 |
| Capital    20 | 15 | | | |
| Total    120 | 110 | | 120 | 110 |

## Test yourself

**Q1.** What is the difference between a retail bank's balance sheet and income statement?

**Q2.** List three key performance ratios used to assess retail banks.

**Q3.** What are the major risks faced by retail banks?

**Q4.** Define 'funding gap'.

**Q5.** What is reinvestment risk?

## Key definitions

**ROA**
Return on Assets.

**ROE**
Return on Equity.

**NII**
Net Interest Income.

**NIM**
Net Interest Margin.

### Cost income ratio

Total costs divided by total incomes.

### 5Cs

Mnemonic used to assess a loan application: Character, Capacity, Capital, Collateral and Conditions.

### Stored liquidity

Refers to that liquidity 'stored' in the balance sheet through traditional bank operations mainly taking in deposits, lending and holding cash. Banks will receive and return money to their customers each day and the overall cash position can be measured, managed and stored.

### Purchased liquidity

Traditionally additional to 'stored' liquidity, this is liquidity that is purchased in the financial markets, such as the interbank or certificate of deposit market.

### Funding gap

This is the gap between average loans and average deposits. It is the gap on a bank's balance sheet that requires funding from the financial markets.

### Refinancing risk

The risk that the cost of rolling over or reborrowing funds could be more than the return earned on asset investments.

### Reinvestment risk

The risk that the returns on funds to be reinvested will fall below the cost of funds.

## Examples & evidence

One way of assessing risk at the large retail banks is to analyse the loan to deposit ratio. Below are two charts, one looking at the loan to deposit ratio in Europe, the UK and United States. The other shows a more detailed position for the largest banks in the UK defined as the Major British Banking Groups.

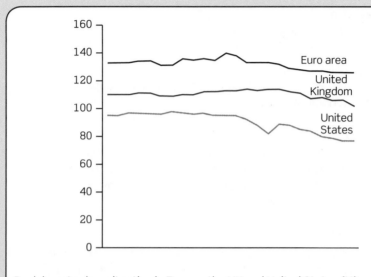

Bank loan-to-deposit ratios in Europe, the UK and United States (%)

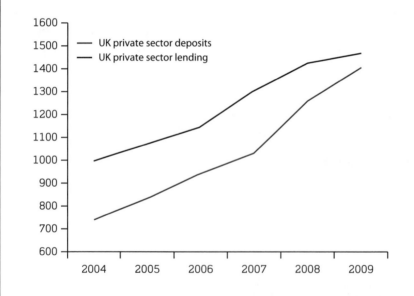

MBBGs core funding and loans, 2001–9 (£bn)

## Questions

What do these graphs show? Why is the loan to deposit ratio important? What is the funding gap and how is it related to the loan to deposit ratio?

## Chapter summary – pulling it all together

By the end of this chapter you should be able to:

| | Confident ✓ | Not confident? |
|---|---|---|
| Understand and explain the rise of the goldsmith and its relevance to banking today | | Revise pages 304–306 |
| Explain fractional reserve banking | | Revise pages 304–306 |
| Define and distinguish between bank liabilities and assets | | Revise pages 304–306 |
| Discuss bank asset transformation including maturity, risk, liquidity and size transformation | | Revise pages 306–309 |
| Explain how banks achieve asset transformation | | Revise pages 309–310 |
| Discuss and show T-accounts examining how banks create credit in a single and multi-bank context | | Revise pages 311–313 |
| Show how reserve requirements and capital to assets, ratios can restrain bank credit creation | | Revise pages 313–317 |
| Distinguish between, and explain, the key features of bank balance sheets and income statements | | Revise pages 320–323 |
| State key bank performance ratios and explain their meaning | | Revise page 324 |
| Explain general risk management in banks and discuss credit, liquidity and interest rate risk | | Revise pages 324–333 |

Now try the sample question at the start of this chapter, using the answer guidelines below.

### Answer guidelines

#### ✳ Assessment question

(a) Examine the theoretical benefits that banks may bring to those undertaking financial transactions. (40 marks)

(b) Explain the risks that banks expose themselves to in their day-to-day operations and any techniques used to manage these risks. (60 marks)

## Approaching the question

Begin this question by explaining the basics. In part (a) you should mention the differences between broker intermediaries and asset transformers. You will also score marks for mentioning the difference between borrowers and lenders. More specifically you should mention how banks transform their liabilities in terms of maturity, risk, liquidity and size and reduce transaction costs. Clear definitions and analysis of these factors will help you to bring borrowers and lenders together and will score highly. Part (b) allows you to show your understanding that the theoretical analysis of banks exposes them to actual day-to-day risks. Introduce each risk including a definition and link the risks to where they arise in the bank. Provide an example of how banks can be exposed to risky situations very quickly with a change in the markets or the liabilities and assets they are holding. Complete your answer by introducing and explaining any techniques that banks utilise to manage risk.

## Important points to include:

- the role of brokers;
- asset transformation, including detailed explanations;
- clear definitions of risk and where they arise in the banks (linked to asset transformation);
- any techniques used by banks to manage risk.

## Make your answer stand out:

- Mention the role of asymmetric information, adverse selection and moral hazard.
- Link any risks to where they directly arise in terms of the asset transformation function.
- Provide examples of how day-to-day bank operations can expose banks to risk of failure.
- Use data and check out large bank websites before the exam. How many deposits do banks have as a proportion of total liabilities? How many loans do they have as a proportion of total assets?

## Read to impress

### Textbooks

There are many books that explain general banking. Worth reading are:

Mishkin, F.S. (2012) *The Economics of Money, Banking and Financial Markets*. Pearson Education.

Santomero, A. and Babbel, D. (2001) *Financial Markets, Instruments and Institutions*. McGraw-Hill.

More specific textbooks will help you to gain extra marks:

Casu, B., Girardone, C. and Molyneux, P. (2013) *Introduction to Banking*. Pearson Education.

Rose, P.S. and Hudgins, S.C. (2012) *Bank Management and Financial Services*. McGraw-Hill.

Saunders, A. and Cornett, M. (2011) *Financial Institution Management*. McGraw-Hill.

### Journal articles

Journal articles are a good source of up-to-date information by key academics. Again, some will make more sense to you than others. Here are a few that link to this chapter well:

Allen, F. and Santomero, A.M. (2001) What do financial intermediaries do? *Journal of Banking and Finance*, Vol. 25, pp. 271–94.

Allen, F. and Santomero, A.M. (1997) The theory of financial intermediation. *Journal of Banking and Finance*, Vol. 21, pp. 1461–85.

Andolfatto, D. and Nosal, E. (2009) Money, intermediation, and Banking. *Journal of Monetary Economics*, Vol. 56 (3), pp. 289–94.

Gorton, G. and Winton, A. (2002) Financial intermediation. Wharton Financial Institutions Centre Working Paper Series, 02-28: **http://fic.wharton.upenn.edu/fic/papers/02/0228.pdf**.

Raff, D.M.G. (2000) Risk management in an age of change. Wharton Financial Institutions Centre Working Paper Series, 01-18: **http://fic.wharton.upenn.edu/fic/papers/01/0118.pdf**.

Scholtans, B. and Wensveen, D. van (2000) A critique on the theory of financial intermediation. *Journal of Banking and Finance*, Vol. 24 (8), pp. 1243–51.

## Websites

Due to the recent financial crisis there are many reports that have been written on banking. Try:

Independent Commission on Banking (2011): **http://bankingcommission .independent.gov.uk/.**

Also try:

Pelkey, A. and Gupta, A. (2012) Eight ways to manage customer and supplier credit risk: credit risk management best practices for corporations. Moody's Analytics.

## Data sources

Check out the websites of the following for data on financial markets and institutions:

Bank of England

Bankscope

British Bankers Association

European Central Bank

Individual bank websites

McKinsey & Company

TheCityUK

## Companion website

Go to the companion website at **www.pearsoned.co.uk/econexpress** to find more revision support online for this topic area.

# Notes

# Notes

# 12 Other financial institutions

- Types of investment bank
- Underwriting
- Trading

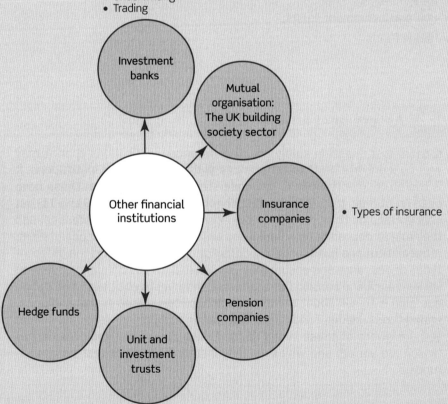

- Types of insurance

A printable version of this topic map is available from **www.pearsoned.co.uk/econexpress**

## Introduction

The previous two chapters introduced the two major financial institutions in an economy – the central bank and the major banks. You will also come across a number of non-bank financial institutions which operate within the economy providing services to both retail and corporate customers. They tend also to play an influential role in the financial markets, investing, for example, many billions of pounds, dollars, euros into the markets, aiding business expansion and the growth of the markets themselves. This chapter looks at these more specialist institutions.

The major non-bank financial institutions are:

- investment banks;
- mutual organisations such as building societies in the UK;
- insurance companies;
- pension companies;
- unit and investment trusts;
- hedge funds.

### ✳ Assessment advice

If there is a question solely on other financial institutions then it may well concentrate on their differences with bank financial institutions. It is therefore important that you understand the differences. These have been mentioned throughout earlier chapters (see Chapters 10 and 11) but concentrate on their position in the economy (hierarchy differences) and their role as deposit takers. Banks and building societies are deposit takers; other institutions fund in slightly different ways. Understand the different types of insurance and ensure that you can explain the difference between life insurance and pension funds and unit and investment trusts. A common question is to ask about the difference between closed-ended and open-ended funds. Hedge funds have also become important recently: ensure you are aware of these types of funds and can define their operations (which are varied) and why they may increase risk for investors in such funds.

**Assessment question**

Explain the role and importance of the non-bank financial intermediaries to the financial services sector of a country.

Can you answer this question? Guidelines on answering the question are presented at the end of this chapter.

## Investment banks

**Investment banks** form a major part of the financial services landscape and they have become increasingly complex in their operations. They can be contrasted to retail banks but delineation has become increasingly difficult as mergers and acquisitions have led to large retail banks integrating investment banking operations into their business. Investment banks' traditional activity was **underwriting**, which is the bringing of an issue of financial securities (debt or equity) to the financial market for a client. These securities are then sold to investors. Investment banks would be involved in all aspects of underwriting including:

- advising clients on their funding needs;
- administration of a new issue, especially the legal aspects;
- underwriting the actual issue;
- distributing the new issue to buyers.

Investment banks have become involved in many other activities including:

- secondary market traders;
- consultants selling financial data;
- agents/advisers/deal makers in mergers and acquisitions;
- investment councillors for high-net-worth individuals;
- brokers;
- money managers for pension funds.

Much of the above activities are undertaken for fee income. More recently investment banks have also become heavily involved in proprietary trading where they trade and invest their own money for profit. Investment banks are known for being opportunistic and innovative and since competition is fierce they need to remain competitive.

## Types of investment bank

There are three main structures that investment banks take:

- Boutique
- Full service
- Financial holding company.

### Boutique

This type of investment bank focuses upon a particular type of business. Some boutique investment banks may concentrate upon underwriting within a section of the market, on which they build up extensive knowledge, for example raising finance for firms in the technology sector, or the mergers and acquisitions market. However, boutique investment banks expose themselves to the greater risks associated with lack of diversification (or being exposed to just one sector).

### Full service

This type of investment bank undertakes the full range of activities listed above, using the knowledge it attains in one area to aid in other areas of investment banking. This type of investment bank would split itself into individual departments to manage the different types of business.

### Financial holding companies

Large financial services firms operate in the majority of banking markets, both commercial and investment, usually throughout the world.

### Recap

Some features of investment banks compared with retail banks:

- The investment banking industry has many small providers or banks, having little or no branch network. Retail banking is dominated by a few large banks with a large branch network.
- Investment banks are intermediaries between investors and issuers of debt and can work on either the buy or sell side. Retail banks also act as intermediaries but transform assets between those wishing to save and those who wish to borrow.
- The majority of transactions in investment banking are completed with knowledgeable corporate clients. Retail banks work with the wider, usually less knowledgeable, general public.
- Investment banks have fewer, very high-value transactions, compared with retail banks which tend towards many transactions of lower worth.
- Investment banking is dominated by foreign currency.

# Underwriting

Underwriting is the bringing of an issue of financial securities (debt or equity) to the financial market for a client. The investment bank guarantees or underwrites the issue, meaning that the bank agrees to buy the securities if demand fails to materialise for the full issue. When undertaking the underwriting function, investment banks can act in a number of capacities. This will include:

- advising the client on the type of security to issue;
- advising on the security's characteristics, when to issue and how much the issue is likely to raise;
- supervising and co-ordinating the legal work required by regulations;
- entering into an agreement with the client to purchase the security for a specified price which will earn the investment bank an underwriting spread.

## Recap

The underwriting spread is the difference between the price that the investment bank receives from the eventual buyers of the issue that it has 'underwritten' and the amount it promised to pay to the client – the issuing firm. This spread is exposed to risk as demand in financial markets is changeable. If the investment bank agrees too high a price it may be unable to sell the securities. If it sets too low a price it will lose the client to a competing investment bank willing to underwrite the issue at a higher price.

Due to the risk that the investment bank may not realise its underwriting spread (which is the profit from underwriting), investment banks attempt to sell the security as soon as possible to reduce the risk of a negative spread. Investment banks keep an extensive client book of wealthy clients, from individuals to institutional investors, and employ a large sales staff who are in frequent contact with their wealthy clients whom they will contact before the issue goes to market to garner interest. If successful the issue of securities may have been resold by the investment bank before it goes to market, taking away the risk of a negative underwriting spread.

The investment bank that has the mandate to administer an issue on behalf of a client is known as the lead manager or **bookrunner**. The investment banks will have to conduct due diligence on the client and then prepare detailed information about the firm and its financial position, all of which will be used to populate the registration statement to be filed with the regulatory authorities (in the United States this would be the Securities Exchange Commission (SEC)). The investment bank will also write the preliminary prospectus and print the stock certificates, and state the listing exchange, for example in London this may be the London Stock Exchange.

In some cases the bank may also involve other investment banks underwriting an issue if it believes the issue is too large or too risky. This is referred to as an **investment bank syndicate** and is led by a lead underwriter who forms an underwriting group, negotiates fees and sorts out any major problems with the client. In addition, after the issue goes public the lead manager acts as a market-maker. A major benefit of creating a syndicate is that it benefits from an expanded client list and so can help increase awareness and demand. The syndicate will share the proceeds of the underwriting spread.

## Key definitions

**Firm commitment**
Where the investment bank agrees to purchase the entire issue and distribute it to both institutional and retail investors.

**Best efforts agreement**
Where the investment bank agrees to sell the securities but does not guarantee the price.

## Trading

Investment banks are also involved in trading. This can be:

- trading on behalf of clients, which involves buying and selling financial securities and will also include providing research;
- proprietary trading, that is buying and selling on its own behalf in order to realise profit. This can include derivatives trading, bonds and/or equity.

It should be noted that many investment banks began to undertake, up to the years preceding the financial crisis, increasing amounts of 'proprietary trading'. They were drawn into trading on their own behalf because they had built up vast experience and information sets on the operation of financial markets and the securities traded within them.

Investment banks are well placed to trade in their own right:

- They are well-known market-makers.
- They have strong relationships with institutional investors.
- They are at the heart of the financial community.

Trading, however, is more risky than underwriting and exposes investment banks to greater risk of insolvency.

## Test yourself

**Q1.** List the three main structural types of investment bank.

**Q2.** Define underwriting.

**Q3.** What is the underwriting spread?

## Key definitions

**Investment bank**

A bank that offers many services to corporate clients, traditionally underwriting new share issues, acting as broker and trading on behalf of clients.

**Underwriting**

The bringing of an issue of financial securities (debt or equity) to the financial market for a client by which (usually) an investment bank guarantees or 'underwrites' the issue, meaning that the bank agrees to buy the securities if demand fails to materialise for the full issue.

**Bookrunner**

The investment bank that has the mandate to administer an issue on behalf of a client.

**Investment bank syndicate**

The involvement of other investment banks to underwrite a debt issue if the bookrunner believes the issue is too large or too risky.

## Mutual organisations: the UK building society sector

UK building societies are **mutually owned organisations** which traditionally offered loans in the form of mortgages to facilitate house purchase. Mutuality means that they are owned by their 'members': that is, those who have purchased shares in the form of deposits or taken out loans usually as mortgages. Until the early 1980s, building societies were the only institutions offering mortgages, and competition was restricted by various agreements and regulations. Competition in this sector has, however, intensified since the early 1980s when deregulation of the retail banking sector allowed banks to offer mortgage finance and thereby to threaten the position of the building societies. This led to demands for deregulation to be extended to the building society sector. Deregulation allows the building societies to compete with the retail banks in the financial markets, where previously they had been restricted. The Building Societies Act of 1986, the subsequent Orders in Council of 1988 and the Building Societies Act 1997 have permitted building societies to offer a whole range of new banking, investment and property-related housing services, in addition to their traditional savings and home loan business.

For example, the Building Societies Act 1997 relaxed restrictions on unsecured lending and permitted building societies, subject to their own prudential controls, to lend out 25% of their assets on an unsecured basis. In addition, it allowed societies to have greater access to the wholesale money markets, permitting up to 50% of their funds (liabilities) to be in the form of borrowings on these markets. This meant that societies did not need to rely as heavily on costly retail deposits from savers to finance their lending, allowing them to compete more aggressively with the banking sector. In fact, by the end of 2007 total wholesale liabilities in the building society sector were over £66 billion.

The 1997 Act, while granting societies more freedom, also ensured that the building societies' main function and basic purpose of attracting savings and making loans for house purchase remained. To this end, societies still have to raise at least 50% of their funds from individual investors (usually in the form of issuing a retail deposit) and remain restricted to having 75% of their commercial assets in the form of loans secured by a mortgage on housing.

## Demutualisation

**Demutualisation** refers to the process of conversion of building societies into bank plcs (which are funded by shareholders purchasing their issued equity). A number of reasons have been suggested for the trend towards demutualisation:

- Banks plcs are in a better position than building societies to compete in the financial services and mortgage markets because they can issue equity. This will provide the funding to permit faster growth and enable speedier diversification into new areas.
- Building societies which convert to banks cannot be acquired for five years, giving them time to establish themselves and compete with the larger banks.
- Building societies which convert can now compete under the same regulatory environment as banks, meaning that they will no longer have strict restrictions on access to the wholesale markets. This provides them with improved access to corporate clients and to cheaper funding.
- Diversification into new and risky areas of business should, it is argued, be undertaken by using newly issued capital raised by newly constituted institutions rather than by using historical capital derived from relatively safe savings and mortgage business.

Such arguments were present in the conversion documents of both the Alliance & Leicester Building Society and the Halifax Building Society. The Alliance & Leicester document (1996) stated that the society intends to expand its commercial lending activities, extend its use of wholesale money markets, and increase its provision of 'personal financial services, such as unsecured lending, telephone banking, life assurance and unit trust products'. This will allow it to reduce its 'dependency on the mature residential mortgage market … and to build new sources of revenue from cross-selling'.

Those who doubt the benefits of conversion have, however, expressed their concern:

- The costs of paying large dividends to shareholders will increase the interest rate to borrowers and decrease the rate for deposit holders (lenders).
- Capital markets have a tendency to be short term in their evaluation of strategy and performance, which may hinder long-term growth.
- There is little evidence that banks are more accountable to their owners than are building societies.
- Takeover threats by other banks still exist. At least one building society waived its right not to be taken over after conversion and in any case the protection from takeover for five years is removed if another building society initiates the takeover, as when Birmingham Midshires was acquired by the Halifax in 1999.
- There are increased costs resulting from conversion, including the cost of compliance with a new regulatory code and the cost of retraining staff.

However, the comparison of building societies with banks and the debate as to the respective advantages and disadvantages of conversion have arguably become redundant issues, having been superseded by events. Those building societies that wish to remain specialist mortgage providers are likely to stay in the building societies sector and, by remaining as mutual institutions, may acquire a competitive edge in offering mortgages at lower interest rates. Much of the rationalisation of this sector may already have occurred, from 481 building societies in 1970 to only 63 by the end of 2005. However, it is worth noting that these societies continue to manage over £270 billion worth of assets.

## Insurance companies

We all live with the uncertainty that future events may occur that are unfavourable. **Insurance companies** exist to help us plan financially for these events which can be wide ranging – from sudden ill health to your house being burgled. Thus insurance companies allow individuals and companies to financially plan for pre-specified adverse events.

Insurance companies do this by selling insurance policies to individuals or companies in return for payment – known as the **insurance premium**. The insurance policy will state the amount of compensation, or payment that the policy holder will receive 'contingent' on a future event occurring, for example having your house burgled or crashing your car. In this way, they assume the financial risk of an event occurring. Key to insurance company success is deciding who to insure and the premium to charge for the insurance. This process is undertaken by underwriters who assess the risk, decide whether they will provide insurance and at what price, or premium, to the customer. The premium will be less for a motorist with no previous insurance claims than for a motorist who has made numerous claims. Insurance companies use the past as a guide to the future: the higher the chance of claiming, the higher the premiums to cover the additional risk.

The risk of events occurring is calculated by an actuary using statistical or actuarial projections to calculate the probability of an event happening in the future. The insurer obviously does not know when an event will occur but, through the law of large numbers and actuarial techniques, they can estimate the probability of something happening accurately, for example the number of house fires that will occur in Manchester in a particular year. This estimate will be used to calculate the premiums required to cover claims from these house fires.

Insurance companies operate within a similar premise to the goldsmith. Just as the goldsmiths knew that not all depositors of gold would return at the same time, so the insurance company knows that not all insurance policies will have to pay out at the same time, and in the case of general insurance may never need to pay out. Either way, they are able to collect premiums today knowing that if they have to pay out on the insurance policy it will be some time in the future. This allows them to accumulate monthly premium payments in a pot, leave a portion of the premiums as cash or near liquid assets ready to pay off claimants and, just like the goldsmith or bank, invest the rest of the pot of money in high-yielding assets. Insurance companies therefore receive:

- income from the premiums on their issued insurance contracts, known as underwriting income; and
- investment income from investing the accumulated premium income on the financial markets.

Income from premiums can be seen as stable and should track the calculated risk of future events occurring. For example, if the world begins to witness more 'acts of God' such as hurricanes, leading to wide-scale damage, or an increase in the incidence of torrential rain, leading to flooding, then premiums will increase over time to reflect higher claims.

The major cost to insurance companies will be the payments they must make on insurance claims.

Investment income will generally reflect the economy: when the world's financial markets are growing then investment income will increase to reflect returns on these markets. This will be dependent on the investment strategy of the insurance company; if it fails to diversify its investment portfolio in an efficient way, it may suffer large losses on this income.

Insurance company profit

Underwriting income (+)

↓

Payment on claims (−)

↓

Investment income (+/−)

↓

Operating expenses (−)

↓

Profit

The balance sheet of insurance companies is dominated on the asset side by investments in bonds and equities. The liability side is largely made up of the **net policy reserve**, which is an estimate of the payments that the company will have to make on its current policy contracts.

## Types of insurance

Insurance is classified slightly differently in each country. In the UK the insurance industry is split into two main types:

- life insurance; and
- **general insurance** (known as property-casualty insurance in the United States).

### Life insurance

This can be referred to as life assurance in some UK textbooks. The term 'insurance' tends to be used when discussing general insurance and insures the policy holder for an event that may happen. Assurance is used in the UK to denote when an event is certain to happen but the timing is unknown – as with death. In the United States, the word 'insurance' is used. There are a variety of types of life insurance, as follows.

## Key definitions

### Types of life insurance

### Whole life

This covers the individual over their entire lifetime as long as they keep paying the insurance premiums. The next of kin receives the value of the life insurance contract, or lump sum, when the policy holder dies.

### Term life

This has a coverage period and therefore matures after a set time. If the premium payments are maintained throughout the coverage period then the next of kin receives a lump sum as long as the individual dies within the time frame covered in the policy. Unfortunately, if the individual dies after the policy has expired then the next of kin receives nothing. The assured is covered for the length of the policy, which can be from 1 to 40 years. It is sometimes referred to as pure life insurance as there is no savings element.

### Endowment life

This combines term life insurance with a savings or investment element. A guaranteed payment is made if the individual dies within the endowment period, but if they live to the end of the endowment they receive a lump sum.

### Annuity

This is the reverse of a life insurance policy in that the individual gives a lump sum to the insurance company and receives a stream of income payments, usually on a monthly basis until death. It comes in varying types including group annuities and husband and wife annuities and can be on either a fixed or varying basis (in which case the payments would be linked to some underlying investment portfolio). Payments can be arranged to start immediately or delayed until retirement and can continue after death or cease after the policy holder dies. These features would be written into the policy document.

## General insurance

This type of insurance is short term, usually for one year and mainly deals with homes; property; motor vehicles and general accident; and aviation and marine insurance. Assessing risk in general insurance can be problematic and profits meagre. This leads to general insurance companies having to increase premiums regularly in line with claims. General insurers are more reliant on their asset investments to increase their annual profits.

## Test yourself

**Q1.** What does the term 'mutuality' mean?

**Q2.** List three reasons why a UK building society may choose to demutualise.

**Q3.** Which two income streams help make up insurance company profits?

**Q4.** What are the two main types of insurance?

**Q5.** What is an annuity?

## Key definitions

**Mutual organisation**

Organisations that are owned by their 'members': that is, those who have purchased shares in the form of deposits or taken out loans usually as mortgages. They have not issued shares into the capital markets.

**Demutualisation**

Refers to the process of conversion of mutual organisations such as building societies into bank plcs which are funded by shareholders purchasing their issued equity.

**Insurance company**

Companies that allow individuals and companies to plan financially for pre-specified adverse events by selling policies to individuals or companies that will pay compensation if the adverse event occurs. Insurance companies assume the financial risk of an event occurring.

**Insurance premium**

A specified payment paid periodically, usually monthly or annually, by a company or individual to provide insurance coverage.

**Net policy reserve**

An estimate of the payments that a company will have to make on its current policy contracts.

**General insurance**

Insurance which is short term, usually for one year and mainly deals with homes; property; motor vehicles and general accident; and aviation and marine insurance.

## Pension companies

**Pension companies** offer the chance for individuals to place regular portions of money into a fund during their working life which is invested in an array (think of this as a pot) of financial securities and which accumulates in size and value over time.

Key features:

- Private pension funds are operated by private companies such as Aviva or AXA.
- Public pension funds are operated by the state or local government.
- The pension plan sets out how the pension fund will operate.
- Pensions offered by life insurance companies are referred to as insured pension funds. This is because, with this type of pension, the incoming funds from investors in the 'insured' pension fund are not invested in a separate pool of assets for each investor. There is no independent fund backing the pension proceeds – all the funds are pooled within the insurance company and invested as identified 'pension assets' along with all other assets of the insurance company. In the UK this is required because of a separate tax regime for pension assets. The proportion of the insurance companies' assets that are put to one side is reported as pension fund reserves on the balance sheet.
- Pensions that are not offered by a life insurance company are referred to as non-insured pensions. These pensions are managed by a trust department within a financial institution. Such pension funds are separate from the assets of the overarching financial institution – the fund underpins the pension fund and funds are invested according to guidelines that the trustee follows. The **trustees** will be appointed by a company, trade union or public sector organisation in order to run the fund for its employees or members. In the UK the fund is controlled and owned by trustees. The financial institution may manage some or all of the funds, but will do so with a mandate from the trustees and in accordance with the instructions of the trustees.
- Pensions funds come in three types:

  - Defined benefit scheme: contributions are made by employees and employers over the working life of the employee. At retirement the employee usually receives a final pension which is a fraction of salary earned at or near retirement, the fraction being based upon the number of years of service with the employer. In this case the contributions will vary to meet the amount required to fund the desired benefit.
  - Defined contribution schemes: in this scheme employees and their employer make monthly contributions which build up and are invested

over the employee's working life. They come in fixed income form, where a minimum pension is guaranteed, and variable income form, in which the pension holder assumes all the risk of the value of the fund declining at the time of retirement. At retirement, the investment fund accumulated is normally used to purchase an **annuity**.

- Hybrid schemes: these offer a combination of the two.

## Insurance companies, pension funds and the financial markets

The insurance companies and pension funds are major investors in the financial markets and exert considerable influence in these markets. They hold large amounts of long-term debt and help absorb ('make markets in') large volumes and values of new issues of various equities, bills and bonds.

Although these insurance companies and pension funds compete strongly against each other in the personal savings market, their portfolio choices differ because the structures of their liabilities differ. For example, the life insurance companies hold a larger proportion of assets as fixed interest securities, because many of their liabilities are expressed in nominal terms (for example, the money value of payments in the future on their policies is known).

However, both these institutions are affected by the volatility of financial markets, both domestic and worldwide. For example, at the beginning of 2000 they held quoted UK company shares to the value of £743 billion, which made up 45% of their total financial assets of £1,657 billion. As the UK share market dropped, the value of their investments in UK company shares halved and by the end of 2002 it was worth only £388 billion. As a result, total financial assets held by insurance companies and pension funds also fell to 1998 levels of around £1,250 billion. The financial crisis has meant that the value of these holdings had dropped to £353 billion by 2009. Importantly, such volatility can affect both premiums and payouts in the sector.

## Unit and investment trusts

Both unit and investment trusts offer lenders a chance to buy into a diversified portfolio of assets and thereby reduce risk while at the same time receiving attractive returns. These institutions achieve this by pooling the funds received from a large number of small investors and then implementing various portfolio management techniques not available to such small investors. Both types of trust have operating expenses which are deducted from the value of the trust at the end of each year; costs are dominated by the management fee, which is the charge for managing the portfolio of assets.

## Unit trusts

There are over 1,400 **unit trusts** in the UK (over 8,000 in the United States where they are known as mutual funds). They are provided by individual companies, banks and insurance companies. A lender looking to buy into a unit trust purchases the number of units they can afford at the current value and then pays up to a further 5% of the purchase price for the management of the fund. The price of each unit is given by the net value of the trust's assets divided by the number of units outstanding. The size of the unit trust fund varies with the amount of units currently in issue, which allows the fund to expand and contract depending on demand; thus unit trusts are termed 'open ended'.

Key features:

- Unit trusts are open ended. This means that the trust increases in size as new investors join, purchasing a 'unit' at the current market price. If those joining the trust outweigh those liquidating their holdings then the trust will grow in size.
- Known as mutual funds in the United States.
- There is no secondary market – units are sold back to the fund management company.
- Investors in a unit trust own a share of the overall portfolio equal to their holding divided by the total size of the trust.
- The value of each unit equals the current market value of the entire fund divided by the number of units in issue. This is also known as net asset value (NAV).
- The value of each unit will vary in price in accordance with the prices of the financial securities that are held within the trust.

## Investment trusts

There are over 300 **investment trusts** in the UK and they undertake a similar role, allowing individuals to benefit from a pooled investment fund. However, investment trusts are plcs and raise funds for investment by issuing equity and debt and by using retained profits. Unlike unit trusts they can also borrow money. If individuals or firms are to buy into an investment trust, they must purchase their shares, which are limited in supply to those in issue; thus investment trusts are termed 'closed ended'.

Key features:

- Shares in investment trusts are much like those for all plcs.
- Shares issued are fixed in amount (or closed). The size of the trust does not grow as shares are purchased, so the trust does not become larger and smaller as with unit trusts – there are set amount of shares that can be traded.

- Once issued the shares of investment trusts are traded on the secondary market.
- The price of an individual share is the interaction of demand and supply as with all shares.
- The value of one share in the investment trust is calculated in the same way as that for unit trusts and equals the current market value of the trust divided by the number of units in issue. However, because the shares are closed ended and finite, the interaction of demand and supply can increase or decrease the price of the shares above the net asset value (NAV). This is referred to as trading at a premium or trading at a discount respectively.
- The initial investors pay for the costs of the initial public offering. Costs are usually above 5% of the total amount raised.

## Hedge funds

The term 'hedge' when related to an investment is used to denote taking a position in an asset that reduces the risk of an adverse price movement (which would lose you money on your investment). An example would be to take out a futures contract to sell your asset at a set price sometime in the future. This allows you to 'lock in' to certainty: whatever the market does you have a contract stating that you will receive a certain price. When used in the context of a fund, the term originally described funds that take long and short positions in financial markets in such a way as to attempt to reduce, eliminate or hedge against adverse movements in those financial markets. Today, the term **hedge fund** denotes a wide variety of funds with differing characteristics and is difficult to define with any certainty. However, Cole *et al.* (2007) define hedge funds as:

- private pools of funds that invest in traded instruments (both cash securities and derivatives);
- employing leverage through various means, including the use of short positions; and
- generally not regulated.

Key features:

- They no longer hedge or prioritise risk; most hedge funds attempt to maximise returns.
- Only the rich investor can invest in hedge funds as the minimum investment is high, perhaps as much as £1 million.
- A variety of trading techniques are utilised in an attempt to gain high returns – this will include: leverage (using borrowed funds to invest); long and short selling (selling a financial security that you do not own); arbitrage

(buying and selling of the same (or very similar) financial instrument on different markets to gain from a slight difference in price).

- Management fees are between 1% and 2% of the total value of the fund.
- Hedge fund managers may take 15% or more share in any profits.
- Derivatives are widely used to leverage positions in markets.
- Funds vary in size from £200 million to billions of pounds.

## Recap

Leverage makes it cheaper for hedgers to hedge, but it also makes it cheaper to speculate. Instead of buying £1 million of Treasury bonds or £1 million of stock, an investor can buy futures contracts on £1 million of the bonds or stocks with only a few thousand pounds of capital committed as margin (the capital commitment is even smaller in the over-the-counter derivatives markets). The returns from holding the stocks or bonds will be the same as holding the futures on the stocks or bonds, but the only outlay would have been the margin requirements of the futures exchange. This allows an investor to earn a much higher rate of return on their capital by taking on a much larger amount of risk. See Chapter 8 regarding futures for a worked example of this effect.

## Test yourself

**Q1.** List the three key features of a pension company.

**Q2.** What are the three main types of pension fund?

**Q3.** What is the main difference between unit trusts and investment trusts?

**Q4.** Define what is meant by the term 'hedge fund'.

## Key definitions

### Pension company

Companies that offer the chance for individuals to place regular portions of money into a fund during their working life which is invested in an array of financial securities which accumulates in size and value over time.

### Pension company trustees

Those that control and, in some countries such as the UK, own the pension fund, where a trustee refers to a person authorised by the Inland Revenue to oversee the management of the pension fund.

### Unit trust

A portfolio of investments in which individuals or companies can purchase units. The trust is classed as open ended, which means that it increases in size as new investors join.

### Investment trust

A separate company which invests in a portfolio of assets but is established as a plc (public limited company) selling shares to those wishing to invest in the trust's future. It is classed as closed ended, which means that the trust is finite as there are set amounts of shares that can be traded.

### Hedge fund

A type of fund where private money is invested in traded instruments (both cash securities and derivatives); leverage is employed through various means, including the use of short positions, and regulation is usually non-existent.

## Examples & evidence

Behind these headlines, a more insidious danger threatens the investment banks. They are finding themselves sidelined by increasingly sophisticated (and, crucially, unregulated) hedge funds and private equity firms, which are happy to avoid the banks' hefty fees and trade directly with one another, or to originate, underwrite and distribute corporate finance deals without allowing the investment banks their usual cut. KKR, for instance, one of the leading private equity firms, has found itself listed along with more traditional investment banks on a number of recent equity offerings, the 2010 bond placement for Manchester United a high-profile example. Citadel, a hedge fund, has become one of the major options market makers. "Boutique" investment banks such as Greenhill are winning mergers and acquisitions business from their larger peers. Given the fear of further lurches in the markets, fewer trades are being done than at any time since the crash, and now the investment banks are finding themselves under threat from erstwhile clients. It is no surprise that earnings at Morgan Stanley and Goldman Sachs – and at the investment banking divisions of other financial houses – have dropped significantly over the past year.

If we are not quite writing the epitaph for the industry yet, the hiring of the retail banker Antony Jenkins as CEO of Barclays – replacing Diamond, with his thuggish investment banker's style – does seem to mark a significant turning point. It was once the case that retail bankers were the unloved stepchildren of the "bulge bracket" institutions, patronised and scorned in equal measure. The CEOs of the big banks were almost always from the investment side of the business; when they weren't (Fred Goodwin, the former boss of the Royal Bank of Scotland, comes to mind), they acted like children allowed to stay up past bedtime when in the presence of their racier, wealthier colleagues. It is clear that, attacked by regulators and nimbler competitors, losing the good staff and firing the bad, the trading floors of the investment banks will look very different in ten years' time. As we mark the fourth anniversary of the financial crisis, it is worth looking back – and forward – and attempting to understand how the banks got here, and where they go next.

*Source:* Preston, A. (2012) '£1m isn't rich anymore': the rise and fall of investment banking. *New Statesman,* October.

This is an extract from the article which places investment banking in context. It is important that you understand the 'culture' of the industry and not just the mechanics. History is important, so that we do not make the same mistakes over and over again. Take time to read this excerpt (and the main article, free online). It will help you to bring some of the things you have learnt into focus.

## Chapter summary – pulling it all together

By the end of this chapter you should be able to:

|  | Confident ✓ | Not confident? |
|---|---|---|
| Understand and explain the role of investment banks and the difference between investment banking and retail banking | | Revise page 343 |
| Explain the different types of investment banks | | Revise page 344 |
| Explain the process of underwriting an issue of financial securities | | Revise pages 345–346 |
| Discuss mutual organisations and the reasons for demutualisation in the UK | | Revise pages 347–349 |

| | Confident ✓ | Not confident? |
|---|---|---|
| Delineate between types of insurance offered to consumers | | Revise pages 349–353 |
| Elucidate the key features of pension companies | | Revise pages 354–355 |
| State the difference between a unit trust and investment trust and define open ended and closed ended | | Revise pages 355–357 |
| State the key features of hedge funds | | Revise pages 357–358 |

Now try the sample question at the start of this chapter, using the answer guidelines below.

## Answer guidelines

### ✳ Assessment question

Explain the role and importance of the non-bank financial intermediaries to the financial services sector of a country.

## Approaching the question

This is a 'catch all' question allowing you to analyse the sector and show your understanding of financial institutions which are not deposit-taking retails banks. Begin by providing an overview of the financial services sector and introduce the main players. Take each of the institutions that you will describe and ensure that you include the basic functioning of each one. Contrasting their operations will help increase your grade as will comparing them with traditional retail banking. Make sure you provide key definitions and show understanding of the differences between life insurance and general insurance or unit and investment trusts. The rise of hedge funds and how they operate will gain marks.

## Important points to include:

- All the main non-bank financial intermediaries.
- Key definitions.

- Differences between institutions.
- Differences between institutions in similar business areas (for example, unit and investment trusts).
- The relationship of the institutions with the financial system; this should include their links, if any, with the central bank, the retail banks and the regulators.

## Make your answer stand out

As always, take time to get the basics correct as many students fail to consider, or overlook, basic definitions. To increase your mark, stating and analysing any data will show that you have undertaken research. Data is widely available in these sectors, for example try Key Note or TheCityUK.

## Read to impress

### Textbooks

There are many books that explain general banking. Worth reading are:

Mishkin, F.S. (2012) *The Economics of Money, Banking and Financial Markets*. Pearson Education.

Pilbeam, K. (2010) *Finance and Financial Markets*. Palgrave Macmillan.

Santomero, A. and Babbel, D. (2001) *Financial Markets, Instruments and Institutions*. McGraw-Hill.

Saunders, A. and Bornett, M. (2012) *Financial Markets and Institutions*. McGraw-Hill.

More specific textbooks will help you to gain extra marks:

Fleuriet, M. (2008) *Investment Banking Explained: An Insider's Guide to the Industry*. McGraw-Hill.

Liaw, K.T. (2011) *The Business of Investment Banking*, 2nd edition. Wiley.

### Periodicals

Accenture (2011) *Top Ten Challenges for Investment Banks*.

*Building Societies Year Book 2011–2012.*

Cole, R., Feldberg, G. and Lynch, D. (2007) Hedge funds, credit risk transfer and financial stability. *Banque de France, Financial Stability Review*, Special Issue on Hedge Funds, No. 10, April.

FSA (2012) Assessing the possible sources of systemic risk from hedge funds. August.

Preston, A. (2012) '£1m isn't rich anymore': the rise and fall of investment banking. *New Statesman*, October.

## Data sources

Check out the websites of the following for data on financial markets and institutions:

Individual websites of investment banks, insurance companies, pension funds, investment and unit trusts, and hedge funds

Try also:

Association of British Insurers

Building Society Association

Chartered Institute of Insurers

Key Note Research

London Stock Exchange

McKinsey & Company

National Association of Pension Funds

Reuters HedgeWorld

The Association of Investment Companies

TheCityUK

The Financial Services Authority

## Companion website

Go to the companion website at **www.pearsoned.co.uk/econexpress** to find more revision support online for this topic area.

# Notes

# And finally, before the assessment . . .

You should by now have developed your skills and knowledge in ways that can help you perform to the best of your ability, whatever the form of assessment used on your course.

At this stage you should be aware that your assessment involves one or more of the following.

- **Assignment** where one or more essay-type question(s) must be answered in your own time and to a specific word limit (e.g. 1,500 words)
- **Examination** where a timed test is set in a specified location with a range of possible questions, such as:
  - *Essay-type questions*
  - *Data response questions*
  - *Multiple choice questions*

Whatever the form of your assessment, the examiners will be looking to award marks for particular skills that you have displayed in your answers.

- **Application** The ability to apply knowledge of economic principles, theories or concepts to data or issues raised in the question. For example, you may be able to use demand, supply and elasticity concepts to explain why the price of gold is so volatile.
- **Analysis** The ability to identify the assumptions on which a particular line of reasoning depends. For example, you may be able to demonstrate that the benefits of a flexible exchange rate in achieving balance of payments equilibrium depend on there being sufficient price elasticity of demand for a country's exports and imports.
- **Evaluation** The ability to make reasoned judgements about the validity of different arguments. For example, you may be able to explain why some argue that austerity measures involving sharp reductions in budget deficits are needed for sustainable economic growth, whilst others argue that austerity measures must be abandoned if sustainable economic growth is to be achieved.

- *Synthesis* The ability to link ideas together in order to form a coherent and logical argument that is not immediately obvious. For example, you may be able to explain why the characteristics of the market in which the firm operates and the objectives the firm is pursuing must be identified if you are to understand the pricing behaviour of a particular firm.

## How to approach and present assignments

Assignments will challenge you to write for different types of task, but the following steps will help you plan, structure and deliver your assignment whatever the task.

- **Realistic time planning:** Check the assignment submission date, work out how long you have from now to that date and allocate a specific amount of time each week to work on your assignment
- **Identify what you need to do:** Make sure you are clear on the word length, on the type of task (e.g. essay/report), on the topic (e.g. firm objective/economic growth) and on the instructions in the questions (e.g. assess/evaluate)

Here are some widely encountered instructions or 'command words' for assignments.

| Instruction word | What you are expected to do |
|---|---|
| *Analyse* | Give an organised answer reviewing all aspects |
| *Assess* | Decide on relative value/importance of issues |
| *Discuss* | Give own thoughts and support your opinions or conclusions |
| *Evaluate* | Decide on merit of situation/argument and give a balanced judgement |
| *Explain* | Give reasons for |
| *Review* | Present facts and arguments |

- **Find and use relevant materials:** Read and make notes on any readings/sources provided on the assignment brief. The 'Read to impress' section at the end of each topic-based chapter in this book will help here.
- **Structure your assignment:** Make sure the following elements are present:
  - **Introduction:** brief explanation of how you intend to approach the question, key definitions etc.

- **Main body of the answer:** a clearly organised set of themes/issues relevant to the question (often using sub-headings)
- **Conclusions:** referring back to the original question, provide a review of the key points raised, perhaps with a balanced judgement
- **Reference accurately:** accurate and full referencing is a key part of any assignment and will help avoid any issue of plagiarism (i.e. taking credit for the work of others)
  - Identify and use a consistent referencing approach, e.g. Harvard style
  - Reference from the text wherever appropriate (e.g. Sloman, J., 2013) and provide full details of the source in your bibliography
  - Identify where you use exact words or sentences from a source using quotation marks or italics, followed by the source reference
- **Redraft your material:** Try to give yourself time in your plan for re-drafting your first attempt. The second or third draft will invariably be better than the first!

## How to approach your examination

- **Plan your revision:** use a calendar to put dates onto your planner and write in the dates of your exams. Fill in your targets for each day. Be realistic when setting the targets, and try your best to stick to them. If you miss a revision period, remember to re-schedule it for another time.
- **Check what will be examined and in what ways:** identify the topics on your syllabus. Get to know the format of the papers – time, number of questions, types of questions.
- **Make a summary** of the key definitions, theories, empirical evidence, case study examples and diagrams relevant for each topic you are revising.
- Read again the chapters in this book for each topic you are revising. Make sure you have worked through all the questions and activities and can tick the 'confident' box for each element in the revision checklist at the end of each chapter.
- Work out the 'minutes per mark' available for each question in your exam. For example, if you have a 2-hour exam, then you can allocate 1.2 minutes for each mark; so you should allocate 12 minutes for a 10-mark question, 24 minutes for a 20-mark question and so on.

## How to tackle your examination

What you do in the exam room depends, in part, on the type of question you are answering.

## Essay questions

- Read every question on the examination paper carefully before deciding which question to answer.
- Answer your 'best' question first, to help gain confidence.
- Make a brief plan for your answer before you begin to write.
- Structure your answer, with an introduction, main body, and conclusion (see earlier) and check that you are answering the question actually set – not the one you wish had been set.
- Throughout your answer bring in relevant economic theory, refer to relevant empirical evidence, draw, label and use relevant diagrams.
- Manage your time effectively. Try not to go over the time allocation for each question. If you have not finished in that time, write a few extra sentences to conclude and leave space to return to the question if you have time later.

## Data response questions

There are different types of stimulus-based or data response questions, but all require the same basic approach. Much of what has been written earlier with respect to essay questions also applies here, though you must remember that the purpose of providing data is to test your understanding of the principles contained in the data.

- Base your answer on the data (numerical or textual) you are provided with. Failure to do this will seriously reduce the mark you are awarded.
- Use economic principles to illustrate your points. Search hard for them. They are not always apparent, especially in real-world data.
- Look for trends and relationships in numerical and statistical data. Manipulate any 'raw' or untreated numerical or statistical data to give it meaning, e.g. find measures of central location or dispersion, trend line etc.
- Try to recognise the limitations of any statistical data you are given and to recognise the assumptions on which any conclusions of some extract you are given are based.

## Multiple choice questions

- Work out the minutes per question; e.g. 50 multiple choice questions in a one and a half hour exam is 1.8 minutes per question.
- Check there is no penalty for wrong answers. If there is no penalty, make sure you attempt all questions.
- Don't spend too much time on any one question – leave it and return later. The following questions may be easier.
- Towards the end of the exam, if you still have some remaining questions unanswered, have an intelligent guess rather than miss them out.

**Final revision checklist**

❑ Have you revised everything in the 'Revision Checklist' at the start of each chapter and topic?

❑ Have you read and made notes on the additional materials in the 'Read to impress' section at the end of each chapter and topic?

❑ Can you see how to structure your answer after working through the 'Answer guidelines' for the question at the end of each chapter and topic?

❑ Have you tried all the questions and activities for each topic in this book and on the companion website?

## Notes

And finally, before the assessment . . .

## Notes

# Glossary

**Annuity**  This is the reverse of a life insurance policy in that the individual gives a lump sum to the insurance company and receives a stream of income payments, usually on a monthly basis until death. It comes in varying types including group annuities and husband and wife annuities and can be on either a fixed or varying basis (in which case the payments would be linked to some underlying investment portfolio). Payments can be arranged to start immediately or delayed until retirement and can continue after death or cease after the policy holder dies. These features would be written into the policy document.

**Asset transformation**  A process that involves banks 'transforming' the characteristics of their liabilities as they become assets. They do this in four ways: risk, size, liquidity and maturity.

**Average/expected return**  The amount expected from an investment that has various known or expected rates of return. It is the average return given these known 'possible' outcomes.

**Bank assets**  Generally what a bank is owed sometime in the future (accepting cash money), the same as its financial investments.

**Bank balance sheet**  A table showing the stock of assets and liabilities in pounds sterling (in the UK) that are held within a bank at a point in time.

**Bank capital**  What is left if a bank sells all its assets and repays all its liabilities.

**Bank income statement**  A table showing the flow of income from held financial assets and expenditure on financial liabilities plus any other income and expenditure.

**Bank interest rate risk**  The risk of loss due to changes in market interest rates affecting either the bank's net interest income or the capital levels of the bank.

**Bank liabilities**  What a bank owes to its customers.

**Bank money multiplier**  Signifies how many deposits can be created given a level of cash and a set cash ratio, remembering that bank deposits are counted as money.

**Bankers' acceptance**  A short-term financial instrument that increases certainty in the buying and selling of goods between two companies because the payment for the goods received by the purchaser is guaranteed by the bank – the bank has 'accepted' the risk that the purchaser of the goods will fail to pay.

**Basis point** A term used to denote changes in interest rates. One basis point change is 1/100th of 1%, so a 1% change = 100 basis points, and 0.01% = 1 basis point.

**Best efforts agreement** Where the investment bank agrees to sell the securities but does not guarantee the price.

**Bond** A fixed interest financial security issued by large companies, financial institutions and governments whereby the investor (lender) gives money to the issuer (borrower) for a defined time period in return for a fixed rate of interest.

**Bond indenture** A written contract between the bondholder and the issuer of the bond specifying the bondholder's rights and privileges and any obligations of the issuer.

**Bond rating** Same as credit rating, a 'rating' given to a company or financial security indicating ability to pay back the debt and chances of defaulting.

**Bond sensitivity** How a bond's current price is affected to changes in underlying factors.

**Bookrunner** The investment bank that has the mandate to administer an issue on behalf of a client.

**Broker** An entity that brings individuals together to enact trades. Brokers do not hold risk.

**Call option** Gives the holder the right but not the obligation to buy an underlying asset at a given price on or before a pre-specified date.

**Callable bond** These are bonds that may be repurchased by the issuer before maturity at a specified call price.

**Capital expenditure** Refers to spending which has the potential to create future benefits for a company and usually involves raising money to purchase fixed assets or to invest more money in an existing fixed asset.

**Capital market** A type of financial market where longer term financial claims are issued and traded. Long-term refers to maturities of more than one year. Typical capital markets are markets for equity (shares) or bonds.

**Capital to assets ratio** The percentage of bank assets covered by capital.

**Cash flow on a bond** The regular payments on a bond as specified by the coupon.

**Central bank** A bank that sits at the top of the financial system and is the 'banker's bank', watching over a nation's financial institutions and overall financial system.

**Certificate of deposit** A short-term financial security mainly issued by large banks wholesale to other market participants. CDs have a stated interest rate, maturity rate and amount.

**Clean bond price** The price of the bond excluding any interest that has accrued.

**Commercial paper** An unsecured, short-term debt issued by a corporation and having a maturity of between 1 and 270 days

**Commodity** A physical product, for example grain or metal, which is interchangeable with another if they are of the same type and quality.

**Common stock or shares** Same as equity providing holders with certain 'rights' such as entitlement to dividends, voting rights, and a share of the net asset value of the company after all other creditors have been paid off.

**Compound interest** The return on an investment taking into account multiple periods and the interest received on the interest in these periods.

**Constant growth model** A model of equity pricing where it is assumed that the dividend grows at a *constant* rate every year.

**Convergence property** The term for the futures price at the maturity date equalling the spot price.

**Convertible bond** These are bonds that the holder may exchange for a specific number of shares.

**Correlation** Very similar to covariance and regularly used as a substitute. The difference is mathematical – correlation is the calculated covariance of the assets in a portfolio divided by each of the assets standard deviations added together.

**Cost income ratio** Total costs divided by total incomes.

**Counterparty** Refers to the other party in a financial transaction such that every financial transaction to sell must have a counterparty who buys and vice versa.

**Counterparty risk** The same as default risk, that is the risk that the buy party will not, or does not, have the capacity to pay or that the sell party does not, or refuses to, deliver the commodity or financial security.

**Coupon** The promised 'cash flow' or interest rate stated on a security when issued, usually paid twice a year.

**Covariance** The related movement of two financial securities given economic conditions and a measure of how much the two financial securities change together. You are asking the question by how much do the returns of the securities move together?

**Covered call** Where an option is used to protect against a decline in price on tangible asset holdings over a period of time.

**Credit creation** The term used to denote how large retail banks can 'create' money by issuing loans based upon deposited money. Note that issuing loans also creates deposits. In banking, liabilities always equal assets.

**Credit rating** A 'rating' given to a company or financial security indicating ability to pay back the debt and chances of defaulting.

**Credit risk** The risk that the borrower will not be able or willing to pay off the loan and therefore default.

**Currency option** An option that gives the holder the right but not the obligation to buy or sell a particular amount of currency at a pre-specified given exchange rate.

**Debt** This usually refers to bonds, which are fixed interest financial security issued by large companies, financial institutions and governments, whereby the investor (lender) gives money to the issuer (borrower) for a defined time period in return for a fixed rate of interest.

**Default risk** The chance that a company or counterparty will not be able to pay back their debt.

**Demutualisation** Refers to the process of conversion of mutual organisations such as building societies into bank plcs which are funded by shareholders purchasing their issued equity.

**Derivative** A financial instrument that 'derives' its value from some other 'underlying' asset.

**Dirty bond price** The clean price plus any accrued interest that the holder of the bond would receive.

**Discount rate or yield to maturity** The rate which equates the present value of each cash flow to be received in the future with the securities' overall present value.

**Diversification** A combination of financial securities with different return characteristics held within a portfolio in order to benefit from a more efficient risk–return trade-off, such that, on average, it will yield higher returns and have lower risk than an individually held financial security.

**Dividend** The portion of a company's yearly earnings that is available to be distributed to shareholders on a per share basis.

**Downside risk** Risk that an investment will move in such a way that the investor will lose money.

**DvP (Delivery versus Payment)** Refers to the settlement procedure where financial securities are traded, paid and delivered at the same time.

**Endowment life** This combines term life insurance with a savings or investment element. A guaranteed payment is made if the individual dies within the endowment period, but if they live to the end of the endowment they receive a lump sum.

**Equity** A type of financial security that in return for cash provides part ownership of a company, with each individual *share* representing individual ownership of a very small portion of the company.

**Eurobond** An international bond that is issued and traded in a currency which is not the currency of the country where it is issued.

**Euromarkets** Where deposits and loans of a domestic country (such as short-term deposits or loans) are held and utilised in a foreign country.

**Exchange Equalisation Account** The account that holds the UK's reserves of gold, foreign currencies and International Monetary Fund (IMF) Special Drawing Rights (SDRs). It was established in 1932 to provide a fund which could be used for 'checking undue fluctuations in the exchange value of sterling'.

**Executive stock option** A long-term call option that is given to executives as part of their compensation package. It gives the executives the right, but not the obligation, to buy or sell shares at an agreed-upon price within a certain period or on a specific date.

**Exercising the option** The act of buying or selling the option at the specific price.

**Expectations theory** A theory that suggests that long-term interest rates are determined by expectations about the path of future short-term (usually one-year) interest rates.

**Expected return**  The amount one would expect to receive from an investment that has various known or expected rates of return. It is the average return given these known 'possible' returns.

**Expiration date**  The maturity date of the option – the option does not exist past this date.

**FCA**  The Financial Conduct Authority.

**Fiat money**  Money that is backed by the government but has no actual value.

**Financial asset**  A financial obligation that somebody owes to you.

**Financial institution**  A general term to cover institutions that deal with those wishing to borrow and those wishing to save and/or offer financial advice.

**Financial liability**  A financial obligation to somebody else.

**Financial market**  This refers to a place, which can be physical or virtual, where IOUs or financial claims are issued and traded.

**Financial Market Operations Division**  The division responsible for planning and conducting the Bank's operations in the core financial markets and banking markets, and for risk analysis and monitoring of the financial system.

**Financial security**  A form of IOU which usually provides a return in exchange for cash today.

**Financial Stability Division**  The division that attempts to maintain the stability of the financial system as a whole.

**Financial Stability Review**  Published twice a year and covering an assessment of the outlook for the stability and resilience of the financial sector.

**Firm commitment**  Where the investment bank agrees to purchase the entire issue and distribute it to both institutional and retail investors.

**Fisher's classical approach to interest rate determination**  A theory based upon three factors: the marginal rate of time preference; levels of income; and the rate of interest or price for deferring spending today.

**Fixed asset**  A long-term physical asset used to operate a part of the business, for example machinery or real estate.

**Fixed income securities**  A type of security where the issuer promises to make fixed payments of a fixed amount during a fixed time scale until maturity.

**Foreign exchange risk**  The risk that exchange rate changes will adversely affect bank assets and liabilities.

**Forward**  A non-negotiable, customised agreement between counterparties to exchange a financial asset of some kind for cash at a future date.

**FRA**  A forward which is locked into an interest rate in the future.

**Fractional reserve banking**  Originally referred to as the system where goldsmiths would keep only a 'fraction' of gold to underpin their issued receipts. In today's banking system, a term used to denote a type of banking whereby institutions only hold a 'fraction' of their liabilities (mainly deposits) as actual ready cash.

**FSA (Financial Services Authority)**  An independent body that regulates the financial services industry in the UK.

**Funding gap**  This is the gap between average loans and average deposits. It is the gap on a bank's balance sheet that requires funding from the financial markets.

**Futures**  Standardised negotiable agreements between counterparties to exchange a financial asset of some kind for a pre-specified amount of cash at a future date

**GEMMs (Gilt-Edged Market-Makers)**  These are the licensed and authorised bodies that trade in UK government bonds on the London Stock Exchange.

**General insurance**  Insurance which is short term, usually for one year and mainly deals with homes; property; motor vehicles and general accident; and aviation and marine insurance.

**Going long on an option**  Buying an option is called taking a long position.

**Going long**  This is where a financial security is bought today in the hope that it goes up in price.

**Going short on an option**  Selling an option is called taking a short position.

**Going short**  This is where you sell a financial security that you do not own, by borrowing it from a counterparty, in the hope that the price will fall. If the security does fall in price you will buy the security at a cheaper price than you borrowed, thus making a profit when you return the security to whom you borrowed it from.

**Goldsmith**  An entity or person who, in the past, would store gold, issue a receipt and charge a fee for this service.

**Hedge fund**  A type of fund where private money is invested in traded instruments (both cash securities and derivatives); leverage is employed through various means, including the use of short positions, and regulation is usually non-existent.

**Hedging**  Taking an offsetting position in a financial security, in which an investment has been made, to reduce or limit risk.

**Holder**  The person who buys an option.

**Income effect in the loanable funds theory**  Increases in the money supply have an expansionary effect on the economy and will raise incomes leading to an increase in interest rates.

**Inflation**  An increase in the price of goods and services in an economy over time.

**Initial margin**  The minimum amount of money the investor must deposit with the exchange per derivative contract.

**Instrumental independence**  Refers to a type of independence that gives freedom to a central bank to use 'instruments' to manipulate the economy, most commonly the setting of interest rates.

**Insurance company**  Companies that allow individuals and companies to plan financially for pre-specified adverse events by selling policies to individuals or companies that will pay compensation if the adverse event occurs. Insurance companies assume the financial risk of an event occurring.

**Insurance premium**  A specified payment paid periodically, usually monthly or annually, by a company or individual to provide insurance coverage.

**Interbank market**  A market where (mainly) banks lend and borrow from each other for short periods of time, usually less than one week but more commonly overnight.

**Interest rate**  The interest rate is the price that a borrower pays to the lender for the use of that money today. The amount of money lent is known as the principal and the price paid for that amount is expressed as a percentage of the principal, namely the interest rate, usually expressed as an annual rate.

**Interest rate option**  An option that gives the holder the right but not the obligation to lend or borrow a given amount at a pre-specified interest rate for a given period of time.

**Interest rate risk**  The risk that unanticipated changes in interest rates will affect the price of debt or returns on investments.

**'In the money' option**  An option is 'in the money' when it is profitable to exercise the option at the given strike price.

**Intrinsic value**  The underlying asset price minus the exercise price.

**Investment bank**  A bank that offers many services to corporate clients, traditionally underwriting new share issues, acting as broker and trading on behalf of clients.

**Investment bank syndicate**  The involvement of other investment banks to underwrite a debt issue if the bookrunner believes the issue is too large or too risky.

**Investment trust**  A separate company which invests in a portfolio of assets but is established as a plc (public limited company) selling shares to those wishing to invest in the trust's future. It is classed as closed ended, which means that the trust is finite as there are set amounts of shares that can be traded.

**Investors**  Those individuals or companies that purchase financial securities.

**Issued at discount**  Issuing financial securities at less than their face value or price on maturity. The 'discount' is the difference between the price received for a financial security at maturity and its issue price.

**Law of large numbers**  A general theorem that asserts that, as sample size increases, the average of these samples moves towards the mean of the whole population. This means that as deposit inflows and outflows increase as a result of a bank holding more deposit accounts (usually via a large bank branch network), then the bank can calculate with more certainty the net cash position.

**Leveraged position**  The degree to which an investor is using borrowed money to invest in financial securities. In derivatives this can be achieved by only having to cover the margin requirement of the derivatives exchange.

**LIBOR**  The London Inter Bank Offer Rate is the average rate that banks will lend to other banks on the London interbank market.

**LIFFE**  London International Financial Futures Exchange, where futures are traded, first opened in the early 1980s.

**Liquidity**  The ease with which a financial security can be exchanged for liquid assets, usually cash.

**Liquidity effect in the loanable funds theory**  As the money supply increases, then interest rates will decline. Interest rates are negatively related to the money supply.

**Liquidity preference theory**  A theory that contends that lenders of funds prefer to lend short, while borrowers normally prefer to borrow long. So borrowers are willing to pay a 'liquidity premium' to lenders to encourage them to lend for longer periods. The size of the liquidity premium normally increases with the time to maturity.

**Liquidity ratio**  The ratio of cash to total or average assets at a bank.

**Liquidity risk**  The risk of the bank being unable to meet its money commitments on time as a result of deposit holders demanding their money, or commitments falling due to the financial markets.

**Loanable funds theory of the determination of interest rates**  An extension of Fisher's classical theory to take account of the role of governments and their demand for funds and their ability to create cash; and individuals and firms holding cash (and not lending or borrowing). The theory contends that economic agents choose to hold their financial wealth either as interest-earning financial assets or as money – or a combination of the two.

**Marginal liquidity rate**  The price at which the central bank will purchase the next 'lot' of money market instruments and provide money.

**Marginal rate of time preference**  The willingness to defer spending now for more future spending.

**Marked to market**  The change in the margin required by the exchange as the price moves against those holding a derivative contract.

**Market model**  A model that states that the return for an individual security and by extension a portfolio will equal systematic return plus unsystematic or specific return of the (weighted) securities within the portfolio.

**Market risk**  The risk that changes in interest rates will affect traded assets or liabilities.

**Market segmentation theory**  This theory views markets for different bonds as completely separate and segmented, and assumes that there are barriers to switching between short-, medium- and long-term investments.

**Market-maker**  Similar to a broker but they smooth the operation of secondary markets by holding an inventory of shares that can be traded when demand for, or supply of, a share changes abruptly. Unlike a broker they bear risk.

**Maturity**  The time it takes for a financial security to pay back in full.

**Monetary Analysis and Statistics Division**  The division responsible for providing the Bank with economic analysis that helps the MPC formulate its monetary policy.

**Monetary policy**  Using techniques, including varying interest rates, to manipulate money and the supply of money.

**Money**  Something tangible that is accepted and can be exchanged for goods and services. Also used as a measure of value.

**Money aggregates**  Definitions of money used by a country (or economic area in the case of the European Union) based upon what is acceptable as a medium of exchange. Money aggregates are defined as being 'narrow' or 'broad'.

**Money market** A type of financial market where short-term financial claims are issued and traded. Short-term refers to maturities of less than one year. Examples of money markets are the Treasury Bill or Interbank market.

**Money markets** Refers to markets that trade short-term securities.

**Money supply** The stock of cash and other liquid instruments in an economy.

**MPC (Monetary Policy Committee)** A committee within the Bank of England that is charged with setting the base interest rate for the UK economy.

**Mutual organisation** Organisations that are owned by their 'members': that is, those who have purchased shares in the form of deposits or taken out loans usually as mortgages. They have not issued shares into the capital markets.

**Negotiable instrument** A piece of paper or document promising to pay a fixed sum of money on demand or at a certain date. As it is a promise (or promissory note), it can be traded between counterparties.

**Net policy reserve** An estimate of the payments that a company will have to make on its current policy contracts.

**NII** Net Interest Income.

**NIM** Net Interest Margin.

**Nominal return** The actual money received, usually expressed as a percentage.

**Non-constant growth model** A model of equity pricing where dividends are assumed to change over time in a non-constant or irregular way.

**Normal distribution** Signifies that the different returns for a given security will be clustered around the expected return and will be symmetrically distributed above and below the expected return.

**Notional principal amount** The amount upon which the swap interest is agreed.

**Off-balance-sheet risk** Risks associated with contingent liabilities such as guarantees, letters of credit or underwriting business.

**Open interest** The amount of outstanding contracts (long or short) that remain on a particular future.

**Open market operations** The buying or selling of government securities such as Tbills to primary participants in order to manipulate the money supply and/or the interest rate.

**Operational risk** The risk that support systems, people or technology fail to operate as expected.

**Option** A contract that gives the holder the right but not the obligation to buy or sell an underlying asset at a fixed price on or before a specified date.

**Option premium, price or fee** The fee that is paid by the purchaser of the option to the writer of the option.

**Order-driven market** A type of market where buy and sell orders are posted to a central location and are subsequently matched. The market price is derived from the interaction of these demand and supply orders.

**OTC** Over The Counter, a term used to denote a type of market that has no physical location, where trading takes place electronically without a formal exchange.

**'Out of the money' option** An option is 'out of the money' when it is not profitable to exercise the option at the given strike price.

**Pension company** Companies that offer the chance for individuals to place regular portions of money into a fund during their working life which is invested in an array of financial securities which accumulates in size and value over time.

**Pension company trustees** Those that control and, in some countries such as the UK, own the pension fund, where a trustee refers to a person authorised by the Inland Revenue to oversee the management of the pension fund.

**Portfolio** A collection of financial securities held together, usually by an individual or group.

**Portfolio theory** The analysis of how investors can use diversification to construct a portfolio to minimise risk and maximise returns.

**Position limits** The maximum number of contracts that an individual trader may hold.

**PRA** The Prudential Regulation Authority.

**Preference shares** Similar to bonds in that preferred stockholders receive a *fixed* return in the form of a dividend every year which takes precedence over common stockholders but does not confer ownership of the company.

**Preferred habitat theory** A theory that contends that investors (lenders) will have a preference for certain time 'windows' or maturities.

**Present value** The value today of a future stream of cash flows, given a specified rate of return.

**Price expectations effect in the loanable funds theory** As expectations of inflation increase, people will demand more money, which in turn will move interest rates upwards.

**Price limits** The maximum and minimum prices that the futures contract can be bought or sold for in any single day.

**Price-level effect in the loanable funds theory** An increase in the money supply will increase the overall price level in an economy and as the price level begins to rise, the cash that individuals held last year will no longer purchase the same amount of goods. Interest rates will rise.

**Primary market** The market where financial securities are first issued.

**Primary participants** Those financial institutions standing by to purchase government-issued securities such as Tbills when issued.

**Protective put** Buying (or already holding) an underlying asset and also buying a put option.

**Purchased liquidity** Traditionally additional to 'stored' liquidity, this is liquidity that is purchased in the financial markets, such as the interbank or certificate of deposit market.

**Put option** Gives the holder of the option the right but not the obligation to sell an underlying asset at a given price on or before a pre-specified date.

**Quote-driven market** So called because quotes of bid (buy) and ask (sell) prices are posted to the market on a continuous basis.

**Real return**  The return having taken account of inflation and any other associated expenses.

**Refinancing risk**  The risk that the cost of rolling over or reborrowing funds could be more than the return earned on asset investments.

**Reinvestment risk**  The risk that the returns on funds to be reinvested will fall below the cost of funds.

**Repurchase agreement or repo**  A transaction in which one party *sells* a financial security to another party and agrees to repurchase an equivalent value of financial securities at some time in the near future.

**Required rate of return**  The minimum acceptable rate of return for a given level of risk; it will equal the risk-free rate of return (usually Treasury Bills) plus the expected inflation rate plus any risk premium that the investor places on the risk of purchasing the equity.

**Reserve ratio**  The percentage amount of total deposits a bank holds as cash money.

**Return**  The amount of money made on a financial security, usually expressed as a percentage.

**Return distribution**  A set of possible outcomes for a financial security with each of the outcomes having a chance of happening.

**Return probability**  The chances of a financial security realising a certain return.

**Reverse repo**  This is where one party *buys* financial securities from another party and agrees to sell equivalent financial securities back at a future date.

**Risk**  The potential for an issuer of financial securities to have inadequate funds to meet their financial obligations; can also be viewed as the variance in return on a financial asset and the potential for loss.

**Risk appetite**  An investor's or company's 'appetite' for risk.

**Risk–return trade-off**  The principle that in most cases as risk increases so does (expected) returns.

**Risk-averse investors**  Will only take on additional risk if they are compensated by additional expected returns.

**Risk-free rate of return**  The rate at which investors can receive a return with certainty. It is usually the Treasury Bill rate.

**Risk-loving investors**  Will seek high returns but will bear greater risk for a relatively lower expected return.

**Risk-neutral investors**  Will concentrate upon expected returns rather than risk, investing in assets for their returns and tend to ignore risk.

**ROA**  Return on Assets.

**ROE**  Return on Equity.

**Secondary market**  The market where financial securities, once issued, are traded.

**Sensitivity**  How a security's price is affected by changes in the discount rate (or YTM).

**Settlement bank** Major retail banks which bank with the Bank and which must maintain a positive balance on their Bank settlement accounts at the end of each day.

**Settlement price** The price used at the end of trading each day to settle trades and call for variation margins if required.

**Short-term** Used when referring to financial securities with a maturity of less than one year.

**Simple interest** The return from an investment for each time period considered, usually one year.

**Speculation** Purchasing financial securities in an attempt to profit from price changes.

**Spot market** This is where a financial security is traded, paid and delivered immediately.

**Standard deviation** A measure of risk equal to the square root of the variance.

**Sterling obligations** Transactions in the economy which require money to be transferred out of one settlement bank into another settlement bank.

**Stock index option** An option that gives the holder the right but not the obligation to buy or sell a stated stock index at a particular price at some time in the future.

**Stock market indexes** A stock market index is a group of financial securities that are grouped together to measure a certain portion of a financial market.

**Stored liquidity** Refers to that liquidity 'stored' in the balance sheet through traditional bank operations mainly taking in deposits, lending and holding cash. Banks will receive and return money to their customers each day and the overall cash position can be measured, managed and stored.

**Strike or exercise price** The price that has been agreed in the option contract to buy or sell the underlying asset.

**Swap** An agreement between two parties (referred to as counterparties) to 'swap' specified cash payments sometime in the future based upon an underlying asset or price

**Systematic risk of security** The influence that outside or economic 'system' events have on the returns of a financial security.

**Tbill** Treasury Bill, a short-term government issued security.

**Term life** This has a coverage period and therefore matures after a set time. If the premium payments are maintained throughout the coverage period then the next of kin receives a lump sum as long as the individual dies within the time frame covered in the policy. Unfortunately, if the individual dies after the policy has expired then the next of kin receives nothing. The assured is covered for the length of the policy, which can be from 1 to 40 years. It is sometimes referred to as pure life insurance as there is no savings element.

**Ticks** The smallest permissible price movement in a futures contract

**Time value**  The option price minus the underlying asset price.

**Transaction costs**  Costs associated with buying and selling financial securities.

**Treasury Bills (Tbills)**  Short-term debt instruments issued by a country's government in order to help finance the country and/or manipulate the amount of cash in the economy. Issued in the UK:

in minimum denominations of £5,000 at a discount to their face value for any period not exceeding one year. Although they are usually issued for three months (91 days), on occasion they have been issued for 28 days, 63 days and 182 days. They are issued:

- by allotment to the highest bidder at a weekly (Friday) tender to a range of counterparties;
- in response to an invitation from the Debt Management Office to a range of counterparties;
- (Bank of England Website) at any time to government departments.

**Tripartite agreement**  An agreement between the Treasury, the Bank of England and the FSA on working together to provide and maintain financial stability.

**Triple A**  The highest rating a company/government can achieve.

**'Twin peaks' approach**  Refers to the new financial stability structure involving the FCA and PRA.

**UK Treasury**  The UK government department responsible for developing and executing the government's public finance policy and economic policy.

**Underwriting**  The bringing of an issue of financial securities (debt or equity) to the financial market for a client by which (usually) an investment bank guarantees or 'underwrites' the issue, meaning that the bank agrees to buy the securities if demand fails to materialise for the full issue.

**Unit trust**  A portfolio of investments in which individuals or companies can purchase units. The trust is classed as open ended, which means that it increases in size as new investors join.

**Unsystematic** *or specific risk of a security*  Risk events that only influence that particular financial security.

**Variance**  A measure of risk which equals the deviations away from the expected or average return (or dispersion around the expected return).

**Warrants**  An option to buy shares from a company at a stipulated price before a set date.

**Whole life**  This covers the individual over their entire lifetime as long as they keep paying the insurance premiums. The next of kin receives the value of the life insurance contract, or lump sum, when the policy holder dies.

**Wholesale markets**  Markets that are used by financial institutions, large companies and governments to transact in large quantities, most commonly hundreds of thousands of currency. These markets are not usually available to private individuals.

**Writer** The person who sells a call or put option.

**Zero growth model** A model used to price equities which assumes that there is zero growth in dividends.

**Zero-sum game** Where the loss to one party is exactly equal to the gain to the other party.

$\alpha$ **(alpha)** Represents a constant and is the expected value of the unsystematic return of the security. That is, if there was no movement in the market, this is the return from this individual security.

$\beta$ **(beta)** A measure of how sensitive an individual security's return is to changes in the market or 'system', describing how the return varies with movements in the market.

$\Sigma$ **(sigma)** Notation used to mean 'sum all'.

**5Cs** Mnemonic used to assess a loan application: Character, Capacity, Capital, Collateral and Conditions.

**Notes**

# Index

Terms in **bold** indicate glossary entries.